CHIEF PETTY OFFICER'S GUIDE

THIRD EDITION

Titles in the Series

The Bluejacket's Manual
Career Compass
Chief Petty Officer's Guide
The Citizen's Guide to the Navy
Command at Sea
Developing the Naval Mind
Dictionary of Modern Strategy and Tactics
Dictionary of Naval Abbreviations
Dictionary of Naval Terms
Division Officer's Guide
Dutton's Nautical Navigation
Farwell's Rules of the Nautical Road
Fighting the Fleet
Fleet Tactics and Naval Operations
General Naval Tactics
International Law for Seagoing Officers
Leadership Embodied, 2nd ed.
Naval Ceremonies, Customs, and Traditions
Naval Innovation for the 21st Century
The Naval Institute Guide to Naval Writing
The Naval Officer's Guide
Naval Officer's Guide to the Pentagon
Naval Shiphandler's Guide
NavCivGuide
Navy Staff Officer's Guide
Newly Commissioned Naval Officer's Guide
Operations Officer's Guide
Petty Officer's Guide
Principles of Naval Engineering
Principles of Naval Weapon Systems
The Professional Naval Officer: A Course to Steer By
Reef Points
A Sailor's History of the U.S. Navy
Saltwater Leadership
Shiphandling Fundamentals for Littoral Combat Ships and the New Frigates
Surface Warfare Officer's Department Head Guide
Watch Officer's Guide

THE U.S. NAVAL INSTITUTE
Blue & Gold Professional Library

For more than one hundred years, U.S. Navy professionals have counted on specialized books published by the Naval Institute Press to prepare them for their responsibilities as they advance in their careers and to serve as ready references and refreshers when needed. From the days of coal-fired battleships to the era of unmanned aerial vehicles and laser weaponry, such perennials as *The Bluejacket's Manual* and the *Watch Officer's Guide* have guided generations of sailors through the complex challenges of naval service. As these books are updated and new ones are added to the list, they will carry the distinctive mark of the Blue & Gold Professional Library series to remind and reassure their users that they have been prepared by naval professionals and meet the exacting standards that sailors have long expected from the U.S. Naval Institute.

CHIEF PETTY OFFICER'S GUIDE

THIRD EDITION

FLTCM PAUL A. KINGSBURY, USN (RET.)

NAVAL INSTITUTE PRESS
ANNAPOLIS, MD

Naval Institute Press
291 Wood Road
Annapolis, MD 21402

© 2025 by the U.S. Naval Institute
All rights reserved. No part of this book may be reproduced or utilized in any form or by any means, electronic or mechanical, including photocopying and recording, or by any information storage and retrieval system, without permission in writing from the publisher.

Library of Congress Cataloging-in-Publication Data is available.

ISBN: 978-1-61251-192-4 (hardcover)
ISBN: 978-1-61251-314-0 (eBook)

♾ Print editions meet the requirements of ANSI/NISO z39.48-1992 (Permanence of Paper). Printed in the United States of America.

9 8 7 6 5 4 3 2 1

Chief Petty Officer's Creed

During the course of this day you have been caused to humbly accept challenge and face adversity. This you have accomplished with rare good grace. Pointless as some of these challenges may have seemed, there were valid, time-honored reasons behind each pointed barb. It was necessary to meet these hurdles with blind faith in the fellowship of Chief Petty Officers. The goal was to instill in you that trust is inherent with the donning of the uniform of a Chief. It was our intent to impress upon you that challenge is good; a great and necessary reality which cannot mar you—which, in fact, strengthens you. In your future as a Chief Petty Officer, you will be forced to endure adversity far beyond that imposed upon you today. You must face each challenge and adversity with the same dignity and good grace you demonstrated today. By experience, by performance, and by testing, you have been this day advanced to Chief Petty Officer. In the United States Navy—and only in the United States Navy—the rank of E-7 carries with it unique responsibilities and privileges you are now bound to observe and expected to fulfill. Your entire way of life is now changed. More will be expected of you; more will be demanded of you. Not because you are an E-7 but because you are now a Chief Petty Officer. You have not merely been promoted one pay-grade, you have joined an exclusive fellowship and, as in all fellowships, you have a special responsibility to your comrades, even as they have a special responsibility to you. This is why we in the United States Navy may maintain with pride our feelings of accomplishment once we have attained the position of Chief Petty Officer. Your new responsibilities and privileges do not appear in print. They have no official standing; they cannot be referred to by name, number, nor file. They have existed for over one hundred years. Chiefs before you have freely accepted responsibility beyond the call of printed assignment. Their actions and their performance demanded the respect of their seniors as well as their juniors. It is now required that you be the fountain of wisdom, the ambassador of goodwill, the authority in personal relations as well as in technical applications. "Ask the Chief" is a household phrase in and out of the Navy. You are now the Chief. The exalted position you have now achieved—and the word *exalted* is used advisedly—exists because of the attitude and performance of the Chiefs before you. It shall exist only as long as you and your fellow Chiefs maintain these standards. It was our intention that you never forget this day. It was our intention to test you, to try you, and to accept you. Your performance has assured us that you will wear "the hat" with the same pride as your comrades in arms before you. We take a deep and sincere pleasure in clasping your hand and accepting you as a Chief Petty Officer in the United States Navy.

Contents

	List of Illustrations	xi
	Foreword	xv
	List of Acronyms and Abbreviations	xix
	Introduction	1
1	Welcome to the Mess! *Understanding and Meeting the Expectations of Being the Chief*	5
2	Leading and Following in the CPO Mess	29
3	Developing and Supporting the Wardroom	51
4	Keeping Your Leadership Cutlass Sharp	74
5	Leading Teams and Navigating Change	114
6	Increasing Your Range of Communication	134
7	Organizational Management Processes and Your Influence on Them	158
8	Helping Your Organizations Manage Risk	190
9	Preparing for and Growing into New Leadership Positions	216
10	Preparing for and Succeeding in Transition/Retirement	242
	Appendix I *"A Short Talk with Chief Petty Officers"*	269
	Appendix II *U.S. Navy and U.S. Coast Guard Service Songs*	276
	Appendix III *"Read, Think, Write, Publish"*	278
	References and Recommended Reading	284
	Index	290

Illustrations

Photographs

1-1	Chief Peter Tomich posthumously presented with the Medal of Honor for heroism	17
1-2	BMCS Terrell Horne, killed in action 2 December 2012	17
1-3	Loretta Perfectus Walsh, the Navy's first female Chief Petty Officer	17
1-4	Master Chief Vincent W. Patton III, the first African American Master Chief Petty Officer of the Coast Guard	17
1-5	MCPON Joe R. Campa Jr. speaks with Sailors during a visit to Pearl Harbor	23
2-1	Chief Petty Officer selectees pose for a photo	35
2-2	Coffee break in the CPO mess, 18 January 1938	43
3-1	Group portrait of USS *Louisville* (CA 28) officers and CPOs, 1931	53
3-2	Chief Petty Officer and ensign observe a weapons exercise	66
3-3	CNO ADM Jonathan Greenert praises MCPON Rick West	72
4-1	Navy Chief supervises a firefighting equipment and hose handling relay	79
5-1	Chief electronics technician briefs Sailors on a maintenance check	116
5-2	U.S. Coast Guardsmen conduct hook-and-ladder climbing drills during a training exercise	124

5-3	MCPON Mike Stevens	131
6-1	Former CNO ADM Jonathan Greenert talks with the Office of Naval Intelligence and Navy Cyber Warfare Development Group commands	138
6-2	MCPOCG Jason Vanderhaden	143
6-3	Commander of the *John C. Stennis* Carrier Strike Group	147
6-4	Coast Guard Force Readiness Command holds a board of advisers meeting	149
7-1	U.S. Navy Chief supervises Sailors as they load ammunition	161
7-2	Flag briefing at Coast Guard Headquarters	183
7-3	Fleet Master Chief takes a photo with Sailors aboard an amphibious dock landing ship	187
8-1	Federal firefighters and a helicopter from Helicopter Sea Combat Squadron 3 combat a fire	193
8-2	Members from a Coast Guard Air Station conduct helicopter rescue training	201
8-3	Quartermaster 2nd class stands lookout watch aboard an aircraft carrier	213
9-1	The author meets with a fleet CPO mess	229
9-2	Chiefs in formation at a pinning ceremony	236
10-1	The Department of Labor principal deputy assistant secretary for policy for veteran's employment and training services meets with transitioning Sailors	254
10-2	The author is piped ashore during his retirement ceremony	262
10-3	Retired MCPON James Herdt, the 9th MCPON	266

Figures

4-1	CPO Power and Influence Model	76

Text Boxes

1-1	Why I Serve	14
1-2	Self-Assessment: Character Attributes of U.S. Navy and Coast Guard Chiefs	21
1-3	The Fouled Anchor	25
2-1	Insights on Training Your Relief	32

2-2	Self-Assessment: "Leading Across" Attributes of Chief Petty Officers	40
3-1	Expectations of Chiefs from a Commanding Officer	58
3-2	Insights on Chief and Officer Relationships	62–63
4-1	Toxic Leadership Self-Assessment	88
4-2	Could My Decision/Conduct . . .	95
6-1	Communication Fundamentals Self-Assessment	135
7-1	Self-Assessment: Managerial Attributes of U.S. Navy Chiefs	159
7-2	Decision-Making Insights	185
7-3	Morale and Commitment Are High in Units Where Your People Believe . . .	188
8-1	The *Eastwind* Collision: The Loss of a Chief's Mess	191
8-2	CPO Activities to Strengthen Safety Policy	195
8-3	CPO Activities to Strengthen Unit Risk Management	197
8-4	CPO Activities to Strengthen Unit Safety Assurance	199
8-5	CPO Activities to Strengthen Unit Safety Promotion	203
8-6	CPO Activities and Functions to Improve Safety Culture	205
9-1	What Does It Take to Become a Gold Badge Command Master Chief?	226–27
10-1	Suggested Timelines for Retirement Ceremonies	259

Foreword

It is with great honor and respect that we introduce the third edition of the *Chief Petty Officer's Guide*—a comprehensive resource designed to help empower, guide, and center esteemed Navy and Coast Guard Chief Petty Officers like you. You may ask yourself, "What purpose does this guide serve?" The seas in which you operate are unforgiving, and in the maritime domain, your role as the chief is pivotal in maintaining the Navy's and Coast Guard's operational excellence, culture of excellence, and customs and traditions. This guide can serve as a kind of personal beacon, illuminating the path for you to navigate the leadership "shoals" and intricate responsibilities and situations that will come with your distinguished position.

Within these pages you will find a wealth of knowledge curated from the collective wisdom of seasoned CPOs, offering insights on leadership principles, professional development, and the unique intricacies of maritime service. The guide is a testament to the enduring commitment of the chief's mess to foster a culture of excellence, self-accountability, and camaraderie. It stands as a companion to many other leadership and management resources you have available and will support you in your journey to lead, mentor, and inspire the people under your charge and within your sphere of influence.

This guide can help you gain a head start in your role as a new Chief, department Chief, executive petty officer, or command Master Chief that would normally take years to learn and grow into. As you know, it is often difficult to reach a mentor while you are at sea; however, the information provided in your guide can help fill that gap and will enhance, validate, or challenge your personal leadership philosophy—any of those outcomes are favorable.

This guide captures the rich history, traditions, values, and expectations that have always defined the Chief Petty Officer rank. Understanding where we come from is crucial in shaping our future. As the stewards of naval and maritime heritage, Chiefs carry the responsibility of preserving our service, leadership, and management legacy while navigating the ever-evolving landscape of modern naval operations. This guide focuses on leadership and management principles that underpin the success of effective Chief Petty Officers and messes and, in turn, their commands and people. Leadership is not just about rank; it is about influence, accountability, and unwavering dedication to the mission, and this guide offers you actionable insights and real-world examples to guide you in honing your leadership skills. The chapters provide easy-to-use and subject-specific talking points that don't require you to remember the guide as whole. It is also a handy reference to help guide and inspire your leadership engagements and speeches.

This guide emphasizes the importance of professional development, continuous learning, and adaptability. Those who go to sea provide a dynamic force, and you must stay ahead of the curve, not only in technical expertise but also in the realms of leadership, management, and professional growth. This guide will help equip you with the tools and resources needed for any naval leader to thrive in a rapidly changing environment. As a Chief, mission accomplishment and warfighting should be your top priorities. And as the chief, your charge—your foremost responsibility—is to lead and manage your people, "your team," to achieve and maintain the highest levels of operational, training, material, personnel, and family readiness within the command assigned. Achieving this will require synergistic and unfaltering leadership inside and outside the Chief's mess. *You must:*

Take Ownership. Maintain your division, department, and command at the highest state of overall readiness through your direct actions and attitude. If something breaks, fix it! You ARE always a leader. Own it . . . set the tone!

Set and Maintain High Standards. If something does not look right or sound right . . . it is not right. Never walk by an issue or problem without taking action to correct it on the spot. If you do not take immediate action, you've just "re-set" the standard for those around you. Set standards early and enforce them daily until they are muscle memory.

Value Integrity. You must have the moral fortitude to always do the right thing; do not take any action on or outside of the command that may dishonor yourself, the command, the U.S. Navy, the U.S. Coast Guard, or our great nation. If you do make a mistake, admit it, study it, learn from it, correct it, and do not make a habit of it.

Continue to Train; Maintain a High Level of Professional Knowledge. Know and understand your job, equipment, platform, and the capability of your team and relate that to mission and readiness. Never miss an opportunity to train. Training is paramount to success individually and collectively. Along with those under your charge, train the junior officers . . . this should be a priority.

Conduct/Utilize Procedural Compliance. There are formal tactics, techniques, and procedures. Know them and follow them exactly! There is no routine day in the maritime domain.

Provide Forceful Backup. Operationally, procedurally, and personally. No one person is infallible. You are the chief instill forceful backup up and down the chain of command. Translate this attitude to those in your charge.

Demand Formal Communications. Engage the warriors by being up front and center and on the deck plates while ensuring they understand the mission, tasks, and orders assigned. Place a high value on two-way communication, and be open to feedback.

Be a Mentor and a Leader. Provide motivation, tools, training, and guidance to succeed. Get your warriors battle ready by being there, being engaged, and challenging them to be better; this applies to both officer and enlisted! Listen, learn, and lead!

Prioritize Qualifications. Both shipboard and watch station qualifications should be a priority and reinforced daily.

Be a Warrior. You are a warrior. Pick up your cutlass, anchor up, and fight!

Finally, as our country, Navy, and Coast Guard navigate the seas of the twenty-first century, your *Chief Petty Officer's Guide* will serve as a compass, helping to guide you through the challenges you will face and the triumphs and setbacks that will define your career. It is a celebration of the indomitable spirit that has characterized the Chief's mess for generations. May this guide inspire, inform, and fortify our Navy and Coast Guard Chief's mess as it continues to lead with honor, courage, and commitment, respect, and devotion to duty. Fair winds and following seas . . . set the tone!

—R. D. West
*12th Master Chief Petty Officer
of the Navy (MCPON)
Semper Fortis*

—J. M. Vanderhaden
*13th Master Chief Petty Officer
of the USCG (MCPOCG)
Semper Paratus*

Acronyms and Abbreviations

AA	acting appointment
ALCOAST	All Coast Guard message
ALNAV	All Navy message
AOR	area of responsibility
ARI	alcohol-related incident
ASNE	American Society of Naval Engineers
BDD	Benefits Delivery at Discharge
BLUF	bottom line up front
BMC	chief boatswain's mate
BMCM	master chief boatswain's mate
CACO	casualty assistance calls officer
CASREP	casualty report
CCC	command career counselor
CCMP	Certified Change Management Professional
CCTI	chiefs call to initiation
CDAR	Command Drug and Alcohol Representative program
CFS	command financial specialist
CGCOOL	Coast Guard Credentialing Opportunities Online
CG-SIS	Coast Guard Safety Information System
CMC	command master chief
CMEO	command managed equal opportunity

CMS	Change Management Specialist
CNA	Center for Naval Analysis
CNIC	Commander, Navy Installations Command
CNO	Chief of Naval Operations
CO	commanding officer
COCOM	combatant commands
COOL	credentialing opportunities online
COS	chief of staff
CPO	chief petty officer
CPO MVGP	CPO mission, vision, and guiding principles
CPOA	Chief Petty Officers' Association
CPOSF	Chief Petty Officer Scholarship Fund
CSB	career status bonus
CSEL	command senior enlisted leader
CVN	nuclear-powered aircraft carrier
CWO	chief warrant officer
CWOPD	Chief Warrant Officer Professional Development course
DAPA	drug and alcohol program adviser
DAV	Disabled American Vets
DDG	guided-missile destroyer
DESRON	destroyer squadron
DFC	detachment for cause
DIVO	division officer
DoD	Department of Defense
DRB	disciplinary review board
EDVR	enlisted duty verification report
EI	emotional intelligence
EMI	extra military instruction
EMIR	enlisted manning inquiry report
EO	Equal Opportunity program
ESAMS	Enterprise Safety Application Management System
ESO	educational services officer
FEDVIP	Federal Employees Dental and Vision Insurance Program
FFSC	Fleet and Family Support Center
FFSP	Fleet and Family Support Program

FLTCM	fleet master chief petty officer	
FOD	foreign object damage	
FRA	Fleet Reserve Association	
GMCM	master chief gunner's mate	
GMT	general military training	
GS	General Schedule	
HQ	headquarters	
HYT	high-year tenure	
ILT	implicit leadership theory	
INJTRACK	Injury Illness Tracker	
INSURV	inspection and survey	
ISIC	immediate superior in command	
JAG	judge advocate general	
JAGMAN	Manual of the Judge Advocate General	
JCS	Joint Chiefs of Staff	
JPME	Joint Professional Military Education	
KAI	Kirton Adaption-Innovation Inventory	
KPI	key performance indicator	
LCPO	leading chief petty officer	
LDO	limited duty officer	
LPO	leading petty officer	
3-M	maintenance and material management	
MCPO	Master Chief Petty Officer	
MCPOC	Master Chief Petty Officers of the Command	
MCPOCG	Master Chief Petty Officer of the Coast Guard	
MCPON	Master Chief Petty Officer of the Navy	
MMC	chief machinist's mate	
MTF	military treatment facility	
MVPGs	mission, vision, and guiding principles	
MWR	morale, welfare, and recreation	
NAMP	Naval Aviation Maintenance Program	
NAVADMIN	naval administrative message	
NAVEDTRA	Navy Education and Training	
NAVSUP	Naval Supply Systems Command	
NJP	nonjudicial punishment	

OIC	officer in charge
OOD	officer of the deck
OODA	[loop] observe, orient, decide, and act
OPNAVINST	Office of the Chief of Naval Operations Instruction
PA	permanent appointment
PAO	public affairs officer
PFM	personal financial management
PME	Professional Military Education
PMI	Project Management Institute
PNOK	primary next of kin
PO	petty officer
POAM	plan of actions and milestones
PPBE	planning, programming, budgeting, and execution
PPE	personal protective equipment
PQS	personnel qualification standards
QMS	quality management system
RFC	relief for cause
RFMC	rating force master chief
RLSO	Region Legal Service Office
ROAD	retired-on-active-duty
SARC	sexual assault response coordinator
SBP	Survivor Benefit Plan
SCPO	senior chief petty officer
SEA	Senior Enlisted Academy
SEA	senior enlisted adviser
SEAC	senior enlisted adviser to the chairman of the Joint Chiefs of Staff
SEL	senior enlisted leader
SELC	Senior Enlisted Leadership Course (USCG)
SELC	Senior Enlisted Legal Course
SES	Senior Executive Service
SIM	shore installation management
SLLC	Senior Leader Legal Course
SMS	safety management system
SNA	Surface Navy Association

SNOK	secondary next of kin
SOCS	chief special warfare operator
SORM	*Standard Organization and Regulations Manual*
SSLC	Senior Shore Leadership Course
TAO	tactical action officer
TAP	Tuition Assistance Program
Transition GPS	Transition Goals, Plans, Success program
TYCOM	type commander
UCMJ	Uniformed Code of Military Justice
USCG	U.S. Coast Guard
USMC	U.S. Marine Corps
USNI	U.S. Naval Institute
USO	United Service Organizations
VA	U.S. Department of Veterans Affairs
VAO	voting assistance officer
VSO	veterans service officer
WESS	Web Enabled Safety System
XO	executive officer
YNC	chief yeoman

Introduction

Chief \'chēf\ (noun): the head or leader of a group, organization, etc.; person of highest title or authority; the most valuable or main part of anything.
—*Webster's New World Dictionary*, Third College Edition

I cherish the years I spent in Chief Petty Officers' (CPO) messes and clubs with fellow Chiefs working through issues to ensure unit warfighting readiness, exploring new ideas and approaches, debating the good and bad of policy change, telling sea stories and jokes, seeking advice and help with personal challenges, and even having the contentious debates and exchanges that are crucial to resolving differences. I have met, and continue to meet, and served with great CPOs, and I have been privileged to have had them in my life, even if only for a short period of time. Throughout my career I observed thousands of Chief Petty Officers at work fulfilling their "make the Navy and Coast Guard run" roles. From my first meeting and subsequent impression of a Chief in a Ft. Lauderdale recruiting station (I still remember thinking how cool his white shoes looked), to the bonds and relationships I enjoy today, many chiefs significantly influenced—and continue to influence—my personal growth, my Navy career, and my work today.

Some believe it is difficult to capture the essence of what Chiefs do in a relevant, unique, and insightful way. The relatively small volume of literature regarding the CPO mess consists of a handful of formally published articles, anecdotal stories and quips, and a handful of books. Over the years

I've found these references useful, but I felt they never fully captured the depth and complexities of the organizational and leadership interactions in which chiefs and CPO messes are key players. This third edition of the *Chief Petty Officer's Guide* strives to build upon the original foundation laid in 2004 and expanded upon with the second edition. But as times change, we needed to "take a fix" on this title in our professional library and update it to ensure relevance. I've brought forward some content from the first and second editions; but with the publication of the new *Petty Officers Guide*, there is an opportunity to broaden the context and approach of this edition to provide Chiefs of all experience levels, aspiring petty officers seeking advancement to Chief, and others interested in understanding the tools and insights regarding CPO success that I often heard them seeking. This edition now offers guidance for the newly selected CPO to the command master chief seeking a position on a flag staff and includes a broader U.S. Coast Guard (USCG) audience. Throughout the guide, the term "Chief" will be used to capture the full range of CPO mess pay grades—Chief Petty Officer, Senior Chief Petty Officer (SCPO), and Master Chief Petty Officer (MCPO). Many petty officers, first and second class, want to better understand how to think like a Chief! Unfortunately, there is no singular model of chief "thinking" that can be captured, so this book works to provide perspectives of how U.S. Navy Chiefs can use power bases, influence tactics, and management competence to advance toward mission success at all levels of Navy and USCG leadership.

This book is my ongoing attempt to augment the key insights from the other literature you may have read concerning Navy and USCG Chiefs and their broader CPO messes. My desire is that this updated edition builds upon and complements the foundation provided by your formal and informal leadership education, life experience, *The Bluejacket's Manual, The Coast Guardsman's Manual, Petty Officer's Guide,* your charge book entries, the coaching and mentoring you receive, and other leadership and management books and podcasts. It aims to help you build your understanding of, and to expand the way you view, the value that Chiefs and the CPO mess bring to your service. Many chapters include lists of attributes, behaviors, and qualities that all chief petty officers (or any leader or manager) should strive for. There is no such thing as a Chief who is consistently strong in ALL these areas, and the intent of these lists is to help you self-assess to get a sense of where you stand and to bring areas requiring improvement to your attention. You should be brutally honest with yourself while completing these self-assessments of how you are doing as a Chief, Senior, or Master Chief Petty Officer. For each item, be thoughtful and objective, taking time to evaluate each as an area you are strong in, that you do about as well as you should, or that you need to work on.

For those in the mess. I'm confident you want to be a more effective Chief, Senior Chief, or Master Chief as you strive to lead and manage strong maintenance and operational teams while increasing productivity in support of mission readiness. You want motivated people and teams who are performing at the highest level of performance and who exceed both your expectations and the expectations they've set for themselves. And I'm confident you'd like to contribute more effectively to the collaborative managerial and leadership efforts and outputs of your Chief's mess. Or perhaps during those trying times you're sure to experience as a Chief Petty Officer this guide will provide you a readily available source of inspiration and reinvigoration.

This book is also for those not currently serving as Chiefs but who are "Chiefs in training," members of a sister service, or supervisors in other organizations. You might have heard about the effectiveness of Navy and USCG Chiefs and would like to gain more insight on how Chiefs think, manage, and lead. If you are going up for advancement, you would probably like to better understand what happens behind the closed doors of the CPO mess so you can contribute more quickly and more effectively upon selection to Chief Petty Officer. Or perhaps you'd like to better leverage organizational networks toward individual and company success.

Finally, for members of the wardroom. I'm sure you'd like to better understand the benefits your division, department, command, or headquarters can enjoy from a highly productive CPO mess and senior enlisted leader. And you probably want to improve your relationships with the Chiefs at your command while better understanding how to harness your CPO mess to achieve your individual and command goals and warfighting readiness requirements.

This revised and updated guide should serve all these audiences well. It is not intended to simply sit on your bookshelf or in a locker—use it! Since 1893, commands, fleets, and our Navy and USCG have successfully completed the missions tasked to them because of strong CPO team leadership and managerial skill. Naval leadership has always had lofty expectations for our CPO mess, as they should. We've historically been expected to deliver "results, not excuses," and "ask the Chief" captures the expectation that we maintain the highest levels of technical and institutional expertise and develop that within our teams and the people who will eventually be our reliefs. Those phrases are easy to put on a T-shirt or coffee mug but are much harder to fulfill daily. This guide is designed to present those concepts to you so that you can reflect on them, acknowledge where you are strong, and improve in areas in which you might be weak. If anything, this guide might even serve to help explain the "why" behind your success to date. These are all things we should reflect on and discuss within our mess. They are in your control to directly influence as Chief Petty Officers.

This book attempts to capture what I've learned from my observations of and interactions with the CPO mess from a variety of perspectives. I've seen CPO leadership and management in action from the perspective of a follower, peer, and mess leader. I've observed it and practiced it on ships; in aviation squadrons; on shore installations and region staffs; and in the offices and meeting rooms of fleet, combatant commands (COCOM), and Pentagon headquarters. This guide is intended to serve as a handy resource to help you think about your role and to offer advice on how you can better lead your service. This guide will never be "complete." Although I offer my perspective and insights, they are and have been shaped (and limited) by my relatively short thirty-one-year career in the Navy. The CPO mess has evolved since 1893, and it will continue to evolve—that is necessary and healthy for our Navy and USCG. Opportunities will arise to add to this book, revise it, and strengthen it. This book is a vessel—it is not full, and it has plenty of room for future replenishment.

I was taught by a wise Master Chief (and friend) that we should reflect on the perceptions we shape because of our behavior at a given command and ask ourselves, "Is my unit, region, force, fleet, or service better because I was there, or is it better because I am leaving?" My wish is that this book helps leave your service and your CPO mess a little bit better in a rapidly changing world. On behalf of all the Chiefs who have influenced me and through their coaching, unique insights, experiences, personalities, and perspectives, I offer you this guide. Fair winds and following seas!

One

Welcome to the Mess!

Understanding and Meeting the Expectations of Being the Chief

> If you're honest with yourself, you're going to question yourself a lot of times. I don't care if you're the captain, the admiral, the CMC, whoever—you will. When I hit the rack last night, I was dead tired, but I lay there worrying—about our ammo, our equipment, our guys. Do they know everything they need to know, is there anything else I need to tell them?
>
> —*U.S. Navy Master Chief*

On the one-hundredth anniversary of the Navy's creation of the rank of CPO, the twenty-fourth Chief of Naval Operations, ADM Frank B. Kelso II, said, "In the United States Navy, the title 'Chief Petty Officer' carries with it responsibilities and privileges no other armed force in the world grants to enlisted people." Today the Navy CPO's mess continues to be lauded as a vital component to mission success. Our CPO Creed states, "In the United States Navy—and only in the United States Navy—the rank of E-7 carries with it unique responsibilities and privileges you are now bound to observe and expected to fulfill."

What is it that makes Navy and USCG Chiefs so unique to be bestowed this prestige, responsibility, and autonomy? What is it about the culture and climate of your servicewide CPO mess that underlies its continued success? In 1893 several hundred Navy men were promoted to the rate of CPO. Since then the Navy's and Coast Guard's messes have expanded, evolved, and matured. In your guide, I'll offer insights, advice, and guidance on how you can and should best utilize your growing power, influence, and management skills in a variety of positions to produce the material, operational, and personnel readiness that enables your service's warfighting, lifesaving, and law enforcement capability.

Your CPO Mess History

Since 1893 the rank of Chief Petty Officer has been a well-respected position of authority. The article "History of the Chief Petty Officer Grade" (Tucker 1993) provides an outstanding synopsis of the establishment and growth of the rate of Chief Petty Officer. Gunner Tucker discovered that "on April 1, 1893, two important steps were taken. First, the grade of Chief Petty Officer was established; secondly, most enlisted men received a pay raise." He believed the earliest use of the term in the Continental Navy occurred when Jacob Wasbie, a cook's mate serving on board *Alfred*, was promoted to chief cook.

Precedence of petty officers was not really introduced until the mid-1850s. Based on pay tables of the period, though, one can infer the rating structure of the time. By the end of the Civil War, precedence of rates was rather clear. Naval Regulations read: "Precedence among Petty Officers of the same rate shall be established by the Commanding Officer of the vessel in which they serve." Precedence by rating was a fact of Navy life for the next 105 years and was substantiated by rating priority and the date of an individual's promotion. Ratings in the seaman branch took precedence over all others, and those with direct responsibility for sailing, navigating, and fighting the ship had higher precedence that those further removed from the Navy's core mission. Precedence of ratings remained in effect until 1968, when a single system for military and nonmilitary matters based on pay grade and time in grade was established.

On 8 January 1885, the Navy classed all enlisted personnel as first, second, or third class for petty officers, and as seaman first, second, or third class non–petty officers. Chief boatswain's mates, Chief quartermasters, and Chief gunner's mates were positioned in the petty officer first-class level within the seaman class; masters-at-arms, apothecaries, yeomen (equipment, paymasters, and engineers), ship's writers, schoolmasters, and band masters were also first-class petty officers but came under the Special Branch.

Finally, machinists were carried at the top grade within the Artificer Branch. Included under the Special Branch at the second-class petty officer level was the rate of Chief musician, who was junior to the band master; that rate was changed to first musician under the 1893 realignment of ratings and carried as a petty officer first class until 1943.

On 1 April 1893, the day the Chief Petty Officer rate was established, the Navy also gave most enlisted men pay raises. Hoary old Chiefs often ask new selectees to find the name of the first Chief Petty Officer. The answer is, flatly, there was no first Chief Petty Officer because nearly all ratings carried as petty officers first class from 1885 were automatically shifted to the Chief Petty Officer level. The Chief Petty Officer grade on 1 April 1893 encompassed nine rates:

- Chief master-at-arms
- Chief boatswain's mate
- Chief gunner's mate
- Chief machinist
- Chief yeoman
- Chief carpenter's mate
- Apothecary
- Chief quartermaster
- Band master

Prior to the establishment of the Chief Petty Officer grade, and for many years thereafter, commanding officers could promote petty officers to acting appointments to fill vacancies in ship's complements. Men served various lengths of time, usually ranging from six months to a year, under acting appointments. If service was satisfactory, the captain recommended to the Bureau of Navigation that an individual be given a permanent appointment for the rate in which he served. Otherwise, the commanding officer could reduce an individual to the grade or rate held prior to promotion if he served under an acting appointment. The change in status from acting to permanent appointment was always a breathe-easier occurrence because the commanding officer could not reduce a Chief Petty Officer without explanation. Only a court-martial and the bureau's approval could reduce a Chief serving under a permanent appointment.

The Chief Petty Officer's status was indicated with PA (permanent appointment) or AA (acting appointment) next to his title. After 8 March 1946, the letter A (acting appointment) was integrated with the rate abbreviation. For example, chief boatswain's mate with an acting appointment was abbreviated CBMA. Pay-grade 1-A no longer signified acting appointment for Chief Petty Officers after 1 October 1949, thanks to the Career Compensation Act of 1949. From that time, CPOs received the same pay regardless of whether they held permanent or acting appointments. On 1 November 1965 acting appointments were dropped from use.

A pay differential existed between permanent and acting appointments until 1949. In 1902 monthly pay for Chief Petty Officers ranged from fifty to seventy dollars, depending upon the specialty held. CPOs holding permanent appointments dated prior to 1 July 1903, the effective date of General Order 134, were required to requalify by standing an examination before a board of three officers. If they passed, they were issued permanent appointments by the Bureau of Navigation. Those who did not requalify remained in the pay and grade level instead of increasing to the seventy-dollar-a-month level.

Pay levels for enlisted men at that time were established by executive order until an act of 13 May 1908 established that the U.S. Congress would set pay for enlisted personnel. In 1920 Congress standardized pay at all levels from the lowest nonrated grade, apprentice seaman, through Chief Petty Officer. Monthly base pay was $126 for permanent appointed chiefs, and $99 for acting appointments. Amazingly, these pay rates remained effective until 1 June 1942, when the act of 16 June 1942 mandated a pay increase to $138 and $126 for CPOs with permanent and acting appointments, respectively.

Congress brought the Coast Guard into full alignment with Navy grades and ratings when it passed "An Act to Increase the Efficiency of the Commissioned and Enlisted Personnel" on 18 May 1920. This legislation decreed, "The grades and ratings of warrant officers, Chief Petty Officers, petty officers and other enlisted persons in the Coast Guard shall be the same as in the Navy, in so far as the duties of the Coast Guard may require." The same day Secretary of the Treasury David F. Houston signed General Order No. 43 authorizing the rate of Chief Petty Officer for eleven enlisted ratings and promoting all acting warrant officers to Chief Petty Officer, the highest enlisted rate one could now achieve. The decades-long delay can be attributed to several factors. The most significant was the volunteer nature of much of the Life Saving Service and the fierce independence of the more militarized Revenue Cutter Service. The latter was regularly at odds with the Navy over issues as seemingly minor as dress uniforms—with documented incidents of Revenue Cutter officers being the envy of their Navy counterparts at dinner parties because of their more ornate jackets and insignia. There was, as there is today, a clear distinction between the sea services, as well as significant levels of pride in both for their unique history and for the duties they performed.

Throughout the war years, Chief Petty Officers were the senior enlisted personnel afloat or ashore. Although it was traditional in the submarine service to identify the most "senior" Chief as "Chief of the Boat," all Chiefs served in pay-grade E-7 throughout World War II and Korea. The current number of ratings of Chief Petty Officers falls far short of the 207 listed at the end of World War II. Only two ratings, boatswain's mate and gunner's mate, have remained in continuous use since 1797.

The Super Chiefs

Navy and Coast Guard senior enlisted rank structure expanded when the pay grades of E-8 (senior chief) and E-9 (Master Chief) were created, effective 1 June 1958 under a 1958 Amendment to the Career Compensation Act of 1949. Eligibility for promotion to E-8, the Senior Chief level, was restricted to permanent-appointment chiefs with a minimum of four years in grade and a total of ten years of service. For elevation from E-7 to Master Chief, E-9, a minimum of six years of service as a Chief Petty Officer with a total of thirteen years of service was required. Servicewide examinations for outstanding Chiefs were held on 5 August 1958, with the first promotions becoming effective 16 November 1958. A few months later a second group of Chiefs from the February 1959 examinations were elevated to E-8 and E-9 on 16 May 1959. Within the Navy, which had not energetically supported the new pay grades, potential nominees were screened by time-in-grade and time-in-service. Since that time, the current promotion progression from chief to Senior Chief to Master Chief has been in place.

One problem immediately facing the Navy was the definition of roles and responsibilities for the new pay grades, then dubbed "super Chiefs," a description not always intended as a compliment. Indeed, for a considerable period, the major distinction among rates was the pay increment only. Particularly on the khaki working uniform, the different grades were identified only by one or two very small stars above the traditional fouled anchor. It was not until the mid-1960s that the present custom of addressing E-8 and E-9 personnel as "Senior Chief" or "Master Chief" began to be practiced and gradually came into general usage.

As explained in *Winds of Change* (Crist 1992), a most significant revision to policy took place in the summer of 1978. After a great deal of study and debate within the command Master Chief community, MCPON Tom Crow persuaded the Chief of Naval Operations to formalize the roles and responsibilities of Chiefs, Senior Chiefs, and Master Chiefs. Chief Petty Officers would be expected to become the top technical authorities and experts within a rating, providing the direct supervision, instruction, and training of lower rated personnel within his or her skill set. Senior Chiefs would be expected to be the senior technical supervisors within a rating and occupational field, providing the total command with technical expertise. And the Master Chief Petty Officer would provide administrative and managerial leadership on issues involving enlisted personnel and would be expected to contribute in matters of policy formulation as well as implementation across the full spectrum of rates. In practical terms, an Information Systems Tech (IT) might be responsible for the ship's transmitter room. A Senior Chief might be responsible for the entire message center, and a Master Chief might take responsibility for development and implementation of the ship's communication plan as well as, perhaps, acting as the leading petty officer for the entire operations department.

The Command Senior Enlisted Leader (CSEL)

It was inevitable that the office of the Master Chief Petty Officer of the Navy (MCPON) would eventually be created. *Winds of Change* (Crist 1992) provides an in-depth look at how the office of the MCPON was established and matured in influence and impact. It all began when the Marine Corps established a billet for a Sergeant Major of the Marine Corps in 1957, with the Army following suit in 1966. And in 1969 the U.S. Coast Guard established a billet for the Master Chief Petty Officer of the Coast Guard; and the U.S. Air Force, Chief Master Sergeant of the Air Force. Members of Congress saw value in creating a position for a senior enlisted member who could act as a representative of a large, untapped contingency, and in 1967 the Navy established the office as part of the personal staff of the Chief of Naval Operations. On 27 August 1969 the office of the Master Chief Petty Officer of the Coast Guard (MCPOCG) was established and MCPO Charles Luther Calhoun was selected as the first MCPOCG.

From there the first MCPONs and MCPOCGs formed and grew their servicewide network of senior enlisted advisers who met with their people to resolve local and cross-command problems while elevating those that appeared to have broader implications. This ad hoc process worked well for several years and is credited with attenuating many of the drug, race, and morale issues that plagued the late-Vietnam and post-Vietnam eras. The lessons learned during this time were valuable in shaping future functional and process changes to the senior enlisted leadership organization.

In 1971 a "Z-gram" was released that formalized the program and identified these senior enlisted leaders as Master Chief Petty Officers of the Command (MCPOC). Twenty-three outstanding master chief petty officers were identified and assigned to major commands ashore and afloat. To further add credibility to these individuals, the Bureau of Personnel changed the specialty mark within their rating badge and permitted the use of a single large gold star in lieu of their rating mark. The two small silver stars above the eagle on the chevron were also replaced with small gold stars. These command master chiefs met frequently to develop policy recommendations regarding enlisted issues. These concerns and recommendations would be routed to the Chief of Naval Operations (CNO) via the MCPON, effectively making the senior enlisted an advisory board to the senior policymakers in the Navy. MCPON Bob Walker revised the organization to a fleet, force, and command master chief structure in 1977. That structure, which has proven to be effective and efficient, has had modifications but remains in place to the present time. Chapter 9 will offer much more guidance and advice on these positions and career opportunities.

Your CPO Mess Legacy

The eleventh Master Chief Petty Officer of the Navy, MCPON Joe Campa, USN (Ret.), would often tell a story about the influence his first Chief had on him. "My first Chief had a big impact on me. I still look at what he did. When he spoke, he spoke with such credibility because he had such a strong knowledge of his ship, his rate, and the people he led; that inspired me to want to do well for him. He planted some seeds—but I have been fortunate throughout my career to have good, strong, deck-plate leaders—those who kept their focus on their people and measured their success through them." We have all had a "first Chief" who impressed on us what a Chief is and does. Some impressions were favorable and positive; others not so much. Many of us remember the first Chief who established our model of what a Chief should be. We never forget them or the impact they leave on us; and not unlike MCPON Campa, many Sailors have been, and continue to be, fortunate to be inspired by strong senior enlisted leadership.

Your experiences with chiefs throughout your career has shaped how you have acted and will act today. Just as you learned from your past chiefs, your Sailors will learn what to do from you; but in some unfortunate cases, they figure out what not to do as well. As a Chief, you translate your beliefs and attitudes through your daily actions and interactions with officers and enlisted Sailors—you never underestimate the lasting impact you can have on your Navy or Coast Guard. You have been and will be many a young Sailor's, Coastie's, and officer's first Chief. Your presence, influence, and behavior impact hundreds, if not thousands, of young Navy and Coast Guard professionals. It is healthy for you, regardless of your time as a Chief, to occasionally pause and reflect on the tone and impressions those first chiefs made on you and to evaluate the kind of first impressions you are making on others as their "first Chief."

Anchor Up!
In your own words, define the term "sense of heritage." How do you use it to connect your teams to their past and to teach values, hence enhancing pride in service to your country?

In today's military-strategic environment, a credible, capable, and competent CPO mess is vital and ensures that your service will maintain its asymmetric advantage—the creativity and experience of its personnel—to help reduce the time in the warfighting observe, orient, decide, and act (OODA) loop. Proactive and effective CPO effort is essential to a command's capability to conduct prompt and sustained naval combat if or when required. You must never forget that your service's mission includes protecting America from attack, conducting offensive naval actions when required, and maintaining strategic influence in key regions of the world. You should maintain awareness of the threats growing worldwide—your teams need to be ready. To this end, you should be interested in the health, focus, and effectiveness of your chief's mess in ensuring that your systems, platforms, and people are ready and able to prevail in all phases of warfare, not only during combat operations but also during "shaping" engagements such as theater security operations or maritime support operations.

Throughout your service's history—from the time John Paul Jones issued his call in 1777 for able-bodied landsmen to today—the role of the enlisted force has remained consistent. They maintain, operate, and support naval warfighting systems and platforms. Over time our warfighting systems have evolved, and in some communities our Sailors and Coasties *are* the warfighting platform. Your service transitioned from ships of sail manned by able-bodied seamen to coal-fueled steel hulls and nuclear-powered submarines. As the technology of naval warfighting platforms improved, so did the technical authority, focus, and expertise of Navy Chiefs. During the Vietnam era, riverine squadrons were established, and the Navy SEALs evolved from their World War II underwater demolition roots. And today Sailors and Coasties are fighting in the cyber domain. None of this would be possible without the leadership of Chiefs who have served and the more than 30,000 CPOs who are currently serving worldwide in the Navy and Coast Guard: all ensuring that the hundreds of ships and cutters, thousands of aircraft, hundreds of bases and information warfare commands, and the hundreds of thousands of enlisted personnel serving in them are ready for war.

1-1 WHY I SERVE

Why do I serve in the Coast Guard? It boils down to a simple phrase—"AYE-AYE"—the correct response to an order, signifying we understand and will comply.

No matter the situation, with little regard for peril or fear of danger, we have answered the calls of our country with a willing "AYE-AYE!" When an earthquake rattled a neighbor ... "AYE-AYE, friends, we will be there." When a storm has flooded our city ... "AYE-AYE, neighbors, we will save you." When we are being threatened from the sea ... "AYE-AYE, Mr. President, we will protect our country."

This is why I serve in our Coast Guard. We don't say it's too hard; we don't say we're too tired; we don't say we can't; we don't say no. We say "AYE-AYE!" Even when we're fatigued, battered, or challenged, we find a way to get to "AYE-AYE!" We understand and will comply. You don't always have to call or tell us—sometimes we see the need and we merely whisper under our breath "AYE-AYE." We are a special breed with a unique heritage. Our work isn't for the faint of heart or weak-willed. We go out when others are heading in; we toil as others rest; we do the impossible while others shrink from the threat.

When you hear a Coastie sing out "AYE-AYE," you know help is on the way! When you hear a Coastie say "AYE-AYE," you know they will stay with the mission until it's complete. When you hear a Coastie say "AYE-AYE," you know you will be safe.

For 223 years, thousands of Coast Guard men and women have taken orders and responded "AYE-AYE!" I am humbled and honored to list my name along with my shipmates, past and present, as a member of this group. "To fight to save or fight and die, Aye! Coast Guard we are for you!" I serve as part of a force that can, will, and does give a hearty "AYE-AYE!" in accepting any challenge to fight to save or fight and die.

—*MCPO Lloyd Pierce, USCG*

Anchor Up!

Your service's CPO mess subscribes to several mantras, including "Results, Not Excuses," "Ask the Chief," "Anchor Up," and "Backbone of the Navy." What beliefs, attitudes, and priorities should you have to fulfill these mantras? What do you and your mess value and believe in, and do these personal beliefs and values align with or conflict with your service's values and principles? How does this impact your (our) effectiveness as a Navy leader(s)?

Some Chiefs have been presented the opportunity to lead in challenging situations in peace and in war: they serve as role models for us all to follow. For example, Chief John W. Finn was at Naval Air Station Kaneohe Bay during the Pearl Harbor attack on 7 December 1941. For his courage and leadership, Chief Finn was awarded the Medal of Honor, and USS *John Finn* (DDG 113) is named in his honor.

Also at Pearl Harbor, Chief Watertender Peter Tomich was at his post in the fire room of USS *Utah* (BB 31) when two torpedoes, seconds apart, pierced the side of *Utah*. He maintained his post and single-handedly began securing all the boilers to prevent a massive explosion and was trapped on the ship with fifty-seven others on board. By preventing the boilers from exploding, he saved the lives of hundreds of men on board and in the water nearby. For such valor and concern for the lives of others, Chief Peter Tomich was posthumously awarded the Medal of Honor. USS *Tomich* (DE 242) was commissioned on 27 July 1943. His medal holds a place of honor at the Senior Enlisted Academy's Tomich Hall located in Newport, Rhode Island.

 Anchor Up!

What does being a proactive leader engaged on the deck plates look like? What are the negative impacts to a command where chiefs are not out leading on the deck plates?

In 2012 USCG Chief Boatswain's Mate Terrell E. Horne III led a boarding team from Coast Guard Cutter *Halibut* to investigate a suspicious vessel near Santa Cruz Island, California. The vessel ignored commands to stop and instead rapidly accelerated directly toward them. The boarding team immediately maneuvered to avoid the oncoming vessel and fired sidearms in self-defense. When impact with the oncoming vessel became unavoidable, Chief Horne disregarded his own safety in order to protect a fellow crew member and firmly pushed the coxswain from the helm, directly exposing himself to the oncoming vessel. The violence of the subsequent collision forcibly ejected him from the boat, and despite immediate recovery from the water and application of first aid by his shipmates, he succumbed to the severe injuries received during the incident. Chief Horne was posthumously presented with the Coast Guard Medal and advanced to the rank of senior chief petty officer (SCPO). USCGC *Terrell E. Horne III* is named in his honor. And on 29 February 2016 Senior SOCS (SEAL) Edward C. Byers Jr. received the Medal of Honor for his heroism serving as a Hostage Rescue Force Team member in Afghanistan in support of Operation Enduring Freedom.

Other Chiefs have overcome cultural challenges and barriers and positively impacted thousands of Sailors. Chief Yeoman (YNC) Loretta Walsh was the first enlisted woman to join the Navy; she demonstrated great resilience and toughness, overcoming stereotypes and ridicule following policy change. Master Chief Gunner's Mate (GMCM) Delbert D. Black, a decorated World War II veteran who had been awarded eight combat ribbons and survived the attack on USS *Maryland* (BB 46) at Pearl Harbor, was selected to be the first MCPON and had to overcome institutional resistance and pushback while establishing the office and showing the value it could provide the Navy. USS *Delbert Black* (DDG 119) is named in his honor. Master Chief Boatswain's Mate (BMCM) Carl Maxie Brashear used a rare combination of grit, determination, and persistence in overcoming formidable hurdles to become the first black Master diver in the U.S. Navy, and Master Chief Vince W. Patton III overcame similar hurdles to become the first African American selected as MCPOCG in 1998. These four Chiefs were instrumental in implementing changes that helped attenuate high attrition rates and in shaping an improved service climate and culture of opportunity.

[1-1] Chief Peter Tomich was posthumously presented with the Medal of Honor for heroism on board USS *Utah* (BB 31) during the 7 December 1941 Japanese air attack on Pearl Harbor.
NAVAL HISTORY AND HERITAGE COMMAND

[1-2] BMCS Terrell Horne was killed 2 December 2012 off Santa Cruz Island while attempting to interdict a panga vessel loaded with marijuana.
U.S. COAST GUARD PHOTO BY PETTY OFFICER 1ST CLASS ADAM EGGERS

[1-3] Loretta Perfectus Walsh was the Navy's first female Chief Petty Officer.
NAVAL HISTORY AND HERITAGE COMMAND

[1-4] Master Chief Vincent W. Patton III overcame formidable hurdles to become the first African American selected as Master Chief Petty Officer of the Coast Guard, serving from 1998 to 2002.
U.S. COAST GUARD PHOTO

Some Chiefs are intellectuals and writers who use those talents to shape their service in a unique way. Chief Machinist's Mate (MMC) Richard McKenna studied creative writing, and—besides winning the Naval Institute's Enlisted Essay Prize for his essay titled "The Post-War Chief Petty Officer: A Closer Look" (McKenna 1948)—he published a major work titled *The Sand Pebbles* (1963), a 597-page novel that won the 1963 Harper Prize and was made into the well-known 1966 film of the same title. And USCG Senior Chief Musician King III took it upon his own initiative to write the service song and march for the U.S. Public Health Service Commissioned Officers Corp.

Anchor Up!
What is the tone you set as a leader in your current position with your leadership, your peers, and your subordinates? What do the attitudes and behaviors in the people around you tell you about the tone you are setting? Is it good or bad?

There are so many more exemplary Chiefs, and you probably have your own personal examples. All Chiefs become a part of this legacy, and you have a responsibility to appreciate and protect it, and you should have a sense of pride regarding it. Your predecessors should inspire you and remind you of the expectations placed upon you and the cost to meet them. As a new Chief, you have much to learn; as a seasoned Chief, you must not lose sight of your place, avoid comfort and complacency, and continue to learn and grow to succeed in positions of increasing scope, influence, and responsibility. Much can be learned from handbooks like this guide and from the study of those who served long before you. But it is the example and wisdom imparted personally, one-on-one, from one generation of CPOs to those who have come to "relieve the watch" that are priceless.

What You Do for Your Service

"When the word 'chief' is used, people, whether officer, enlisted, or civilian, look and listen. Nowhere else is a word so diversified yet still so pure in meaning. In a nautical context the word 'chief' is given to the top three enlisted ranks: chief petty officer, senior chief petty officer, and master chief petty officer" (Stewart 2004). These are a distinct group of naval elders accorded a high level of respect and admiration due in large part to seniority in their respective ratings and within the organization. Because of their seniority they are recognized as leaders and are positioned and empowered to influence individuals, commands, and the service (Stewart 2004).

The importance and empowerment of CPOs, SCPOs, and MCPOs has never been greater than it is today. You have considerable influence through the general authorities you possess. Consider the following general responsibilities you have the authority to fulfill:

- Scheduling, coordination, and supervision of work
- Inspection of personnel, assets, and facilities
- Unit-level training and formal school planning
- Enlisted employee reviews
- Good order and discipline oversight
- Award recommendations
- Supervisory watchstanding
- Officer development

You are expected to hold a considerable amount of knowledge and experience. You are expected to know yourself; your rating; your boat, cutter, aircraft, or systems; and your people. You should know your strengths and weaknesses and play to these strengths to compensate for or correct your weaknesses. Although you may never have served on the type of platform to which you receive orders, you must quickly learn the new command and your responsibilities within it to be successful in your position. You must also be familiar with, and stay up to date on, the multitude of policies, programs, and resources available that you may need to reference or use to meet a mission requirement or to take care of a personnel issue.

You are expected to maintain your rating knowledge—as a CPO, SCPO, or MCPO, maintaining technical expertise is paramount. Considering the pace of technological change and frequent and continuous updates to personnel programs, if you don't invest time to stay educated and knowledgeable on those things, you will quickly find yourself obsolete due to the erosion of your expert power base and perceived lack of competence. Professional military knowledge is only strengthened by completing Professional Military Education (PME), Senior Enlisted Academies (SEAs), and Joint Professional Military Education (JPME) courses. And when military training obligations are fulfilled, there is an expectation of continued growth, including pursuing educational opportunities that build depth in or complement rating expertise such as college degrees and professional certifications.

Equally important is proficiency in your role as a manager. As a CPO you will often find yourself resource limited—there are never enough people, parts, tools, time, or opportunities to do the job quite the way it should be done. Given these limitations, management is the skill that enables you to attain organizational goals efficiently and effectively. The objectives, actions, and activities of any organization must be directed and managed, and although you possess some amount of leadership competence, you must also possess keen management skills. These fundamental skills include planning and organizing, decision-making, problem solving, time management, and effective communication, as discussed in depth in the *Petty Officer's Guide* (Kingsbury 2022).

Furthermore, it is vital that you understand how Chiefs (and the collective CPO mess) work to influence successful outcomes. A clear understanding of such successes must start with an understanding of what you do for the Navy and Coast Guard. There are many CPO leadership and management roles and activities that enable and ensure unit warfighting readiness and mission success. Furthermore, these competencies reinforce the strong culture(s) within the mess that underpin the success that in turn enables our Navy's diverse mission sets. CPO mess culture—the collection of CPO mess behaviors—is shaped by a foundation of strong values, beliefs, and attitudes; thus, it is important for all Navy leaders to understand them and how they shape our individual and collective mess behaviors.

Over time, a narrative has developed regarding your role and importance as the Chief. Some of that narrative is based in fact, some in fiction and lore; but in some way or another, collectively they capture the values, beliefs, and expectations of individual Chiefs and the broader CPO mess. This embodiment is important: it translates the beliefs and value systems into a set of behavioral outcomes the people in our Navy and USCG can achieve.

1-2 SELF-ASSESSMENT:
CHARACTER ATTRIBUTES OF U.S. NAVY AND COAST GUARD CHIEFS

- Consistently uphold standards over the full spectrum—uniforms, grooming, military courtesies, watchstanding, log-taking, recordkeeping, personal and professional conduct, and cleanliness
- Uphold standards for people not directly assigned to them
- Take responsibility when things go wrong, and give full credit to others when they go right
- Are transparent, keep their word, and never promise things they cannot deliver
- Master self-awareness and emotional intelligence
- Look out for their people's best interests, even when it means holding them accountable for something
- Stand up for their people, even when it means they conflict with the chain of command
- Make their feelings known in an appropriate venue when they do not agree with a decision or policy handed down
- Report problems and serious issues to the chain of command rather than covering them up to avoid trouble
- Take their people at their word unless they have a good reason to doubt it
- Do not "pass the buck" for unpopular orders. They do not say to their Sailors, "The department head wants..."
- Do not tolerate criticism of officers, CPOs, or any part of the chain of command in front of their people
- Encourage their people to have pride in their service to their country

Anchor Up!
Outline three of the best leadership and visibility practices you have seen put into action by chiefs at past commands. How can you integrate these practices into your own leadership style?

CPO Mess Guiding Principles

A variety of mantras try to capture and express the core of what Chiefs do: "Ask the Chief," "Results, Not Excuses," and "Anchor Up" are just a few. These slogans are easy to print on a T-shirt but much harder to fulfill day-to-day. This guide will work to connect these mantras with the underlying beliefs, attitudes, behaviors, competencies, and activities that sustain the favorable reputation of Navy and USCG Chiefs.

First, you belong to the broader profession of arms, so it is important that you understand and embrace the obligations that go with being a professional. As explained in *The Noncommissioned Officer and Petty Officer: Backbone of the Armed Forces*, "a profession generally has four basic elements: a specialized practical expertise, an acknowledged responsibility to society, a sense of 'corporateness,' and a 'professional ethos'" (Office of the Senior Enlisted Advisor 2013). As members of the profession of arms, you should understand the importance of professionalism and being a professional. The *Petty Officers Guide* offers more insight and a professionalism self-assessment checklist you can refer to.

Second, there is an important and distinguishing aspect of naval service and culture that makes Navy and Coast Guard Chiefs stand apart. Because each service's organization and culture developed at sea, the notion of self-sufficiency and use of one's own skill and wits are highly prized—and necessary! From this stance developed the culture of doing what needs to be done without being ordered or told. In the age of wooden ships and iron men—the "Master and Commander" Navy—the commanding officer and the entire chain of command did not wait to be told to hone their gun crews, correctly handle sails, or pay close attention to ship's maintenance. They had to self-assess, self-correct, and be self-sufficient because they were far away from their "home" support. In the naval services this translates into control by negation—you do what is right and required without waiting to be ordered. You should act and are expected to act before being ordered. Navy and USCG leaders often use control by negation, compared to Army leaders who give orders. There are good reasons for this difference, a difference that has strong bearing on what it means to serve as a Chief at sea or deployed.

"A Short Talk with Chief Petty Officers" provides some of the earliest written insight into the expectations of the Navy Chief (see appendix I) (Van Der Veer 1918). The concepts and expectations captured in this "short talk" reach across generations and services and are extremely applicable today. The expectations and roles include

- Expert knowledge of every detail that applies to your branch of the profession;
- The training and instruction of lower ratings;
- Conduct entirely above reproach, and a daily life such as to set an example in both personal as well as professional life;

[1-5] MCPON Joe R. Campa Jr., author of *Chief Petty Officer Mission, Vision, and Guiding Principles*, speaks with Sailors of the *Ticonderoga*-class guided-missile cruiser USS *Chosin* (CG 65) during a visit to Pearl Harbor. U.S. NAVY PHOTO BY MASS COMMUNICATION SPECIALIST 1ST CLASS JAMES E. FOEHL/RELEASED

- Strict compliance with the formalities of military life and requiring the same of your juniors; and
- Work done from a sense of duty while requiring thoroughness and military exactitude from your Sailors.

Review appendix I and reflect on how these words, insights, and expectations apply to you today. Simply update a few words to reflect the structure and social context of your modern CPO mess and you have a solid base of advice to apply today.

Third, unique to the CPO mess is the *Chief Petty Officer's Creed*. For those in the mess, the beliefs and expectations captured in the book are familiar and help guide their actions while providing a source of inspiration during trying times. In the Navy, new Chief selectees will attend Teaching to the Creed sessions to help translate the words to the expected outcomes. For those Chiefs in training, reading the creed will help reinforce the expectations the Navy has for them.

In 2001 a panel of fleet and force Master Chiefs updated and refined the CPO competencies, giving these qualifications for CPOs:

enlisted members, in pay-grades E-7 through E-9, who lead and manage Sailors. . . . They are responsible for, have the authority to accomplish, and are held accountable for leading Sailors and applying their skills to tasks that enable mission accomplishment for the U.S. Navy; developing enlisted Sailors and junior officers; communicating the core values, standards, and information of our Navy that empower Sailors to be successful in all they attempt; and supporting with loyalty the endeavors of the chain-of-command they serve and those of fellow Chief Petty Officers with whom they serve. (Herdt 2001)

Finally, you are also guided by (and, in the Navy, evaluated on) the attributes captured in the CPO mission, vision, and guiding principles (CPO MVGP) first drafted in 2007 (Campa 2016). Campa explained, "We developed the CPO MVGP shortly after I became MCPON. It goes to the heart of the services a chief should always provide no matter what the title." The CPO MVGP was revised by MCPON James Honea in 2023 (Honea 2023)

1-3 THE FOULED ANCHOR

The fouled anchor is the emblem of the rate of Chief Petty Officer of the United States Navy. The fouled anchor has long been the symbol of the CPO. In terms of the Chief, the fouled anchor symbolizes the trials and tribulations every CPO must endure on a daily basis. Attached to the anchor is a length of chain and the letters U.S.N. To the novice, the anchor, chain and letters only identify a CPO of the United States Navy, but to a Chief, these have a more noble and glorious meaning. The U stands for Unity, which reminds us of cooperation, maintaining harmony, and continuity of purpose and action. The S stands for Service, which reminds us of service to our God, our fellow man, and our Navy. The N stands for Navigation, which reminds us to keep ourselves on a true course so that we may walk upright before God and man in our transactions with all mankind, but especially with our fellow Chiefs. The Chain is symbolic of flexibility and reminds us of the chain of life that we forge day by day, link by link, and may it be forged with Honor, Morality, and Virtue. The Anchor is emblematic of the hope and glory of the fulfillment of all God's promises to our souls. The golden or precious Anchor by which we must be kept steadfast in faith and encouraged to abide in our proper station amidst the storm of temptation, affliction, and persecution.

—*Author Unknown*

and lays out the expectations concerning where your focus and energy should be directed and the values that should guide you.

Your mission is delivering combat-credible naval forces by providing leadership to our naval warriors and advice and counsel to senior leaders. The vision is that you are senior enlisted leaders who develop naval warriors needed to build tough, resilient, and effective combat teams to fight and win; cultivate a culture of excellence rooted in trust, respect, and transparency; continually assess themselves, their teams, and teammates; drive toward the best possible outcome while staying aligned to leadership and connected with Sailors; conduct themselves in a consistently professional, ethical, and traditional manner. And your guiding principles are as follows:

1. *Technical Mastery.* Chiefs are technical experts in their profession. Chiefs use technical knowledge and experience to produce a well-trained enlisted and officer team. Chiefs apply their knowledge, skills, and abilities to meet any mission.
2. *Institutional Expertise.* Chiefs understand how their unit mission and the Naval mission support the National Military Strategy. Chiefs recognize and engage at the point of friction to ensure mission success.
3. *Professionalism.* Chiefs understand and promote the attributes and behaviors that define the profession of arms. Chiefs' conduct is in direct alignment with the Navy core values. Chiefs actively teach, uphold, and enforce standards. Chiefs measure themselves by the success of their Sailors and are the role model of good order and discipline.
4. *Integrity.* Chiefs abide by an uncompromising code of integrity, take full responsibility for their actions, and keep their word. Chiefs set a positive tone, unify the mess, and build trust within the command to create esprit de corps.
5. *Accountability.* Chiefs are mission focused. Chiefs clearly define the problem and are accountable for the outcomes. Chiefs continuously assess with an unbiased, learning mindset and provide solutions that are well founded, thought out, and thoroughly considered. Chiefs provide forceful backup and take prompt action to learn from mistakes. Chiefs know what right looks like and are their own toughest critics. Chiefs hold themselves and their peers accountable.
6. *Deck-Plate Leadership.* You are a visible leader who sets the tone. You will know the mission, know your people, and develop them beyond their expectations as a team and as individuals.

7. *Team Effectiveness*. Chiefs are proactive leaders who are invested in all Sailors. Chiefs understand the power of inclusion to promote connectedness, which expands competency and strengthens character. Chiefs cultivate seasoned teams who anticipate problems, overcome challenges, and deliver best outcomes.

It is easy to see the similarities in expectations captured in the guiding documents, but it is harder to determine how well you are fulfilling them. This guide will help you achieve that goal. Take time now to read the CPO mission, vision, and guiding principles. Which principles are you strong at and why? Which are your weakest and why? What can you do to better execute these guiding principles?

Anchor Up!
The CPO Creed emphasizes duties and responsibilities that CPOs fulfill that are not outlined in writing. What are three examples of responsibilities you fulfill or should be fulfilling that are not outlined in organizational directives?

Translating values and belief sets and the accompanying verbalization about them may appear easy, but if intent is misunderstood, misaligned behavior can occur. Furthermore, as a person wishing to be a more effective chief, you must strive to possess many other activities and skill sets, such as setting lofty goals; using your experience, creativity, and CPO mess network to ensure organizational learning and problem solving occur; and using keen analytical skills to conduct rigorous self-assessment. To be effective in achieving organizational goals, you must have and continue to develop keen management skills and a working knowledge of how to use your growing power bases and influence in a variety of new positions. This book offers much more guidance on your relationships and role within the Chief's mess in the next chapter, "Leading and Following in the CPO Mess."

Just as your service's warfighting systems and platforms have evolved, its people and CPO mess have as well. The shift to an all-volunteer force, along with more technically designed and oriented systems as well as policies, education, and resources implemented during the 1970s and 1980s, all have shaped a more professional, educated, informed, and capable enlisted force and CPO mess. As the Navy has evolved, it has shaped and evolved the CPO mess. And as the CPO mess evolves, it continues to shape the effectiveness and capability of our Navy.

To effectively lead up, down, and across in growing positions of influence, you must maintain and build upon your communication and time management skills. More importantly, you will need to maintain the credibility you have earned through your demonstrated leadership and management skill to date. This guide will offer insight and advice on how to best be successful using increased power and influence, and how to develop and use increasingly complex management and communication skills to achieve warfighting readiness and mission success in a variety of new positions and roles. Combined with what you learn during your service's initiation process and through the experiences you have had to date, the insights in this "short talk" should give you a strong sense of the expectations your service and your peers have of you.

Two

Leading and Following in the CPO Mess

> You have not merely been promoted one pay grade—you have joined an exclusive fraternity, and as in all fraternities, you have a responsibility to your brothers, even as they have a responsibility to you.
>
> —*CPO Creed*

Aboard a ship or cutter, the mess is the Chief's home. Underway, nothing is more valued than the opportunity to enjoy a delicious meal and a warm, dry place to sleep, relax, or just hang out. Indeed, for centuries, groups of mariners have joined together, either voluntarily or by watch assignment, in ad hoc dining rooms. These ship's messes—the word derives from the Latin "mensa," meaning table—long precede the present cafeteria-style food service found on most ships today.

On one level, the CPO mess is a physical space. In a submarine or on board a small vessel, it may be as humble as one small table with a few bench seats in a corner compartment adjacent to CPO berthing, or it may be as impressive as the spacious, well-equipped dining area and grandly decorated lounge facilities on a CVN. It may be as unorthodox, humble, and mobile as a tent in a Seabee battalion deployment site or as nondescript as a room in the training command ashore. It's home, nonetheless.

Most seasoned veterans of the mess understand that membership in the chief's mess comes with obligations that are not subject to personal interest but to the CPO community itself. Today's Chief's mess exists to provide you and your peers a venue to improve cohesion and to provide and receive training in "chiefing." It also provides you with a visual reminder of the distinct and unique nature of your community and serves as a place for you and your peers to discuss common problems and seek solutions from the collective wisdom of the entire group. In this chapter we discuss how you can best integrate into and contribute to whatever CPO mess you find yourself in.

Welcome to the Mess! Tested, Tried, and Accepted

In many organizations the process for selecting leaders is based on tradition and the provisions within a legal document or organizational policy. Your journey and advancement to Chief, Senior Chief, and Master Chief started at boot camp. You were selected for advancement to new pay grades not only due to your achievements using management skills and influence in prior leadership positions but also because of your potential to lead in the next pay grade. Over your career you were vetted by Chiefs—they recognized your potential, provided you with assignments to leadership and management positions, shaped your evaluations and rankings, and ultimately "approved" your selection at a board composed primarily of Master and Senior Chief Petty Officers. Over these years you have been tested and tried, and your service has authorized your advancement.

Your official integration into the CPO mess starts with your selection as a CPO. Your initiation (Chiefs call to initiation, or CCTI in the U.S. Coast Guard) process provides the final instruction and evaluation needed for you to successfully perform as a CPO. During your time as a petty officer first or second class, you may have been encouraged to engage with your CPO mess, give and receive formal training, conduct physical training events, and participate in community service events. Participation in these events should have offered you a sense of the role the CPO mess plays in command effectiveness and to help build your knowledge of Navy programs, policies, heritage and tradition, and leadership fundamentals. It is important that, now that you have been selected as a CPO, you (and your CPO mess) understand the goals of initiation/CCTI and acceptance into the CPO mess. Although your guide won't and can't offer you details in every aspect of your unit's initiation process, it can pull the curtain back a little bit to help you understand what this process is about.

Activities such as your initiation play a rite-of-passage role, marking your progress from one status to another. Rites of passage, often ceremonies surrounding events such as other milestones, demonstrate how the social hierarchies, values, and beliefs are important in specific cultures. Although it may not appear this way, your CPO initiation is a professional training and socialization process in which you will effectively be socialized into the CPO mess network.

Fundamentally, the process is designed to

- Introduce you to the values, beliefs, and expectations you must have to contribute effectively to, and succeed within, the CPO mess and help you gain an appreciation of the CPO mess legacy and your role to protect it;
- Test your ability to work with and contribute to a diverse team to achieve goals while under stress and time constraints;
- Evaluate and test a variety of essential leadership attributes including reliability, loyalty, confidence, humility, resiliency, and physical fitness;
- Eliminate the apprehension you may have regarding the CPO mess so you can effectively contribute to it once your mess accepts you; and
- Provide you with coaching and feedback when deficiencies are discovered.

Through the completion of CPO mess-supervised and -executed formal training sessions, the challenges of informal training and of team building, the charge books, and the personnel qualification standards (PQS), your mess will work to achieve these training objectives. *A Tradition of Change* (Leuci 2015) summarizes the history and evolution of the process of accepting new Chiefs into the CPO mess; it is an excellent resource for both Navy and Coast Guard Chiefs for understanding the evolution of the initiation process and what it is designed to achieve. I recommend that you read it.

2-1 INSIGHTS ON TRAINING YOUR RELIEF

One of the most profound of all experiences serving as a Navy Chief came from the opportunity to train my successors. It was a journey that not only contributed to shaping the future of the deck-plate leadership community but also left an indelible mark on my own professional and personal growth. A few thoughts on why proactively and positively training our reliefs is an investment well worth the time and focus:

1. *Passing the Torch with Purpose*: Training someone to take over your responsibilities is more than a transition; it's a legacy. The experience is all about passing on knowledge, values, and the nuances of excellence that define the role of a deck-plate leader. The satisfaction of seeing "Chiefs in training" thrive and carry forward the dedication to Navy core values and professionalism is unmatched.
2. *A Mirror to Our Professional Journey*: Teaching others allows fellow Chiefs to reflect on their own journey, appreciate how much we've all accomplished, and recognize the breadth of expertise gained through service. Engaging with other CPO mess teams provides for a moment of pride and introspection and reminds us of our growth and the hurdles we've overcome.
3. *Cultivating Leadership Skills*: I believe that the act of training someone is a leadership role in itself. It hones our abilities to guide, inspire, and motivate. The challenges and successes in this process are invaluable lessons in leadership and communication.
4. *Strengthening Team Dynamics*: When we invest in preparing our reliefs, we're not just facilitating a smooth transition; we're strengthening the fabric of our teams. It fosters an environment of learning, support, and collective growth, making our teams more adaptive.
5. *The Gift of Continuous Learning*: The process is a two-way street. In training our successors, we often find ourselves learning anew. Whether it's a fresh perspective, a novel approach, or simply the reinforcement of gained knowledge, the experience becomes a catalyst for continuous personal and professional development.

—CMC Glenn Mallo, USN (Ret.)

One of the most important things to understand is that hazing during initiation/CCTI is unacceptable. Unlike what you've probably heard or thought, the MCPON and MCPOCG put forth specific guidance each year that specifically prohibits any form of hazing or situations that would put you in any physical danger. Over time, and with guidance from the office of the MCPON, a more mature and focused process has developed. Today, as in the past, activities of accepting new Chiefs include congratulating, welcoming, inspiring, improving, instilling trust, and motivating the CPO selectee while teaching leadership, building esprit de corps, promoting unity, building teamwork—and having some fun in the process.

Your command senior enlisted leader will ensure you are guided through your season. In addition to the technical aspects of your rating and your general Navy responsibilities, Chiefs will task and talk to you about leadership, accountability, support of the chain of command, and other professional subject matter, often using personal experiences to illustrate how something should (or should not) be done. You can expect to be given tasks to prepare and present a variety of in-person training sessions and complete a command issued PQS. Some of these are designed to be formal and others are designed to be fun, team-building events. Through your charge book, training, and social activities of the season, experienced CPOs will offer you advice, inspiration, and guidance to help you step off strong in your new role. These are also vehicles used to introduce you to members of the mess who will be your new peers. Regardless of the task given, don't take anything lightly, and definitely don't be late!

Early in the process you will complete the *Teaching to the Creed* modules. Upon completion of this block of instruction, you will have a clearer understanding of the necessity of leadership in a dynamic environment, understand your role in advocacy, learn the traditions of Chief Petty Officer leadership, and reflect on the importance of trust behaviors and their relationship to the CPO Creed. You will be equipped with knowledge and skills necessary to apply yourself confidently as a new Chief and adapt to the diverse environments at different command levels.

One of the first tasks you will be assigned as a CPO selectee is to build your CPO charge book. The charge book is steeped in tradition evolving from what were known as "memory books." As explained in *Ask the Chief*:

These books were a combination journal, scrapbook, and diary of their Navy experiences to take home and share with family. During WWII, CPO hopefuls carried a more formal logbook, recording the wisdom and advice collected from chiefs in preparation for advancement into the Chiefs' Mess. For many years after the war, the contents of a charge book were seldom worth preserving. . . . Today's charge books are made with such creativity and skill that many qualify as a new genre of folk art and instantly acquire status as family heirlooms. (Leahy 2004, 40)

Your charge book represents and signifies your pride in Navy service, entrance into the CPO mess, and your patriotism. Today's reinvigorated charge books tap the roots of early traditions of pride in accomplishment and knowledge, providing yet another example of a tradition evolving in strength from the old practice.

You will be tasked with guidance on how to organize and present the charge book to every CPO in the mess and with soliciting their wisdom and guidance. You will use your charge book to collect notes and words of wisdom as a future reference guide, but you should understand that the charge book is one of the key tactics used to help introduce new Chiefs into the CPO mess. The charge and signature are not the goal; sitting down with each Chief in your mess and taking time to learn about their personal and professional experiences while sharing yours is! Also, focus on meeting the Chiefs in *your unit's* mess first before venturing out to secure charges from Chiefs outside your command or that prized entry from your fleet or force Master Chief. You want to focus on building relationships with the Chiefs you will live and work with day to day. Chief-selects should prioritize this activity, and members of the mess should as well. By the time your season is complete and you are at final night, all the charges in your book should have been signed.

You will also be assigned a sponsor who is your "go-to" person to help you navigate the challenges of the process and to answer questions when you do not understand the intent behind training activities, to help you piece together the lessons each activity is trying to teach, and to help you keep a positive attitude when times get tough. Your sponsor is chosen not only due

[2-1] CPO selectees pose for a photo with their charge book vessels. U.S. NAVY PHOTO BY MC1 SARAH VILLEGAS

to seniority and experience but also by how their strengths complement you as a selectee. Consider your sponsor as your guide for the "Chief season" to aid in the transition from Chief-select to Chief. They also continue to mentor you for your first year in the mess with the purpose of offering an outlet for guidance from someone with different career experience outside of the select's chain of command.

Your season will conclude with a final night and pinning ceremony. The procedures for these are different throughout the Navy and Coast Guard, but all of them have commonalities. For many years CPO initiations and final nights were rowdy and boisterous—but closely guarded—private events. Only CPOs participated, and even the CO required a personal invitation. For the selectee, exactly what lay ahead was a closely held secret. Selectees looked forward to the initiation with a mixture of genuine anticipation, anxiety, and dread, all the while casually maintaining a feigned bring-it-on attitude. Several variations of colorful, creative, and scripted pageants were produced that provided a memorable entry into the mess.

Your initiation process is important because it will help you understand and reinforce your obligation to your command, your CPO mess, and your

Sailors in the demanding and unforgiving operating environment of naval warfare. But this process is not just about training and welcoming new Chiefs into your mess. The season is also a time for Chiefs of any experience level to reflect on their roles in ensuring that the CPO mess remains strong and that they are fulfilling their duties and living up to the high expectations and exacting standards of Navy and Coast Guard Chiefs. In the following sections we will explore the role of the CPO mess you are now a part of or have been a part of and how to effectively continue to thrive in and contribute to it.

The Role and Influence of the CPO Mess

The challenge of running an effective and efficient Navy or Coast Guard unit or command can be paralleled to conducting an orchestra or producing a play, a dynamic environment consisting of many leadership interactions working synergistically to consistently produce not just success but excellence. The day-to-day routine of running your command is complex. If one piece of the command is not doing its part, other pieces are affected, synergy is lost, and your command does not perform to its potential.

Your CPO mess is a part of the team, but it is not a stand-alone entity. It fits into your unit's structure and should work to enhance productivity, climate, and communication. It *should not* work against the command's goals. Your CPO mess must be developed, leveraged, and given the support required to ensure your command leaders can effectively leverage it toward achieving command excellence. In *Charting the Course to Command Excellence* (Department of the Navy 1989, 10), an important section discusses the characteristics of superior CPO messes and explains that "in superior commands, the chiefs quarters function as a tight-knit team. The chiefs coordinate well, seek inputs from each other, help with personal problems, identify with the command's philosophy and goals, and treat each other with professional respect."

The relationships among your fellow Chiefs are invaluable and must not be allowed to erode or the command will struggle. Your CPO mess serves as a force multiplier, and true success is achieved when each Chief Petty Officer has ownership and claims responsibility for the condition and readiness of *all* personnel, *all* spaces, and *all* officers on board when they not only strive for vertical effectiveness but command-wide success as well. Your CPO mess network also extends outside the lifelines of your command, which only serves to increase the capability of each Chief even further.

Your CPO mess should also be leveraged as a tool to effectively manage good unit order and discipline. Your CO and wardroom should empower your mess to handle discipline and performance issues with the tools of discipline readily available to you. Although there should be clearly defined and communicated offenses that should go directly to nonjudicial punishment (NJP), many can and should be handled by your mess using tools such as coaching and feedback, praise, performance counseling, extra military instruction (EMI), removal of privileges, or disciplinary review board (DRB).

Anchor Up!

How well does your mess work together to manage command-wide requirements and hold each other accountable to the highest standards of warfighting readiness and the expectations captured in the mission, vision, and guiding principles (MVGP)?

An aligned CPO mess also brings consistency to commands. As you know, senior enlisted tours are longer than those of officers, but this is what brings the leadership continuity that your command needs to succeed. Additionally, you will serve as the lynchpin between officer and enlisted and are in the best position to translate policy to their Sailors while bringing forth issues (and solutions) arising from those policies. You are expected and encouraged to harness your command-wide influence in the best interest of your division, department, and command. The horizontal influence and impact of your mess should be manifested in the consistent application of standards across all departments in your command and, to some extent, interdepartmental alignment, support, and integration. Furthermore, it's important not to confuse the role and influence of the broader CPO mess with the roles and responsibilities of each individual Chief. Rather, one should seek to understand how the two complement each other.

Your CPO mess also possesses unique power assigned to it via the variety of deliberative forums such as ranking and award boards and DRBs. Your mess naturally contains a diverse range of backgrounds and experiences that, when positively unleashed in open forums like these, can strengthen your command's policies, programs, and warfighting readiness and capability.

Foundations for Successful Deliberation

As a Chief you will typically spend most of your time leading down, but your energy within the *collective* CPO mess serves to strengthen its networking power, which is then harnessed to help manage larger command evolutions and projects, align standards of good order and discipline, act as a body of self-accountability, and provide insight and perspective via policy working groups and boards. The attributes of teamwork, accountability, and respect underlie a strong mess and must be developed and maintained. And to maintain the strength of your CPO mess network, you and your peers must develop and nurture productive relationships within your mess.

The CPO mess MVGPs sets the expectation that you should demonstrate *loyalty* and engage in *active communication*. Furthermore, a strong CPO mess invests not only in building a strong network but in nurturing the *relationships* that are crucial to information exchange. Developing networks is important, but nurturing the relationships is vital. You and your peers must commit time daily toward relationship-building, on- and off-duty. The time spent having discussions over a meal or cup of coffee in the mess is extremely invaluable, and the discussions provide the opportunity for you to learn about leadership and influence tactics, your command, broader Navy policy insights and implications, and—most importantly—about your fellow chiefs. In your mess you will share laughter, disappointment, and personal heartache; as a result, the trust among you and your peers will be deepened. It's also where "rudder" is given and received when you or one of your peer's focus, attitude, or performance is not up to par.

Without a baseline amount of *trust, humility,* and *loyalty*, those important interactions may not happen, or if they do, they will not yield the depth of candor required to be fully effective. This also weakens the overall effectiveness of your CPO mess. The members of your mess should strive to establish and maintain high levels of trust among yourselves. Although there is a certain amount of trust associated with being a Chief, trust is further strengthened by each Chief demonstrating competence, character, and loyalty as they conduct their day-to-day business. Weakness in or an absence of any of these quickly becomes apparent to members of the mess and impacts credibility and trust.

Another necessary attribute of a strong mess is a *sense of loyalty* of members of your mess to each other. Loyalty is important to demonstrate to your Sailors and leadership, but it is equally important to demonstrate to the members of your mess. Your loyalty manifests itself in your ability to have hard discussions about the effectiveness of your mess or individual chief and about areas that require improvement. It's always easy to work with those you get along with (although too much agreement can introduce its own harmful dynamics), but it is more important to handle relationships with those we don't get along with quite so well. You should expect that your fellow Chiefs won't always like each other or agree, but they know they must be professional and positive and keep their working relationships constructive. As frustrating as it can be, they know to keep focused on the task at hand rather than let personality differences or conflicts interfere with mission readiness—they don't let these issues fester. Through one-on-one or group discussions, your CPO mess should work to adjust poor peer attitudes and behaviors that can infect and erode the connection power base of your mess. It's crucial that you and your peers are willing and able to proactively hold each other accountable for personal and professional excellence. In this way you reinforce the strength of the collective CPO mess and ensure its value to the command is maintained.

Like other deliberative bodies, the candid discussions required to get to "right" can and should be contentious. Deliberations that too easily lead to agreement should raise your eyebrow and invite a questioning attitude to consider whether your mess or working group has fallen into the trap of groupthink. These discussions and debates can easily become emotional. Because Chiefs have traditionally embraced the role of Sailor advocacy and have often personally experienced the effects of poorly thought-out policy, they come to the table prepared to ensure these negative outcomes are avoided. However, if certain values are lacking within your CPO mess, these discussions can result in lingering frustration or fractures within your mess. Your CPO mess also requires—and you should expect—strong leadership from your command senior enlisted leader (CSEL) and other "senior" Chiefs to inspire cooperation, spur controversy and healthy debate, and serve as a moderating force.

Anchor Up!
How do you communicate your opinion if it differs from what is being discussed in a CPO mess meeting? What is meant by "Acceptance is not agreement"?

The best CPO messes take time away from work to improve upon and strengthen their networks and relationships. You have an obligation to your peers to attend hail and farewells, promotions, and retirements not because the CSEL tells you to but because it is the right thing to do, it comes with being a member of the CPO mess, it demonstrates solidarity, and it strengthens your network.

Your CPO mess is a place where military protocol can be relaxed. Although you are expected to say what's on your mind—there is immense value in free and open conversation about all things work and social—this doesn't translate into "anything goes." It's very important to ensure that the Navy core values you embrace are not in any way compromised behind the

SELF-ASSESSMENT:
"LEADING ACROSS" ATTRIBUTES OF CHIEF PETTY OFFICERS

- Have a sense of ownership about the entire ship, squadron, platoon, submarine, or base.
- Assist other Chiefs in maintaining the guidance they have assigned to Sailors
- Be considered a team player by other members in the mess.
- Take full advantage of opportunities to learn from other chiefs in the mess.
- Be able to be counted on to support other Chiefs' efforts, particularly in the performance of their assigned duties.
- Work with other chiefs to demonstrate a united front to the crew; keep criticisms and disagreements inside the mess.

closed doors of your CPO mess by any false perception of personal privilege or some reckless interpretation of the freedom from normal protocol. Taken to its extreme, the concept of "What's Said in Here, Stays in Here" could yield counterproductive or unethical behavior. Although the connection power of your CPO mess can serve as a unit force multiplier, it does have boundaries. Some perceive that the CPO mess provides access to a "black market" of resources and mafia-like behaviors, but that misrepresents how the CPO mess should use its connection power.

Firsts among Equals

A unique paradox that exists within the CPO mess is the existence of two coexisting organizational constructs. On one hand, there is a hierarchical structure. There are Master Chiefs, Senior Chiefs, and Chiefs. Prior to the establishment of these rank and pay-grade differences, the seniority construct in the mess would have been based on time in service or time in pay grade. It's easy to envision a handful of "crusty" Chiefs "running herd" over the collective body of Chiefs, providing the institutional and life experience required to keep the CPO mess focused, productive, and credible.

Coexisting with this hierarchical structure is an egalitarian construct and philosophy. This egalitarian structure supports and enables the connection power base that the CPO mess brings to a command—a recognition that regardless of pay grade, each Chief brings unique and diverse experiences, backgrounds, and potential resource access that strengthen their connection power base. As we've discussed, one of the proudest moments in any enlisted Sailor's life is when he or she become a Chief Petty Officer. The newly advanced Chief may have as little as six years of service, or as many as nineteen. The new Chief may be entering a mess—without knocking!—filled with many experienced Chiefs, Senior and Master Chiefs; but on every level, even the newest CPO is accepted as an equal. Your CPO mess is much like a family with a keen sense of equality among its members. No one member is more important than the next. Members have a healthy respect for and sensitivity to the needs of other members. The success of one is celebrated by all. Forgiveness for errors and omissions is a given, and genuine concern for the well-being of others is translated into actions when there is a need.

Anchor Up!
Your mess is made up of many personality types. Some are involved in the details of things while others tend to "not sweat the small stuff." How well do you know these personalities, and how each is serving as either a force multiplier or a liability to the broader efforts of the CPO mess? How can you help your peers to more effectively balance the spectrum of personalities toward warfighting readiness?

It's important to know your peers to a significant degree to build the trust required to develop and maintain a solid CPO mess network, but these two leadership structures must be balanced. If your mess leans toward the hierarchical structure too much, it risks stifling open communication, camaraderie, and the free flow of ideas. Conversely, if your mess "levels out" too much and dismisses pay-grade differences, it risks allowing the good order and discipline within your mess to erode. The best messes find the "sweet spot" between the two. They know not to de-emphasize or dismiss pay-grade differences within the mess or only address each other as "brother" and "sister" or solely on a first name basis.

You should understand and accept that accountability from Master Chief to Senior Chief, Senior Chief to Chief, or Chief to Chief must occur to ensure that good order and discipline exists within your CPO mess. You should be cautious to never become too familiar or hesitant to confront infractions made by your peers. The misperception that "we're all the same behind the doors of the CPO mess" could distort the reality that there *is* a military structure in the mess, and it needs to be respected and used to hold each other accountable. The additional stars on the anchors of Senior Chiefs and Master Chiefs represent the increased responsibility, authority, and accountability earned due to their demonstrated management and leadership competence. It's an earned privilege to be addressed as "Chief," "Senior," or "Master Chief," and you should embrace those titles, the respect they infer, and the limited time you have on active duty to use the power and influence they provide you while enjoying the prestige that accompanies them.

As one of my former command Master Chiefs explained to our mess, "Master Chiefs may call me Bob; Senior Chiefs and Chiefs may call me

[2-2] Coffee break in the CPO mess, 18 January 1938. Note the cold-storage locker in the background. NAVAL HISTORY AND HERITAGE COMMAND

Master Chief." Many in the mess took his message as an affront to their egalitarian structure, but he was simply trying to reemphasize the hierarchical structure that must exist in the mess to ensure that CPO mess self-accountability and good order and discipline remained intact.

Finally, as a member of the mess you will have significant input to processes and recommendations. In some cases, you will have the opportunity to cast a vote on a motion or for a ranking or award recommendation. You are expected to strongly bring your insights, experience, and advocacy to those situations and be able to substantiate them to the strongest degree you can. However, you must realize and accept there will be times when your individual or collective CPO mess recommendation or vote is trumped by your senior enlisted leader. You may have heard that the CMC gets "51 percent of the vote." When a decision does not go your way, you must understand that your input was just that, an input, and there are typically many other inputs into the decision-making process. That 51 percent given to your CSEL represents their experience, access to information, and access to other perspectives regarding the decision that you usually don't have. It also represents the accountability they have for their recommendation and input to the final decision, and it gives them the right to make the best decision on behalf of the command.

In these instances, I've always found it to be a good idea to take time to explain the reason they went with an input that ran counter to the collective CPO mess input. This conversation serves to both help educate the mess on the bigger factors in the decision but also helps mitigate any sense of mystery or beliefs about hidden agendas that are likely to arise. At the end of the day, part of your growth is learning that you won't always get what you want in the mess, your command, or life; it's all about compromise, fully understanding the decision, and then accepting it and communicating it as your own.

CPO Mess Accountability

The importance of self-accountability has been mentioned several times in your guide because it's such an important function of your CPO mess. Strong CPO messes utilize "watch-team backup" to hold themselves accountable to standards and expectations. For example, when selected and accepted into the CPO mess, you must understand that this is now your new peer group. Although you are encouraged to spend time with your people, your selection as a Chief now introduces you to a new category of fraternization.

Your peers in the mess typically are (and should be) "in the know" regarding those peers most at risk for professional or personal failure. Because your mess serves as a self-correcting body for those who fail to demonstrate competence and character, it's important for your mess to reflect on its capabilities of fulfilling this function of performance feedback. If a Chief is falling short in divisional standards or in the training of their Sailors, a fellow Chief should be the first to engage to make the deficient Chief aware of those shortfalls and provide advice and guidance on how to improve. In effective messes, the larger community of Chiefs should easily be able to overcome the weaknesses of one or two. Contrary to the impression some periodicals might give, CPO misbehavior accounts for less than 0.005 percent of the Navy-wide CPO population. However, the negative effects on CPO mess and Navy credibility—even for this small percentage—are too severe to not take this role seriously.

Your CPO mess should have mechanisms of self-accountability to ensure all members are setting a solid tone and example for the crew. Your collective mess should easily be able to overcome your weakest chief(s). Your mess must be able to engage those struggling peers and get them back on course and not fail to meet this obligation—the credibility and reputation of the CPO mess erodes when this is not done. Chiefs must have the courage and tactics to handle these situations; unfortunately, this does not happen consistently across the Navy and Coast Guard.

When you or a peer fails to demonstrate the competence and character required to remain effective, your command leaders, officer and enlisted, have a plethora of tools at their disposal to improve the faltering performance. For those CSELs reading this, you will weigh in heavily on these situations and you must have the determination to use them and advise on their impacts. Although your commanding officer is ultimately responsible for the performance of your command, horizontal alignment is the leadership challenge of your executive officer and SEL. Collaboratively, the XO and SEL can help enable mission readiness by overseeing the effective functioning of the wardroom and CPO mess, respectively. The culture and climate of your unit's CPO mess is greatly shaped by the leadership of the CO and SEL. In most cases, strong command leadership, visible support, and CPO mess self-accountability can easily mitigate most of the behavioral challenges experienced.

Anchor Up!
What is meant by, "What is said in the mess, seen in the mess, and heard in the mess . . . stays in the mess"? How does loyalty factor into this saying?

The "ownership" of CPO accountability depends on the vector of influence you are trying to affect. In the vertical direction of influence, the responsibility more directly falls onto departmental leadership, primarily the department head and leading Chief Petty Officer (LCPO). And although the CSEL can engage to correct deficiencies, they must ensure that they do not do so in a way that subverts the authority of the department head. There are many tactics CSELs can use to address these issues, but they should be discussed and understood by the wardroom and CPO mess. On the other hand, the CSEL and other more senior CPOs have strong influence on the CPO mess effectiveness and conduct in the horizontal vector.

Rather than go it alone, CSELs should strive to build a strong core team of senior CPOs who can work together to promote the climate, communication, and camaraderie that determine CPO mess effectiveness. Ultimately, the CSEL and other senior members of the mess must develop tactics and techniques to ensure that CPO mess discipline is in place and effective. They must be leaders who encourage mess collaboration and self-accountability—they set the tone for the mess. They should be firm but fair and demand self-accountability and discipline while remaining approachable to their chiefs.

> *Anchor Up!*
> Does your mess foster an "if you see something, say something" attitude? Furthermore, is your mess actively addressing challenges and attempting to overcome them or is it more likely that you complain about them?

Command and Immediate Superior in Command Relationships

Earlier in the chapter I discussed the relationships between mess members in a unit. This concept extends beyond the command for the unit's SEL and their relationship with their immediate superior in command (ISIC) Command Master Chief (CMC) or a unit-level chief and their relationship with a chief on a staff ashore. The ISIC is the officer to whom the commander, CO, or Officer in Charge (OIC) reports—basically the next officer up the chain of command.

Although the unit CMC works for their CO, who gives them priorities and direction and signs their evaluations and recommendation letters, the ISIC CMC is a source of guidance, advice, and direction and has influence on recommendations for career opportunities and nominative positions of the subordinate CMC. And though the unit CMC doesn't work for the ISIC CMC, they should understand the nature of and how to take advantage of the supported–supporting relationship that exists between them. In this relationship, the ISIC should work to ensure information flow up and down the chain and make their CMC team aware of resources and policies that serve the interest of the Sailors under their area of responsibility. The unit CMC works to keep the ISIC CMC aware of challenges to the unit that require external support and can reinforce requests and needs that the unit CO is passing to their ISIC or staff. Furthermore, each should understand and discuss how their respective CO and commander think about their roles and how they expect to benefit from a productive ISIC to unit CMC relationship. For those CMCs assigned to a flag or general officer staff, there are several best practices you should consider to develop a healthy subordinate–ISIC relationship.

First, review chapter 10 of Navy Regulations, *Precedence, Authority, and Command* (Department of the Navy 1990) and the Navy's and your command's *Standard Organization and Regulations Manual* (SORM) (Department of the Navy 2012) to ensure you understand the roles and authorities of your CO or commander and their staff. This goes beyond just knowing the Sailor aspect of things. Does your commander have operational, tactical, or administrative control, and how do the units assigned fall into that control? Can your commander assign or attach forces? Has a support command authority relationship been established by your commander between subordinate commanders when one organization should aid, protect, complement, or sustain another force? With this knowledge you will be in a better position to understand how the units below you are being used, where you should pulse to check for effectiveness or the level of resource support, and how the CO and CMC of the unit may be thinking and prioritizing things.

Next, set up a one-on-one meeting when you and the newly reported unit CMC will discuss the nature of the relationship, expected communication, and performance expectations. These expectations flow both ways. It is also recommended that you set up meetings and introductions with your commander and the unit CO to discuss and align expectations. From there you should schedule periodic touchpoint calls or meetings to check in on how the unit CMC is doing and to lend an ear or offer guidance and advice as needed. As an ISIC CMC, you should be a source of coaching and performance feedback for your unit CMCs. And make sure to check in with the unit COs from time to time to see where you can be of assistance.

Finally, you should develop a communication plan for your drumbeat and vehicles of communication. Take time to consider how to use all available channels of communication including emails, newsletters, and in-person meetings. Think about what you want to communicate, why you want to communicate it, how often it should be communicated, and how to get the information out. Seek feedback from your CMC team on what they need for information flow. You should also think about holding educational and informational meetings to keep the team informed of policy and resource changes, to solicit feedback on those, to help build competency in your CMC team, and to prepare them to succeed as your relief.

Chief Petty Officer Associations

Each command usually has a private organization separate and distinct from the CPO mess, which provides for the welfare and recreation of its members, family members, and, in some cases, their crew. In the case of the Coast Guard, there is a national Chief Petty Officers' Association (CPOA), which assists members and dependents in urgent need of assistance, assists in recruiting for the Coast Guard, engages in community affairs, and keeps its members informed of Coast Guard matters. The Navy Memorial's Delbert D. Black National Chief's Mess tells the unique story and important role of the Navy CPO and provides an opportunity for active duty and retired Chiefs around the Navy to stay connected. The National Chief's Mess was dedicated in September 2017 in memory of Delbert D. Black, the first MCPON.

There is also the Navy's Chief Petty Officer Scholarship Program. In November 1994, the USS *Chief* (MCM-14) was commissioned in honor of the dedicated service of the Chief Petty Officers of the U.S. Navy. The planning and all subsequent activities leading up to the commissioning were the work of a small group of Chief Petty Officers who took the initiative to put out "The CALL" across the nation for Chiefs to donate just $5 in honor of the ship. The response was so overwhelming that not only was the cost of the commissioning ceremony covered but there were enough leftover funds to bring the scholarship fund to fruition. In 1998, with MCPON Bob Walker's and MCPON Duane Bushey's guidance, the charter of the Chief Petty Officer Scholarship Fund (CPOSF) was signed, and four $500 scholarships were awarded that year.

The CPOSF is 100 percent supported by charitable donations, volunteers, and fundraising and in twenty-five years has awarded over $1.7 million in scholarships to 902 spouses and children of U.S. Navy Chiefs, Senior Chiefs, and Master Chiefs across the nation and overseas. Specific events hosted as fundraisers and team builders include The Best of the Mess Culinary Competition, annual golf tournaments in various regions across the nation, the MCPON Walker Legacy Ride, and a variety of online and in-person coin auctions. You can learn more or donate at https://www.cposf.org/scholarship.

CPOAs can elect officers, collect fees, assess monthly dues, and spend the money any way members choose. The CPOA is defined as a category VI morale, welfare, and recreation (MWR) program. The commanding officer gives written permission for the CPOA to use base or shipboard facilities to conduct meetings. It's important to note:

- The CPOA may not operate as a business. The Navy strictly prohibits making loans of money from operating capital.
- The CPOA may raise operating capital from dues or by selling merchandise to members only. Many associations sell T-shirts, CPO challenge coins, or similar items.
- The CPOA may not receive non-appropriated funding from MWR funds.

CPOAs follow Navy financial accounting procedures. The MWR Office is normally assigned to advise and assist the CPOA in financial procedures, and the CPOA may be subject to an annual informal audit by the commanding officer when operating on a naval base or ship.

It's sometimes hard for newly selected Chiefs to remember or understand the difference between messes afloat, ashore, and CPOAs. The mess, which consists of all personnel E-7 through E-9, provides dining and berthing at sea and dining facilities ashore. The CPOA, which consists of members who pay dues, supports recreational activities such as parties, outings, and unique events like initiations and khaki balls. Your personal support funds the CPOA. If you are called on to serve as an officer of the CPO mess, perhaps even as a treasurer or caterer, you should consult and become intimately familiar with all the pertinent instructions governing their overall operation.

Finally, although participation in association-related activities is important and encouraged, your CPO mess must balance how much time it spends on "feel good" activities such as fundraising or group physical training and on those more productive and mission-critical leadership and management functions. In a resource-constrained Navy and Coast Guard, CPO messes feel pressure to meet mission readiness requirements with fewer or dwindling resources. So, although these team-building activities have a place, they must not displace your command, departmental, and divisional management and leadership activities and responsibilities. CPO messes that allow this to happen will soon see negative impacts to mission readiness and increased scrutiny and criticism.

Command leaders should take time to consider, discuss, and manage the various influencers that may be affecting their CPO mess effectiveness. For example, they should take time to examine how different personality interactions in the CPO mess impact effectiveness. As much as we would like to think that professionalism trumps human behavior, it may not be the case. Additionally, there are also other external factors that can impact CPO mess effectiveness such as command-wide rankings that can serve to yield behavior counter to what effective CPO messes strive for. It is crucial that the CSEL understands how their leadership contributes to command-wide effectiveness in the vertical and horizontal vectors of influence. Far too often we undervalue the impact unit leadership has, too easily excusing poor CPO mess performance because of organizational or process woes. Although these factors do have influence, in many cases, they can be countered by strong command leadership.

Three

Developing and Supporting the Wardroom

> That man was my Chief when I was an Ensign, and no one before or after taught me as much about ships or men as he did. You civilians don't understand. You go down to Long Beach, and you see those battleships sitting there, and you think that they float on the water, don't you? You are wrong, they are carried to sea on the backs of those Chief Petty Officers!
>
> —ADM William "Bull" Halsey

The above quote from ADM Bull Halsey is a well-known anecdote regarding the reputation of the CPO mess. There are also others that are a bit cheekier. For example, "As a division officer, my chief was a great mentor. One day I was sketching systems in my notebook and he took away my pen. He then went on to say, 'Sir, use a pencil. You don't know enough yet to use a pen!'" Although many senior officers tout the impact a great chief had on them as a junior officer, little has been written regarding the importance of a healthy wardroom–CPO mess relationship. If the two bodies operate too independently, they will miss opportunities to collaborate and reinforce each other. Although the wardroom has several written guides to help prepare them for their roles such as the *Naval Officer's Guide* (McComas 2019) and the *Division Officer's Guide* (Stavridis et al. 2017), it's helpful to offer insights on how to develop and nurture healthy relationships between the wardroom and CPO mess. Because it's been said that "a strong CPO mess can overcome a weak wardroom, but a strong wardroom cannot overcome a weak CPO mess," it's important to understand how the CPO mess and wardroom strengthen and support each other.

Expectations, Roles, and Responsibilities

U.S. naval officers have empowered, supported, and maintained high expectations for Chiefs. Many senior officers will tell you that the CPO mess has directly contributed to the success of their commands, departments, divisions, and careers. You should understand the roles of the wardroom and the characteristics that underpin wardroom success. As captured in *Charting the Course to Command Excellence*,

> the wardroom is the interface between the senior officers of the command, who make the policy, and the senior enlisted, who carry out the tasks of the command. The wardroom is responsible for developing and implementing plans that achieve the goals set by the CO and XO [executive officer]. In top commands, the department heads and division officers make sure these plans are specific, deciding who is to do what, when, and how. They gather information from their chiefs and other relevant sources, and are careful to coordinate their department's or division's activities with other work going on. (Department of the Navy 1989)

So like you, naval officers should have ample leadership and management capability and skill. Furthermore, wardrooms in the best commands are cohesive, take initiative, effectively perform detailed planning, and take responsibility for work-group performance. You should be mindful of this and work to help ensure your wardroom is fulfilling its roles and functions.

Think for a moment about what the former Chief of Naval Operations, ADM Mike Boorda, had to say on such Navy expectations during the commissioning of USS *Chief* (MCM 14) on 5 November 1994:

> The title "Chief" raises so many memories for all Sailors. Every one of us who has served for any length of time can tell you about his or her special Chief, indeed, most of us have more than one—a salty

[3-1] Group portrait of USS *Louisville* (CA 28) officers and CPOs, 1931. The ship's CO, CAPT E. J. Marquart, is in front, right center; XO CDR L. F. Thebalt is in front center. NAVAL HISTORY AND HERITAGE COMMAND

individual who took care of them, who taught them all the important things, who set the example, who cared about them and was not afraid to show it in so many ways. We officers have our special Chiefs, too: usually somewhat older than we, always wiser in the ways of the Navy than we could possibly be as we started out on our careers, ready with advice, with counsel, and with the knowhow to make it happen, to get it done, no matter how difficult. And through it all, those great Chiefs were and are also great teachers. They know, as only Chief Petty Officers can know, that getting the job done today is important, but that the task of helping a new officer in the finest sense of the term, is part of the job. It's a key part, a critical role that Chief Petty Officers have been playing for over one hundred years now. Our Navy depends upon them, and the Chiefs know that and they thrive on the challenge.

I am a lucky man for I have served as a new seaman, a petty officer, and an officer. In each phase of my career a great Chief Petty Officer appeared at just the right time, guiding me, pushing me when necessary, leading me, and when appropriate, letting me think I was leading him. There have been many Chiefs in my life, all important, many personal friends, all professionals. And I know, as every Sailor knows, that the word leadership and the title "Chief Petty Officer" go together.

You cannot say one without thinking of the other. In war and in peace, they teach, they provide technical expertise, they know how to get the job done, and they know how to make all the right things happen. They know that combat readiness is based on taking care of people, on keeping their ship requirement-ready at all times.

But all of that is just a preamble to leadership in war. No Chief, no Sailor, wants to fight in wars. We want to deter them. But when our nation calls, when the fight is no longer optional, no longer avoidable, but now is required, when "now" is the order of the day, that is when all that Chief Petty Officer leadership—honor, courage, and commitment—really pays off. For deep down, each and every Chief Petty Officer knows that we are warriors and that he or she is a leader of warriors as well. In the smoke and fury and, yes, the confusion of battle at sea, it is then that the Chief Petty Officer proves again and again that everything else was simply preparation for the moment of truth, the moment when all that work pays off. When young Sailors do what is required, they do it almost instinctively, and they look to the Chief for the example of all that is great in our Navy.

Wow . . . pause at the enormity of that charge; but ever since 1893, U.S. Navy CPOs have lived—and will continue to live—up to these expectations.

Your access to and influence over every level of the chain of command will come with significant benefits but also demanding and varied expectations. The twenty-fourth commandant of the Coast Guard, ADM Robert Papp, described these expectations well:

> We have wonderful men and women who are performing heroic deeds on a near daily basis, but they need your leadership, chief petty officer hands-on leadership, to ensure they perform their challenging maritime missions safely, professionally and effectively. . . . You are unique in that you have the ability to influence the largest number of crew members in our Service. . . . Chiefs must take a keen interest in their shipmates' well being and professional development. Senior leaders look to Chiefs to be engaged in the issues of the day and mentor both enlisted and officers. You should be proactive and approachable for the shipmates you lead. . . . So assert yourselves, grab the reins and lead.

Admiral Papp would often recall the story of a young ensign who was called into the Chief's mess where the assembled Chiefs told him that he could do better, and they wanted him to be successful. They advised him that, in pursuit of getting better, he must be comfortable enough to come to the Chief's mess and ask for guidance. They knew that if Ensign Papp was successful, their ship would be successful, and the service would be successful. "That's foundational chief petty officer leadership—reaching out to junior officers and petty officers when they are headed in the wrong direction," said Papp, adding, "Your deck plate and hangar deck leadership is vitally important, because you forge your shipmates into leaders."

The wardroom expects your CPO mess to bring deck-plate leadership, experience, good order and discipline, continuity, and execution of policy and requirements to the team. Without an engaged, effective, and fully functioning Chief's mess, your command simply will not perform to its potential, and it may even fail. In return, your Chief's mess expects to be empowered and supported by your officers. To state the philosophy of one commanding officer,

> Officers may have grand ideas, formulate strategy and think tactics. But without a Chief to carry the water for him, to take the rubber to the road, to see the tactics through to execution, everything he thinks or says or writes is so much finger-painting, so much vaporing, so much ephemera. With the chief's mess on your side, all things are possible. If they turn against you, because you can't live up to their expectations of an officer (these are, thankfully, much less stringent than their expectations for themselves), you will fail. It is exactly that simple.

Those observations ring true today. Like all effective relationships, communication and trust are paramount. Your officers should be embracing opportunities to engage with your mess in meaningful ways and should reflect on how well they empower and support it. Questions should include the following:

- Do the tools of good order and discipline really reside in the hands of our Chief(s)?
- Do we accept our Chief's input on NJP, awards, evaluations as my/our own because we know our chiefs know what's best, or do we take that input simply as a recommendation?

- Do our senior officers lurk at the quarterdeck and monitor liberty call rather than accepting that their chiefs have things under control?
- Are we adding or removing administrative processes and bureaucratic obstacles that distract our chiefs from fulfilling their primary duties—providing material and personnel readiness for combat?

Poor officer leadership and management can cause your CPO mess to become resentful and disengaged; conversely, great wardroom leadership empowers your mess and makes wonderful things happen for your command. Wardrooms that fail to consider and implement recommendations (when appropriate) from the CPO mess can hinder division, department, or command effectiveness. Furthermore, a CPO mess that does not feel supported by the commanding officer and wardroom will not perform to its full potential. The wise commanding officer understands this and strives to fully empower and leverage the influence of their Chiefs. They use the experience and influence of their CSEL to strengthen the effectiveness of the CPO mess. Chiefs will deliver results, but they want to know they're trusted and supported and that the CO has their back when the heat comes.

But, when empowered and supported, you now have the obligation and responsibility to deliver results. Before you claim that your power has been "taken away," pause to consider:

- Is my power-base use, influence, management skill, and networking serving the best interests of my division, department, and command?
- Am I taking ownership for the performance of my division, department, and command?
- Am I holding effective quarters and walking my spaces?
- Am I providing well-written evaluations and awards to my chain of command?
- Am I looking for opportunities to invite my division officer, department head, XO, or skipper down to the mess for a meal or a cup of coffee so I can build trust and the commitment and support that follow?

Unfortunately, the CPO mess that becomes complacent or disengaged will be micromanaged. And, even more unfortunate, the price for that complacency falls directly on the backs of Sailors. As stated earlier, phrases like

"Chiefs make the Navy run" and "Backbone of the Navy" must be earned. You can't just print them on a T-shirt and expect results. You should understand that, ultimately, the wardroom is responsible for oversight of unit policy and programs that you have the responsibility to execute. Your CPO mess does not function as an autonomous body that serves to undermine the chain of command and that should be void of wardroom oversight. Wardrooms that allow and promote that philosophy risk inviting failure. Commanding officers and CSELs have been relieved for the poor command climate resulting from negative CPO mess influence on command processes and climate.

Anchor Up!
Is there a minimum frequency for "All Khaki" calls/meetings? Discuss where your command could better leverage these meetings to improve its communication, climate, efficiency, and effectiveness.

Many of us have heard the term "Chiefs run the Navy." Although it sounds impressive, it's a fallacy and misrepresents the role of the Chief and the CPO mess. The verbiage that more accurately captures the roles and relationships of the wardroom and CPO mess is "Officers run the Navy, and chiefs make the Navy run." The officers are responsible for creating command goals and policy, managing performance and climate, and ensuring that mechanisms are in place to evaluate/inspect the command's level of readiness. The pitfall of using ambiguous catchphrases such as "Backbone of the Navy" is the risk of misinterpretation of roles and responsibilities. Lanes can get crossed, confusion can develop, and command effectiveness can be reduced.

CSELs must recognize that one of their functions is to ensure that the relationship between the wardroom and CPO mess team remains healthy. Because they have the unique access and perspective to see this relationship from both sides and to gauge its impact on command effectiveness, they should be the catalyst that facilitates an ongoing and healthy dialogue between the two. It will be strained on occasion, but when the relationship between the wardroom and CPO mess is strong, the warfighting readiness of the command and its Sailors will follow.

3-1 EXPECTATIONS OF CHIEFS FROM A COMMANDING OFFICER

- Support their division officer and contribute to their professional development.
- Cooperate and promote teamwork both within and external to the Chief's quarters.
- Take responsibility for their work groups both personally and professionally, and take care of their Sailors.
- Manage by walking around; get around the unit to maintain a visible presence, set a personal example, monitor work in progress and start new work, monitor morale and solve problems, get the word to the Sailors, and represent their Sailors up the chain of command.
- Take initiative individually or as a group to develop programs, anticipate problems, and recommend new procedures.
- Use outside resources for help or advice from any other group or individual that can help them get the job done.
- Represent the command always and their CO in certain circumstances.
- Always keep themselves sensitive to situations where they represent self, command, or CO, and adjust their actions accordingly.
- Know that there is a time and place for everything: a time to act and a time to react, a time to speak and a time to be silent, and a time to unite or act alone.
- Know that they are the link in the chain of command that can make or break a team effort.

Developing Power and Influence in Naval Officers

The role of training the division officer (DIVO) was not captured in the *Short Talk with Chief Petty Officers*, but at some point, it became an expected—although unwritten—activity (responsibility?) of the Chief. Many things make your role as a Chief Petty Officer unique. One is that you have the absolute obligation to participate in the development of junior officers at the same time as you are being the best, most loyal subordinate possible. Indeed, no role you play is more important or more special than the development of junior officers. It's a role so important that it's expected as one of your core competencies. It's an unusual relationship—business managers aren't expected to develop their executives; and plumbers aren't expected to develop their foremen; and ballplayers aren't responsible for the professional growth of their coaches and managers. Only in the sea services do senior enlisted readily and willingly take responsibility for the development of their own leaders. Just as you do with your Sailors, you should work to recognize unique qualities in these young men and women and become vested in their successful development as naval officers. Developing junior officers, like developing junior enlisted, is not easy, but this role is extremely important.

Consider that somewhere in Japan, a young ensign eagerly reports to their first forward-deployed ship. And thousands of miles away, a lieutenant, recently graduated from flight school, arrives at an East Coast aviation squadron. Both are anxious and excited to start their careers, and both have been counseled to engage with and listen to their Chief. You should make it a point to envision these young officers as future commanding officers and flag officers, and then treat them and train them in a way that will help them succeed in these positions of leadership. Although many discuss the importance of division officer "training," you and your peers should fully understand the intent that this education, advice, and development strives to achieve.

Anchor Up

What is your division officer's / department head's "golden path" to command? What are five activities you could/should do daily to develop them toward success in that path? Should these activities change for limited duty officers who serve as your division officer?

As explained in "Tapping the Power of the Chiefs" (Kingsbury 2017), young officers must understand and learn how to effectively develop and use power, and you should work to help them do this. This is especially important in the warfighting domain and has relevance at the tactical through strategic levels of leadership. Although it's not usually discussed this way, it's useful to view junior officer "training" through the lens of power-base development.

The collective strength of a person's power base is derived from their position, character, experience, and span of the personal network of the individual, and the sooner young officers learn this and start to develop their power bases, the more quickly they will become relevant and effective as leaders. Although young naval officers are assigned to positions of leadership (positional power), they typically lack the requisite development of their other power bases that are commensurate with their position and that build the credibility they need to lead. Let's consider the types and depth of the power bases available to young officers.

- *Expert power.* Although young officers have some level of educational foundation, they lack the technical, institutional, and life experience (knowledge of Navy policies, processes, and warfighting tactics and systems) that provides them with the competence required to effectively lead and manage.
- *Personal power.* The fact that these young leaders were selected to receive commissions reflects that they have a solid foundation of character development but still require growth and must demonstrate and earn the trust of their people by their actions.
- *Reward and coercive power.* Small-unit officer leaders will have some degree of reward and coercive power, but they typically lack knowledge of the tools available to them, and they do not have situational leadership experience for applying them.
- *Information and connection power.* These days young officers have much more access to information than prior generations of leaders; however, they may not be familiar with the most valuable and efficient sources of information naval leaders have at their disposal. And since they are new to the Navy, the extent of their personal networks is limited.

Given this perspective, your goal for DIVO education should be to help young officers develop all their power bases commensurate with their positional authority as quickly as possible so they can lead their units competently and effectively. Most importantly, you should guide young officers in the development of their expert power (competence) and personal power (character). These power bases, more than any others, yield the credibility required to gain trust with their Chiefs and divisions—trust that is vital to successfully leveraging influence.

To do this, you should work to explain to the young officer everything happening in the division and explain why they do things a certain way and why processes occur the way they do. You should also strive to make the DIVO a subject matter expert in all things related to their division and connect them to other Chiefs in your command to help the DIVO understand how the CPO mess works and help them build connection power. Finally, you should be respectfully but brutally honest with the young DIVO to help identify and correct weak areas.

Because their power bases are immature, new naval officers rightfully rely on your experience prior to making decisions. These young officers will give orders that you will see through to execution—orders that may involve risk; decisions that could result in sacrificing the lives of your people. Although you lack the positional authority the division officer has, your other power bases are much more fully developed and influential. You have much more expert power gained through years of institutional, technical, and life experience along with formal education. You should have a solid base of character and benefit from a "connection" with your people that junior officers typically won't have unless they were prior enlisted. And you have had years of experience observing and using reward and coercive-based influence tactics. You also have access to additional reward and coercive power, which is vested in your CPO mess in the form of recognition, advancement, and disciplinary boards. Furthermore, through your relationships with the broader CPO mess, your expert and information power bases are amplified, which enables you to shape command-wide behaviors and standards. Through a strong, positive relationship with you, your division officer can access the collective knowledge, experience, and networking power of the CPO mess. Since you serve in key developmental and advisory roles to your division officer, you will find that approaching officer "training" from the context of power-base development can help you better tie their effort to expected outcomes.

3-2 INSIGHTS ON CHIEF AND OFFICER RELATIONSHIPS

You've heard all the rhetoric about how you are now expected to be the fountain of wisdom. Every word of this is true. But I stand here today to charge you with the greatest challenge and the most important task that you, as a Chief, will ever undertake.

I expect that each of you will fulfill your duty as a mentor and leader of your enlisted charges. But, this is the easy part of being a Chief. It has been drilled into them, just as it was drilled into each of you, that, when in doubt, "Ask the Chief."

I wish I could say the same for our junior officers but, alas, I cannot.

Based upon my own experience, junior officers are far too cocksure of their own abilities and unwilling to admit their own shortcomings. Their training has been long on the technicalities of warfare, but pitifully short on the realities of leadership. And this is where you come in. The single most important task you will ever undertake is in the training of our junior officers.

This will, without doubt, be the most difficult task which you will ever undertake. Yet, you cannot shirk from it. I cannot . . . indeed [neither] the Navy, nor the country can afford your abandonment of this responsibility. The stakes are, simply, far too high.

You will be constantly frustrated in this role. You will find yourself battling an individual who writes your fitness report. You will find yourself at odds with someone who has a mere fraction of your knowledge and practical experience. You will find yourselves at odds with someone who is half your age, and is somehow convinced that he is right, and you are wrong.

This will be, for many of you, a no-win situation. And, you will ask yourselves, "Can I afford to stand up to the person who writes my evaluation?" My answer to this is simple and direct: You can't afford not to.

Each of you is a specialist in your field. There is no one, officer or enlisted, who has been where you have been or done what you have done. Draw upon this experience. Choose your battles carefully. But never back down when your arguments are sound.

You will, no doubt, encounter the prototypical "Salty" Ensign. He will be your nemesis. He will assert his authority. And you will support him. But after quarters is done, you will seek him out and attempt to set him right. If he is potentially a good naval officer, he will listen to you. If he is wise, he will seek your council. If he is none of these things it is your responsibility . . . indeed, it is your duty, to confront him, and the consequences be damned. You must, when the time comes, be willing to put everything on the line.

I had it put to me, in no uncertain terms, from a grizzled old Chief Boatswain's Mate, when I was a young first lieutenant. "Sir," he said. "Let me put it this way. I am a Chief Petty Officer. I will retire as a Chief Petty Officer. Nothing that you can say or do will change that fact. My career is winding down. Your career is just starting. This makes me a very dangerous person. I can do you a whole lot more damage than you can do me. Do we understand each other?"

I charge each of you to emulate my old Chief. In my career, I can think of no individual, officer or enlisted, who had the impact that he did. I consider him both my mentor and my friend. I went on to learn from him, not just about his rate, but about life, leadership, and responsibility. Often, to this day, when I encounter a problem I'll ask myself, "What would the Chief have said?"

—*Commodore Felkins, commander, Fleet Training Group,*
Guantanamo Bay, Cuba, 1982

Developing junior officers, like developing junior enlisted, is not an easy task. They all have personalities and beliefs that shape their attitudes and behaviors. But you strive to develop successful division officers who have a willingness to learn and the proper attitude. These officers take time to know their stuff, develop mutual professional and personal respect, take a genuine interest in their people, communicate well, do things right, set realistic goals, and serve as positive examples. Some officers come to their first command with many of these attributes well developed. However, some officers don't, and their personalities and lack of maturity may exhibit behaviors and attitudes that are counterproductive to their current and future success, so you will have to engage each accordingly.

For example, some will fail to consult with you or fail to heed your advice freely and prudently given. Junior officers have been taught to act decisively and to be leaders, but some lack the maturity and wisdom to understand that experience is a harsh mistress—and that lessons learned through experience are much stronger than those learned through books. You should note this situation and be nonthreatening and helpful to this junior officer. Furthermore, you should let the young officer know that you're there to help, not overrule or embarrass, and take time to explain that listening to the voice of experience can reduce, rather than increase, whatever stressors the young officer may be feeling.

Other junior officers fraternize with or become unduly familiar with junior enlisted. Most junior officers are about the same age as second- and third-class petty officers and share generational cultures. In small commands where the wardroom is not large, junior officers (and some Chiefs) might think they can expand their circle of friends through the enlisted community. Your job here is to remind the officer and their subordinates that it is never appropriate to cross the line with their officers, emphasizing that no long-term good is likely to result from flouting the clear and oft-stated rules regarding fraternization.

Others may perform end-runs around you or the chain of command. Few situations are more frustrating than finding out that your division officer or other officers in your chain of command are passing instructions, orders, or information directly to your subordinates without including you in the information flow. It's a situation fraught with peril because the chain of command is designed to work downward as well as upward. A short, direct conversation with the offending officer typically alleviates this situation. If the behaviors continue, you should discuss the situation with your LCPO, who can in turn take the matter directly to the department head. Conversely, there are those officers who inadvertently act as a cutout, failing to pass the word. The first time this happens, it is the division officer's fault, but it is your first signal to take some firm but respectful action to ensure that the junior officer takes this seemingly routine duty of officer's call seriously.

And yet others may usurp the role of the CPO because of their energy level, desire to help the Chief, or genuine concern for their people. Your best way to handle this situation is to gently remind the erring junior officer that his or her plate is no doubt full, and taking responsibility for things outside the job description just leaves less time for things that need to be accomplished at their own level. On the opposite end of the spectrum is the officer who is self-centered and overly concerned with obtaining his or her own qualifications and promotion. Sometimes junior officers see their division or collateral responsibilities as less important than driving submarines and ships or flying fighter jets. Take time to remind the junior officer of their responsibilities in addition to helping the junior officer meet their required qualifications.

The knowledge, skills, and abilities that make a young officer successful do not develop overnight, and your feedback—behind closed doors—can make all the difference. Newly commissioned officers may have a college degree, may be smart, and may know how to relate to the baseball team they captained, but not all of them immediately relate to the people they lead. They need the benefit of your experience, and they need to understand and relate to their people—who come from diverse backgrounds. As one former executive officer explains,

> So, if you can understand the person you are working with better, there is a better chance of coming to common goals and being able to get there. And I think for a brand-new junior officer showing up on a ship, well, he or she really doesn't understand all of that. A chief

petty officer is probably the same age as his or her father, and that officer/subordinate relationship is really a pretty complicated thing for a junior officer to work through. But the sooner they can develop that, the better their tour of duty will be. (CAPT Dennis G. Watson, quoted in Leahy 2004, 90)

As discussed in the beginning of the book, there is no such thing as a chief who is consistently strong in all areas. The same is true for officers. It was also said that you will be a young service member and officer's first chief. You will need to help division officers who need the benefit of your experience. Respect and trust are critical, and the worst thing you can do is to watch your DIVO fail. An important aspect of the Navy is forceful support and backup. Forceful support means you must speak up to correct a situation—even if it is difficult to do. When it comes to the DIVO, you must communicate and use your expertise to help the DIVO succeed and develop. The easy thing to do is to generalize about officers and complain in the Goat Locker or show disrespect. If you do this, you have failed.

[3-2] Chief Petty Officer and ensign observe a weapons exercise on board the USS *Mitscher* (DDG 57).
U.S. NAVY PHOTO BY DEVEN B. KING

Anchor Up
Review the personality types discussed in this section. Do you see any of these types in junior officers in your unit? If so, what are you and your peers doing to mentor them?

Wardroom training and development continues well beyond the junior officer level. Department LCPOs and CSELs have considerable influence on the decision-making and policy of department heads, executive officers, and commanding officers. CSELs possess many unique attributes that the wardroom should strive to take advantage of. They have decades of experience dealing with enlisted policy issues from a variety of perspectives and positions within the chain of command. Unlike senior officers, who cycle in and out of command positions over the course of their careers, CSELs have consistent "front office" experience because they are consecutively assigned at the command level of leadership.

CSELs also occupy a unique position outside the chain of command that allows them to stand back from the organization, figure out what works and what doesn't, and then influence change. They can access, observe, and advise all officers and enlisted personnel within their boss's sphere of influence. CSELs have been promoted to their highest pay grade, so they no longer have promotion boards acting as potential behavioral barriers to unfettered advice. Many have degrees in fields such as business and leadership or have attended advanced professional military education and executive education courses and seminars and understand how organizations function at the strategic level. Furthermore, senior enlisted are also well networked, which contributes to increasing their command's connection and information power bases, thus improving the command's capacity for effective communication. Their influence can provide a method of "checking and balancing" policy development and command climate.

The Navy's officer corps, regardless of commissioning source, is the finest in the world. Regrettably, however, there are officers who fail to meet their moral responsibilities, just as there are Sailors, Chiefs, and civilians who do the same. Chiefs who notice minor failings like poor uniform appearance, inappropriate personal conduct, or inattention to detail should have a quite word with the young officer. The Chief should let them know that they have observed or know of the behavior, and they want to help the officer excel, while suggesting the most appropriate course of action. In more serious circumstances—those involving egregious violations of our core values—should be reported without fear or favor through the chain of command. Chiefs who fail to report this egregious behavior have compromised their own honor.

Anchor Up

How healthy is your relationship with your division officer or department head? What are your metrics of success of your focus and energy with this relationship? What should you continue doing and what should you start doing to improve it?

Handling a Toxic Boss

Unfortunately, every year there are several news headlines about a commanding officer or officer in charge (and occasionally an XO) who was relieved from their position due to a toxic climate or toxic leadership. Stories of cultivating cultures of fear, bullying, screaming, and assault may make some shake their heads and wonder how these things can happen, but they do; and you may find yourself in a position to have to engage to mitigate the damage these leaders can inflict.

Before you feel the need to take any action, you will have to be able to identify a toxic leader in action. Chapter 4 of this guide provides a toxic leadership checklist you can use to assess your boss (and yourself), but in most cases the behaviors of egregious toxic leaders are readily apparent. The behaviors usually consist of verbal assaults and screaming that go beyond the boundaries of professional performance coaching expectations (raising your voice to make a point is OK, but screaming, name calling, and belittling are inappropriate), assault, abuse of punishment measures, bullying/hazing, or extreme micromanagement are not OK. In one instance, a toxic commanding officer put a senior enlisted in time out like a child being punished. In most cases these behaviors are directed toward members of the wardroom, but the crew sees these interactions, and they have a tremendous negative impact on climate. Beyond the physical symptoms, these leaders are often identified in command climate surveys. Yes, some amount of mild discontent can be expected, but toxic command leaders are often cited extensively in these surveys.

Once you observe one or several of these behaviors occurring and see a pattern being established or beginning to evolve, you have a responsibility to act. Although it may be easy to turn a blind eye or empathize with this kind of leader, your real loyalty is toward the Navy and your command, not your boss. Also, you and your people can't just get up and quit to solve the issue, so you will have to address this head on. This is "leading up" performance counseling—it takes courage but is a responsibility that comes with senior enlisted leader positions.

First, meet with them one-on-one and discuss your observations and the impacts their behavior is having on the command or department. This kind of conversation can also be helpful in determining whether your boss is truly toxic or their management style is simply misaligned with what you and the crew are used to. In many cases, the person may not even be aware of their behavior and the negative impacts of it. During this discussion use your active listening skills and try to learn and understand why they need to exercise so much control over others or where they are feeling performance pressure from. Once you understand what is shaping their beliefs and attitudes (and fears/insecurities), you can then work to offer advice and reassurance. If the behaviors are egregious, you should make a point to highlight the legal and career ramifications of their behaviors. Don't threaten them—remind them that the behaviors are not within the boundaries of acceptable behavior or the Navy's core values. Remind them that serving in their position is a privilege, not a right. Chances are the toxic leader isn't exhibiting their problematic behavior just to you. There may be others who are ready (or responsible) to engage the behavior, including the executive officer, chaplain, and legal officer, so you should consider a coalition influence tactic as a way to emphasize the issue. You may want to consider drafting a "memorandum for the record" to document that you engaged to correct the behavior.

Next, give them time to adjust, and engage and coach them daily. Again, this is the same approach you would take with performance feedback and adjustment of the people working on your teams. The goal is to see the behavior adjusted in the best interest of the command and the boss—that's the win-win you are looking to achieve. If they are feeling pressure from their boss, encourage them to set up a meeting with their ISIC, ISIC CMC, and you to openly discuss where expectations are misaligned or perceived pressure exists. In the case of a DH, the meeting should be with the XO, LCPO, and you. You can help broker this conversation by presenting your observations to your ISIC CMC. Also, encourage them to seek out the advice of a mentor or to reach out to one of the instructors at the Navy Leadership and Ethics Center.

At some point you should encourage the toxic boss to own the behavior and acknowledge they are wrong, they are aware of it, they understand the negative impacts to the crew, and they are working to change. If the behaviors were called out in a command climate survey, then those should be addressed in an all-hands debrief of the survey. In many cases toxic behavior is rooted in narcissism, and the feedback you give your boss might go unacknowledged. So you'll want to gauge if their reaction and plan to adjust to your professional feedback is sincere or indifferent so that you have a better sense of how to proceed. If your boss's behavior improves, that's a win. If it doesn't, then it's time to take a more formal approach. Again, consider documenting these evolving steps in a memorandum for the record.

If the above steps aren't working and toxic behaviors persist, it's time to take more formal action. When you're working for a toxic person, you only have so much individual power to change their behavior. First, before it gets to be too much to handle, turn to someone else for advice on how to navigate the situation. Once you're ready, formally notify your boss that their behavior and lack of willingness (or ability) to change has forced you to take formal action. I would start by notifying your ISIC CMC (or unit CMC for DH issues) of the issue and highlight what's been done to address it. Provide your documented and specific instances of your boss's abusive behavior. If the CMC was involved in a prior performance coaching discussion, they will be aware, and your feedback should help encourage them to initiate the next level of formal engagement. You may want to find others who will substantiate your observations, such as the executive officer, but expect that fear of reprisal may hinder their willingness to take this approach. If you find the ISIC is unsupportive or unresponsive, you may have to use other tools and resources such as the Navy Inspector General's Office. There are also several Uniform Code of Military Justice (UCMJ) articles in place to hold leaders accountable for this kind of behavior, including Article 93: Cruelty, Oppression, or Maltreatment; Article 138: Complaint of Wrongs Against the Commanding Officer; Article 133: Conduct Unbecoming an Officer and Gentleman; and Article 132: Retaliation. Always consult with a legal officer when considering bringing these charges forward.

Finally, there may be pushback or accusations/perceptions of disloyalty on your part. However, if you follow the guidance offered above, you will rest easy knowing you worked to be loyal to all the parties involved at the right time needed for each. And although navigating this situation will bring apprehension, stress, or other potential emotional consequences, the same is true of doing nothing, and your people and command will be extremely grateful for your leadership and advocacy on their behalf. Doing something is honor, courage, and commitment in action.

Working Together

Officers and their Chiefs must understand, respect, and reinforce the role each plays in warfighting readiness while understanding the strengths (and weaknesses) each brings to the relationship. They should prioritize this relationship, set aside time to develop it, and communicate with each other candidly and frequently. Mess training and mentoring can be effective and powerful tools to capitalize upon the experience of the mess to the benefit of the junior officers in a command. There are many factors that can influence the health of this relationship, and both leaders should understand these dynamics and mitigate the negative impacts they may have. Furthermore, the roles and responsibilities of each must be continuously reevaluated and adjusted appropriately as young officers grow into their leadership role.

Infantilizing young officers is counterproductive and does not serve the interests of the Navy or the division well, and Chiefs who insist on performing division officer duties allow their primary roles to atrophy. Conversely, young officers who try to "take over" Chief functions risk disenfranchising their chief and may find themselves "on their own." As a result, young officers can risk failing to build expert power or miss opportunities to exercise the influence tactics successful leaders use. Unfortunately, some young officers are more than willing to pass their responsibilities to the Chief so they can focus on tactical warfighting skills, and many Chiefs are more than willing to fulfill division officer roles, typically at the expense of their more important deck-plate management and leadership roles and activities.

Successful Chief–officer relationships build competence. You should use a variety of education tactics, including discussions, walk-arounds, modeling, and paperwork reviews, to expose officers to situations that require the use of power and influence. You should also consider how you define successful officer development and support. One metric you could use is that, because of your advice and guidance, a young officer can stand in front of your division without you present, speak confidently and competently, and be received with credibility by your people. Another metric of success is that the officer can successfully and competently assess their division's material and personnel readiness and can brief their department head or commanding officer on both without you present.

[3-3] CNO ADM Jonathan Greenert praises MCPON Rick West, the twelfth MCPON, on board the amphibious dock-landing ship USS *Fort McHenry* (LSD 43) during an all-hands call.
U.S. NAVY PHOTO BY MC1 PETER D. LAWLOR/RELEASED

The effectiveness of the Chief–officer relationship also directly shapes the perception and valuing of the CPO mess. It is well known that young officers who are fortunate to work with a strong Chief will be those department heads, executive officers, or commanding officers who continue to recognize the value Chiefs bring and who provide the support their Chiefs need to be as confident and assertive as required to maintain their units at the highest levels of warfighting readiness. And it is more likely they will advocate for and encourage the CPO mess to fulfill their important officer development obligations.

Anchor Up
Are there officers in your unit who appear to have an unfavorable opinion of chiefs or the mess? What are the existing barriers to changing or negative influences shaping these opinions? List five ways your mess can improve relationships with the wardroom in the next month.

Junior and senior officers alike can benefit from understanding power and influence and need to be taught how to plan, organize, and assess material and personnel readiness while learning the complex dynamics of naval situational leadership. You have ownership for this key task. You must understand the importance of your role in developing and supporting the success of confident leaders who have the knowledge, skills, and abilities to lead their divisions, commands, and fleets. And you must work to build officer leaders who can make the hard and effective risk decisions needed to win in denied and contested naval environments during high-end warfighting scenarios.

Four

Keeping Your Leadership Cutlass Sharp

I believe a good leader is one who cares for his people and can act as a compass for those in his/her unit. I always looked up to leaders who I felt I could talk with, and I think that's particularly important to young people. Particularly in my new role, where I am their voice to the Commandant, it's important that those on the deckplates see me as approachable and a leader they can trust. I don't ever want to be seen as unapproachable.

—MCPOCG *Steven W. Cantrell*

Why do I refer to a leadership cutlass? The cutlass is historically known as the Sailor's weapon of choice. Although less ornate and requiring less formal training than the officer's sword, the cutlass was robust enough to use for the fighting and heavy cutting work required on ships of sail and short enough to be used in close quarters and belowdecks. Simple in construction but sturdy and versatile, it could be used in a variety of routine and combat applications. The characteristics of the cutlass reflect a few fundamental attributes of the best leaders and managers I've observed and that you should work to develop in your teams: sturdiness, versatility, and credibility. There is a reason the cutlass is the ceremonial weapon for Navy Chief Petty Officers.

Good leaders are able to apply the theories of the social and psychological science of leadership, the experiences and insights of others, and their own personal experiences to help them improve their leadership skills to best achieve their organizational goals while bringing out the best in their people and teams. The *Petty Officer's Guide* (Kingsbury 2022) introduces readers to a set of guidelines they can use to focus their leadership development efforts:

1. Develop and harness eight personal/organizational power bases
2. Understand and become proficient at using eleven influence tactics
3. Develop proficiency with a strong suite of communication skills
4. Learn and apply situational leadership theory
5. Solicit feedback from team, peers, leaders, and mentors

At this point in your career, you should have a fairly firm grasp on fundamental leadership approaches and these guidelines with one-on-one and small-team interactions. But leadership has as much art to it as it has science, and it must be practiced. As an advanced leader you must now apply existing knowledge and skills but also learn new skills and concepts to achieve higher productivity, ensure clearer communications, resolve conflicts effectively, build and retain strong teams, and understand and lead change in growing spheres of influence. As you move into positions of increased influence, responsibility, and authority, you will start to consider how the organizations you are or will be a part of harness power and influence and how you integrate into those power and influence structures. You will find yourself working with the wardroom and CPO mess to build high performance teams; build trust and increase productivity; help your division, department, and command adapt to change; facilitate conflict resolution solutions; enhance work relationships; and develop organizational negotiating and problem-solving skills.

Beyond fundamental leadership and management skills, you will need other skills to succeed at the top levels of your service. You may be experienced in setting strategy, prioritizing, and managing others, but leading at the executive and strategic levels requires that you are able to help influence and drive large initiatives or culture change. In this chapter I explain how to

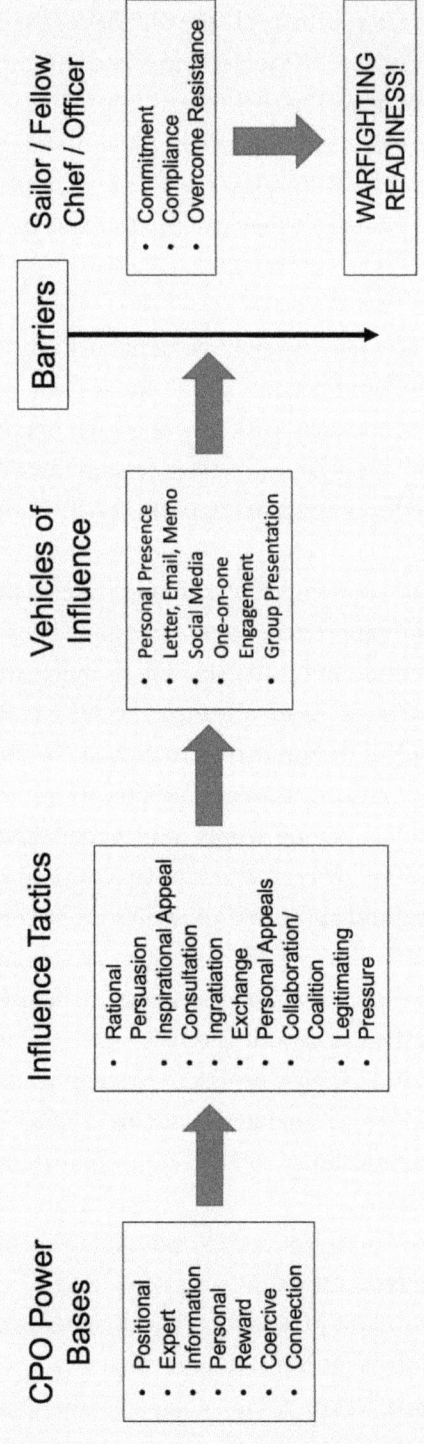

Figure 2-1 CPO Power and Influence Model

adjust and grow as you move into new positions of responsibility and influence in your service. You should work daily to build your competence as a senior enlisted leader and constantly seek opportunities to use your power bases and influence and those of your service and organization to better your units and your Navy or Coast Guard.

Your Expanding Power Bases

Your advancement to the highest enlisted ranks within the service affirms that you know how to leverage power and influence, but as a career professional committed to the success of your service, you will need to continue the work to develop your influence-based knowledge, skills, and abilities to your full potential and be able to apply them in expanding spheres of influence. There is much to learn and improve on with your influence tactics. You still have power bases from which to draw to influence team and individual behavior, but they expand and change as you advance or take on new positions.

Legitimate/Positional Power

The power you possess due to your position within the organization grew with your advancement to CPO and will continue to grow as you progress in your career. As a Chief, your legitimate power enables you to give direction and adjust resources toward the accomplishment of your leadership's goals. Your fouled anchor collar device recognizes your performance, but it is simply a symbol of your positional power and represents the trust and confidence your service has in you to lead and manage in a positive and effective way. Symbols such as these provide you with a significant amount of influence and respect. During boot camp your people are taught—and hopefully internalize—the need to obey you as an authority figure; comply with rules, regulations, and your direction; and adhere to service courtesies, customs, and traditions. When you report to a new command as a Chief, no one usually gives any thought to how long you've "worn khakis." They will simply respond to the fact that you are a Chief Petty Officer, and you enjoy being able to immediately influence results simply because of the respect and reputation that accompanies your positional power.

You will also have ceremonial roles that involve traditional and symbolic activities for your department or command, such as serving as the honors boatswain's mate at official ceremonies. You should understand that your positional power symbols—your hat, your uniform, your position standing in front of your people—is not the job. These symbols are the rewards for doing your job and doing it well to help your unit accomplish its mission as efficiently and effectively as possible. I dive more into how to prepare for and succeed in new positions later in your guide.

Anchor Up

When is the last time you reviewed the responsibilities and authorities associated with your current position? Your next desired or expected position? What are you doing to prepare for or strengthen the knowledge, skills, and qualities expected of those positions?

Expert and Information Power

A *competency* is defined as a behavior or set of behaviors characteristic of excellent performance in a work context. You are expected to be the expert in your field and use that expertise to help produce a well-trained enlisted and officer team. As a Chief, maintaining your baseline of technical expertise is paramount, but you must also learn more about your rating community and broader processes. Considering the pace of technological change and frequent and continuous updates to personnel programs, you will quickly find yourself ineffective due to the erosion of your expert power base and your perceived lack of competence if you don't invest the time to stay educated and knowledgeable on those things. As you advance to SCPO or MCPO, your technical and institutional expertise still matter, but you will have to develop competence in new areas of leadership and management. You should also have a growth mindset and consider other educational opportunities that build depth or complement your rating expertise, such as college degrees or professional certifications.

Crews have come to learn to "Ask the Chief" due to a legacy of CPOs demonstrating strong bases of expert, personal, and informational knowledge, and connection powers. They understand that you have technical, institutional, and life experience and that you couple these with a base of character that makes you approachable for help and advice. Although officers have similar power, your experience as a deck-plate leader provides a perspective and connection that most officers will never enjoy.

You are expected to hold a considerable amount of knowledge and experience, but you are also expected to have a growth mindset. You are expected to know yourself; your rating; your cutter, platform, and systems; and your crew, but you should also be learning about how your force, fleet, Navy, and Coast Guard operate within the broader Department of Defense (DoD) organization. You must know these to maintain the respect of your people. You may never have served on the type of cutter or unit to which you receive orders, but you should know that you must quickly learn the new command and your specific responsibilities within it to be successful in your position. You must also be familiar with the multitude of policies, programs, and resources available that you may need to reference or use to meet a mission requirement or to take care of a personnel issue.

[4-1] A Navy Chief supervises a firefighting equipment and hose-handling relay during the damage-control Olympics on board an aircraft carrier.
U.S. NAVY PHOTO BY MC2 GREGORY WHITE/RELEASED

Being an agile learner is an important skill you will need to value and harness at senior levels of leadership. As an experienced leader, applying your experience in new ways is crucial to you and your command's success. My commanding officers and commanders always valued the perspectives and values I brought from the nuclear power community.

Furthermore, understanding the limits of your own experience and point of view becomes even more important as the scope of your role increases. You can expect to be assigned in communities you have never experienced, and although you will bring a new perspective, you will have to learn about the unique attributes of this new unit. For some, this has become second nature. But you should avoid overreliance on what worked in the past or assume you have what it takes to be successful in a new community or on a flag staff. Although I brought my own experiences, I was always mindful to work with my command triad and CPO mess to figure out how to best apply those best practices in a new community. Your challenge will be knowing when to change course, developing a growth mindset to learn and adapt, and helping others on your team to do the same. Are you taking time to reflect on and learn from experience? Are you continuing to seek opportunities to learn even if you have been promoted to MCPO? Are you staying open to others' perspectives, ideas, and insights? Refer to the *Petty Officer's Guide* (Kingsbury 2022) for advice on ways to build and demonstrate your expert power.

Personal/Referent Power

At this point in your career you should have a sound base of character. You are a professional and have internalized the service's core values. You are disciplined and lead in a fair way. Every act of your leadership should make your organization or team feel that if they are doing their best to follow, they will be secure and their efforts will be appreciated. Just as there are ways to encourage crews, there are ways to demotivate them too. Being arbitrary, playing favorites, or relying heavily on draconian threats may get immediate obedience, but the damage done by these toxic approaches will soon negate your authority as a leader. Doing so may even negatively impact your career or end your time in the service. Later in this chapter I delve more into how you can protect the sound base of personal power that you have developed to this point.

Connection Power

You develop connection power through the CPO mess and other external networks and resources to increase the depth of your other power bases. Associations and social media networks are resources you can leverage to help you build this base. This power base is discussed in depth in chapter 2 of this guide and in chapter 6 of the *Petty Officer's Guide*.

Reward Power

You have a variety of awards available to help shape behavior, and you should be aware of available award programs to increase the number of options you have to incentivize and recognize your people's performance. You have considerable influence to submit recommendations and make subordinate organizations aware of external award program opportunities. You will sit on boards that make recommendations for unit and personal awards, recognition programs such as Sailor or Coastguardsman of the Quarter and Year, or awards available through civilian or professional organizations such as the Navy League and United Service Organizations (USO). As you progress up the ranks, you will have the privilege to attend and participate in a wide variety of award programs and ceremonies. In many cases just knowing that the opportunities exist provides your command a competitive advantage. Here are a few to consider:

- *U.S. Navy League Awards.* The Navy League has many national and chapter awards that honor those serving in the sea services, so you'll want to know where those local chapters are. National awards are handed out at the annual Navy League convention, held in the summer. Submission dates and criteria are announced via ALNAV, so keep an eye out for those. More information can be found at https://www.navyleague.org/programs/awards/.
- *GEICO Military Service Awards Program.* This program honors one currently serving enlisted member from each of the six armed services (Army, Navy, Marine Corps, Air Force, Coast Guard, and Space Force), and one enlisted member from the National Guard for their achievements and contributions on duty and off duty for their military and civilian communities. The achievements or contributions

must be made in the areas of leadership (on-duty accomplishments) or community involvement (off-duty accomplishments). The active duty / Reserve and National Guard recipients will be recognized annually and receive a certificate to commemorate their accomplishments as well as a cash honorarium of $2,500 from the GEICO Philanthropic Foundation. Nomination packages are due to GEICO no later than 30 December each year. More information is found at https://www.geico.com/information/military/returning-the-favor/service-awards/.

- *Del Black Leadership Award.* This award is hosted by the Navy Memorial's National Chiefs Mess and recognizes a first-tour Command Master Chief, Chief of the Boat, or Command Senior Chief who exhibits the ideal of service with sacrifice as demonstrated by MCPON Delbert D. Black. Submission information is communicated via NAVADMIN (naval administrative message). The award recipient is announced by the MCPON's office, and a recognition banquet is held by the Navy Memorial in Washington, DC, in November. Find more information at https://www.navymemorial.org/chiefs-mess-programs.
- *Surface Navy Association awards.* The Surface Navy Association hosts a dynamic awards program to award our Sailors, cuttermen, dependents, future Sailors, and civilian military supporters through a wide spectrum of opportunities, including recognition and monetary awards. Recognition takes place annually, with major awards presented at the annual symposium held in Alexandria, Virginia. These awards recognize some members of our community whose achievements, in a variety of pursuits, have warranted individual recognition for their contribution to the legacy of surface warriors. Submission information is communicated via ALNAV (All Navy message). Find more information at https://www.navy league.org/programs/awards/.
- *The Ancients.* The USCG recognizes distinguished senior leaders who epitomize the very best in career fields that are both inherently dangerous and richly rewarding. The tradition of naming the Coast Guard community's "Ancient" dates back to 1966, when aviators

created the Ancient Albatross, a title that recognizes the longest-serving pilot in the Coast Guard. In 1978 the cutter community followed suit by naming the Gold (officer) and the Silver (enlisted) Ancient Mariners to honor the officer and enlisted member with the earliest qualifications as a permanent cutterman. In 1988 aviators established the Enlisted Ancient Albatross. In 2003 the Ancient Keeper was developed to honor the member with the most experience in the small-boat community. And, finally, in 2016 the Gold and Silver Ancient Trident was created to honor those longest-serving members in the Marine Safety community.

There are many other award program opportunities available, so as a command senior enlisted leader, you should ask around and get smart on what local and national opportunities there are for team recognition. And keep an eye on ALNAV and ALCOAST (All Coast Guard) messages that will announce these opportunities and the criteria for submission.

It is interesting that many people are more motivated by recognition than by money. However, if you asked them, many people serving would probably acknowledge that their supervisors and unit leaders do not provide enough recognition. You should understand by this point in your career that organizations that fail to provide appropriate recognition see tangible negative impacts on their climate and retention. When used correctly, praise, appreciation, and recognition are powerful tools to increase productivity and buy-in. You will also feel good using this power base . . . believe me, rewarding people feels good. Recognition and award ceremonies develop and introduce positive energy into any organization.

Ecological Power

Ecological power is manifested in your capability to shape the physical environment, organization, and processes of a group. For example, you have ample leeway in determining how tasks are assigned so individuals are enabled to grow their skill sets and gain experience while simultaneously meeting service performance targets and goals. You will also have input into liberty risk programs and recommendations for punishment that may restrict your people to the ship or base. Furthermore, you will learn that money is a form of ecological power—it can enable or restrain organizational effectiveness, so you should be aware of the budgetary decisions being made and the impact they have on the resources your people need to do their jobs effectively and safely.

Coercive Power (Punishment and Legal Processes)

Coercive power is your potential, capability, and willingness to use threats or punishment, including negative administrative/evaluation remarks or reports of offense, to shape behavior and hold people accountable. You should use this power sparingly to align "high-resistance" individuals toward team objectives or when timelines are short, when potential outcomes are severe, or when all your tools of positive discipline have been used and have failed to achieve the desired behaviors. The *Petty Officer's Guide* offers in-depth information and guidance on things such as legal resources, report chits, extra military instruction, and withholding of privileges.

At this point in your career you should understand the fundamental processes and may have been involved in an investigation in some capacity. As you move up the ranks, you will be confronted with new situations that will require you to have knowledge of legal processes, limits, and rights, and your role and involvement in those processes will change. Topics you will need to be familiar with include investigations, nonpunitive measures, nonjudicial punishment, administrative separations, government ethics, gifts, fundraising, military justice, sexual harassment, sexual assault, legal assistance, overseas legal issues, freedom of expression, political activities, religious accommodation, and grievances/FOIA.

Your commanding officer will seek your guidance during investigations and punishment, so you will need to have a solid foundation of knowledge to offer concrete insight and advice. Opinions won't work in the legal realm. And your people will seek your counsel and advice on a variety of legal issues or when being punished. For example, as a CMC you will have to know whether it is legal and appropriate to confiscate the military identification cards for personnel assigned to restriction or liberty risk. Or you will have to understand the role and limits of the Disciplinary Review Board and manage it. As a division Chief, you will have to know when and why you can extend working hours. And all chiefs should know their people's rights to appeal nonjudicial punishment.

There are too many topics with too many nuances to cover in this guide, but there are educational resources and opportunities for you to know. First, you have the *USN/USMC Commander's Quick Reference Legal Handbook* (Naval Justice School 2009). This guide provides procedural information to assist commanders with legal matters within their command. While this guide serves as a useful tool to spot and develop solutions for legal issues, it is not a substitute for the informed advice of a judge advocate. This reference, like all reference material, is meant as a guide and is not, by itself, authoritative legal or regulatory information. Statutes and service regulations always supersede contradictory guidance that may be contained in this reference. Under all circumstances, commanders—whether using this guide or not—are strongly urged to contact a judge advocate to seek personal guidance in handling all legal issues that may arise in execution of command responsibilities.

The second resource is the Senior Leader Legal Course (SLLC), which is a three-day course designed by the Naval Justice School to prepare O-5 and O-6 commanding officers, executive officers, and senior enlisted leaders/advisers (SEL/SEA) for the legal issues they will likely face as a command triad and team. Previously, the SLLC was called the Senior Officer Course (SOC). The SOC has been integrated with the Senior Enlisted Legal Course (SELC) to form the SLLC. For personnel who are unable to attend the in-person course, several virtual SLLC courses are offered throughout the year. These are dedicated online courses, specially tailored to the virtual environment to take advantage of the tools it provides and to overcome the challenges typically associated with online instruction.

The third resource is the *Manual of the Judge Advocate General* (or JAGMAN; Office of the Judge Advocate General 2007). This handbook is designed to assist commanding officers and investigating officers with the administrative investigation process. There is no substitute for a working knowledge of chapter 2 of the JAGMAN; this handbook is not designed to replace reference to, and study of, the source document. Rather, this publication gives you a simplified "nuts and bolts" summary to initially orient your approach to the investigative process.

I highly encourage you to invest time in learning about legal situations and resources so you can be best prepared when they arise—and, believe me, they are sure to arise.

Your Role as the Ambassador of Goodwill

As you know, each year the U.S. Navy and Coast Guard advances thousands of new Chiefs, and each Chief goes through a service process called initiation or Chiefs call to initiation. One significant line of effort with the process is to indoctrinate selectees on the new expectations and roles that accompany their advancement. Many of these expectations are found in the Chief Petty Officer's Creed, and among them is the charge to be the "ambassador of goodwill." Although this charge is directed toward new and tenured Chiefs, the necessity for any naval or civilian leader—from leading deck seaman to the Chief of Naval Operations, shift supervisor to chief executive officer—to embrace and execute their role as an ambassador of goodwill cannot be overstated. Outcomes such as the Glenn Defense Marine scandal, liberty incidents overseas and stateside, public hearings on the impacts of infrastructure shortfalls, and recent expressions by Sailors indicating their growing mistrust of the CPO mess all have caustic impacts on organizational reputation, morale, and performance. Yet, despite the charge from senior naval leaders to commissioned and enlisted naval professionals to serve as ambassadors, there is little formal education or guidance on ambassadorship. In turn, individuals are left to determine who or what they represent, and when and how to manage loyalty conflicts that are certain to arise with the role of ambassadorship.

An ambassador is a person who represents, speaks for, or advises an organization, a brand, or a group of people. In this role, you represent many things, including your country, your Navy, your command, your rating and warfare community, and your Sailors. The second word, "goodwill," is more important and finds its roots in the old English words of "good," which means virtuous, and "villa," which means wish. It is having friendly, helpful, or cooperative feelings or attitudes or a disposition of kindness and compassion. The opposites of goodwill include hostility, apathy, meanness, or disagreement (attributes commonly associated with toxic leadership).

Serving effectively in this role requires the development of a suite of skills and attributes, not just a warm smile and a cache of mantras and platitudes. Ambassadors must possess a deep base of knowledge of their brand, their organization, and their people; a high a level of professionalism; solid speaking, listening, and writing skills; the ability and willingness to gather feedback and offer insight on behalf of people; and a keen ability to influence people and compel action toward organizational goals. Another fundamental requirement of great ambassadors is to have a belief in, passion for, and loyalty to people and relationships. And it is in these areas that those in positions of leadership should be particularly reflective, asking themselves questions such as, "Is there implicit bias shaping my attitude toward my junior personnel?"; "Do I view younger teammates as adults capable of making decisions (and mistakes) or as children I must constantly supervise?"; and "Do I have an attitude grounded in a belief that people gravitate toward personal success and development, or do I think they have an inherent bias toward irresponsibility, inaction, and failure?"

Because your leadership behaviors and approach toward your people reflect your underlying beliefs and attitudes, taking time to reflect on these questions can help you determine whether you are leaning toward goodwill or hostility. I think it's important to note here that having an attitude of goodwill does not mean you can't express frustration, disappointment, or anger as you pursue high levels of team excellence. But you should not be engaging in or condoning harassing or abusive conduct (derogatory remarks, insults, or physical intimidation) or bullying (using threats, humiliation, or intimidation tactics) with or within your teams. You may have heard of stories of prior chiefs using "bulkhead or fan room counseling" techniques to adjust the attitudes of their people, but those days are long gone. This also applies to your interactions in the digital space such as comments on social media pages. You should be professional and take time to evaluate how you are being perceived and the tone you are setting. Unfortunately, there are those in the mess who subscribe to these kinds of attitudes and behaviors, and they are negatively impacting the reputation of the mess.

As an ambassador, you will have a multitude of loyalties—to your organization, to your brand, to your peers/colleagues, and to your people. You will often represent many brands (sometimes called "wearing different

4-1 TOXIC LEADERSHIP SELF-ASSESSMENT

- Am I boastful and arrogant? Do I feel I'm always right and expect others to accept my word as the absolute truth? Do I fail to help others? Do I react negatively when someone dares to correct me, especially one of my subordinates?
- Do I frequently reject opinions other than my own? Do I expect others to quietly follow my directions without encouraging a questioning attitude in my team?
- Am I perceived as highly irritable by my peers and people? Do I react negatively when asked to help with anything?
- Do I present a tough or arrogant appearance to hide my insecurities or fear of change? Do I find that I am inflexible to change and the most vocal opponent of any changes in my unit?
- Do I act supremely confident but know that I have no confidence in my abilities and contribution to the team? Do I find it difficult to trust and delegate to team members and peers? Do I hide issues that I should communicate and resolve to avoid being scrutinized?
- Am I incompetent or do I often struggle to make easy decisions or complete the simplest of tasks? Does my sense of importance and usefulness come from criticizing others and highlighting my own positional worth?
- Do I find myself often using positional authority and seniority to control team members?
- Do I set objectives that are unfair and unrealistic? Do I see the impacts of this, such as team members struggling with unachievable goals and appearing demoralized?
- Am I overly reliant on positional power symbols and perks such as parking spaces, access to resources, and decorating my entire workplace with my own symbols of accomplishment, rank symbols, and recognition?
- Am I often discriminatory, and do I allow my biases and prejudices to manifest in the form of sexism, racism, or other discriminatory behavior?

hats") and represent/wear them twenty-four hours a day and seven days a week whether you want to or not. In some roles you will wear one hat at a time; in others you will wear several at once; and sometimes these different simultaneous roles will bring one or more of your loyalties into conflict. It's great when all your loyalties are aligned, but it's important that you consider which organization or brand you are expected to represent in given situations, and understand that if you knowingly or unknowingly choose loyalty to the "wrong" brand or group, there is usually a cost. One frequent example is in your role as a change agent helping to manage the introduction of an unpopular policy, decision, or order that brings disagreement or discomfort into the team (longer working hours, fewer resources, etc.). In this situation your loyalty to your organization/command may conflict with your loyalty to your people. When this happens, you should understand why the decision was made and the trade-offs, communicate the policy down including the why and the understanding of the cost of the decision by leadership, actively solicit feedback from your team, communicate impacts and attitudes up and encourage decision-makers to adjust when they can or clarify, and continue to support and communicate up and down and engage resistance to resolve conflicts—taking time to teach others about loyalty. If you find yourself resistant to the change or unable to advocate for it, take time to examine your own personal attitudes, values, and beliefs, and talk to a mentor who can help you reconcile your position. Another example is when the behavior or attitude of a peer or colleague runs counter to group norms. In this case you will find your loyalty to your organization and peer group in conflict with your loyalty to your peer, friend, or colleague.

In these kinds of situations, you may choose to represent the "wrong" thing, for example choosing personal values over organizational values. A recent illustrative example of this is the relief of U.S. Navy captain Brett Crozier for his approach to handling the COVID-19 breakout aboard his ship. And as we see all too often, we are all susceptible to choosing misplaced loyalty to our own selfish motives at the expense of organizational or team loyalty. In 2017 there was a CPO mess scandal on board USS *Hue City* in which a large portion of the CPO mess was disciplined for misconduct—an example of choosing loyalty to the CPO mess brand over loyalty to organizational values and commitment to Sailors. Only you (or your group) can make the decision, but understand and accept that there may be a cost to your personal reputation and career prospects. When you are experiencing these kinds of loyalty conflicts, get advice, experience, and insight before you make the decision of who or what you are going to represent.

The more you invest in and maintain your ambassadorship skills and attributes, the stronger your ambassador effectiveness will be, and your personal and organizational reputation will improve. I encourage you to take time today to pause and reflect on your relationship with your teams and seek feedback on your effectiveness as their ambassador of goodwill. Ask yourself what you believe about your people. Are they "kids" you must manage, or do you see them as future leaders you want to help develop to their full potential? If you are doing this right, keep doing it right and help those colleagues who are falling short. If you find you are falling short, take time now to understand why and fix it. Talk to a mentor and take some time off, reset, and reengage in a positive way. When you develop the right mindset and embrace your role as an ambassador of goodwill, I promise your connection with your teams and people will improve.

Keeping Your Followership Sharp

Like most leaders and managers, you work to improve the skills and attributes that improve your influence, effectiveness, and efficiency to make things better. But when is the last time you paused to reflect on how well you're being a good follower in your current leadership position, regardless of your time in service or position? Most discussions on leadership development and improvement focus on our influence leading "down." But, face it, regardless of your role or position of influence, and as much as you would like to have complete autonomy or ownership, you work for and are accountable to others (bosses, boards, business partners, laws, etc.). In turn, you must continue to be a good follower and hone your skills leading "up."

Perhaps in your current position you are more "senior" by age and experience than your boss, or you find yourself in a position of working for a friend or close acquaintance and you're struggling to embrace his or her vision. In situations like these, you must be able to check any feelings of resentment or frustration and work for, rather than against, your boss toward achieving their goals. So, what are some of those attributes of a good follower?

In his article "Ten Good Rules of Followership" (2008), Phillip Meilinger provides some great insight to help us understand the importance of, and relationship between, followership and leadership. His rules for followership include not blaming your boss for an unpopular decision or policy, fighting with your boss if necessary but not publicly, making decisions then running them past your boss, doing your homework to give your boss all the information needed to make the best possible decision, and keeping your boss informed on what's going on.

Interestingly, many of the goals of both leader and follower success are similar. Both roles require you to strive to create harmony, togetherness, and a sense of belonging within your team. As a follower, you demonstrate harmony with your positive and supportive attitude, your spirit of cooperativeness, and sense of esprit de corps. When engaging in your leadership role, you promote harmony through the positive use of your power bases and the mindful use of your influence tactics. So, being aware of which role you are filling—follower or leader—can help you determine how to better use your influence skills when leading up. Furthermore, it's important to reflect on how your understanding and development of personal attributes such as humility, reliability, loyalty, and accountability are impacting your level of followership.

At this point in your career, you should understand followership fundamentals, but you should also understand more complex follower theory. Implicit leadership theory (ILT) is a cognitive theory of leadership developed by Robert Lord and colleagues. It is based on the idea that people create mind models of their world and use these models to interpret their surroundings and control their behaviors. This theory suggests that as much as leaders have expectations of what makes a good follower, your people have implicit expectations and assumptions about the personal characteristics, traits, and qualities inherent in what they consider a good and effective leader. These assumptions are known as leader prototypes, and they guide your peoples' perceptions and responses to you as a leader based on their past experiences and how they compare to their experiences with new leaders.

Why does this matter? Because it is important for you to understand that when a leader does not match his or her followers' expectations, that leader may be met with resistance, regardless of actual leadership competence.

Like it or not, your leadership effectiveness is determined not by what you think your effectiveness is but by the experiences and expectations of your people. Studies have found that employees who find their mental models of effective leadership align with their actual leader at work feel greater satisfaction with their position, experience higher commitment toward their group, and increase the individual's well-being. So take some time today to ask your people what they think makes a good leader, Chief, or senior enlisted leader. Reflect on what you learn, and align your behavior and activities to the most important attributes identified. You should also ask what they don't like and make a point to ensure you are not representing any of those behaviors.

Make sure to conduct your own personal self-assessment of your followership attributes, skills, and attitude. Then take what you learn to improve where needed and make a positive difference in your personal and professional life.

Leading and Managing Self and Avoiding Career Derailment

As you advance within the service, the risks and challenges to your focus and career increase. You may feel competing pressure from a variety of sources. You are human and susceptible to burnout, fatigue, or creeping cynicism, and you need to manage your leadership "villains." Throughout this book you'll learn about the tremendous professional pressures that come with the responsibility of being a chief in your service. But you also have personal obligations to fulfill and must strive to find balance or risk becoming unhealthy in your professional and personal life. You must also take time to pause and reflect to ensure your personal values and beliefs have not become misaligned from those expected of you by your service, your fellow CPOs, and your family.

Your *morals* are the principles, standards, or habits that help you determine what conduct is right or wrong. As a leader, you must adhere to your service's core values. Just as old-time quartermasters took frequent sightings off Polaris and other fixed heavenly bodies, so you too should take frequent moral fixes off the values that guide your service. *Ethics* is your or your profession's generally accepted notions of good behavior by which you act and expect others to act. They are less straightforward than laws since they are based on your personal consideration and judgment instead of legal requirements. Ethical guidelines include things like honesty, openness, fairness, and commitment and are very situational.

You will likely encounter professional *and* personal situations involving ethical conflicts. Sometimes the solution will be immediately obvious. In other cases just sorting out right from wrong will be a significant challenge, and deciding exactly how to react will be even more difficult. Since you are a significant role model, your ethical decision-making is even more critical. In today's Navy and Coast Guard, there is little tolerance for leaders who engage in or exhibit behaviors on or off duty that are inconsistent with policies and core values.

You may be able to momentarily ignore the ethical implications of your decisions and actions, but you cannot prevent them from becoming part of you, and you can never escape them. In situations that are not outlined in policy, regulations, or laws, you should pause and ask yourself some questions to help you determine the right thing to do, including these:

- Is what I am doing good?
- Is what I am doing right and appropriate?
- Is what I am doing legal?
- How will doing this make me feel about myself?
- How will doing this be perceived by a reasonable person?

Usually, if it doesn't feel right, it isn't the right thing to do. But you can also bounce your situation off your leadership or a legal officer to get more clarification on the ethical or legal boundaries. Your personal example is the manifestation of real integrity. In striving for good order and discipline, you must remember that people admire a leader who lives in accordance with values that are enforced. Nothing but resentment can result when a leader demands behavior from followers that is not expected of the boss. Understand that if you expect unflinching obedience and cooperation from a crew, you must give the same obedience and cooperation. If you combine this attitude with your abilities and a genuine interest in the well-being of your team, you will avoid many problems.

Anchor Up
Consider an ethical decision you made at a previous point in your career and use the guidance provided in this chapter to evaluate whether you made the right choice. What should or could you have done differently?

Positions of greater authority will also expose you to ethical challenges and scenarios, such as giving and receiving gifts, travel, and interactions with private organizations, so it's important to become familiar with the specific rules and guidelines covering these actions. Furthermore, as you get older, you may find yourself in personal relationships that are unhealthy and, if not properly handled, could impact your career.

Because you have influence on section, department, and commandwide processes, your behavior must be above board, and the relationships with your crew must not put you into a position where you are perceived to make recommendations in favor of an individual based on an unduly familiar relationship. A quick review of your service's inappropriate relationships and fraternization policies provides the requisite guidance and insight you need to ensure you maintain healthy and professional relationships with your crew. Conduct is prejudicial to good order and discipline if it calls into question your objectivity, results in actual or an appearance of preferential treatment, undermines your authority, or compromises the chain of command. Specific examples of relationships and activities that may be prejudicial to good order and discipline include dating, shared living accommodations, sexual relations, commercial solicitations, private business partnerships, gambling, and borrowing money.

As a leader, you are being watched all the time. What you say matters. Set the example by making sure your statements and actions are sending the desired message. You will make decisions daily. Most will be mundane, but some will make you feel pulled between two or more options. It is critical to set the example and rely on the service's core values to help you get to the right solution. People most admire leaders with clear and strong beliefs. Be clear about what you stand for, believe in, and value. Align your values with those shared by the entire service.

COULD MY DECISION/CONDUCT . . .

- Have an adverse impact on the mission or readiness of my unit or family?
- Result in decisions made by superiors that would be based on an inaccurate picture of my team's actual achievements or capabilities?
- Abuse the public trust? If this matter became public knowledge, would I be proud of my actions, or would they result in potential damage to the public support of and trust in the Navy or Coast Guard and its members? Would my family be proud of it?
- Set an example for subordinates? What would be the long-term effect on my service's ability to defend the United States if every subordinate petty officer used my actions in this matter as a guide?
- Result in selfishness or personal gain? Does this matter involve career advancement or financial aspects that are outside the expected conduct to further my career or to avoid censure for my own shortcomings?
- Involve a cover-up of the real or apparent failure of myself, my unit, or my subordinates to attain prescribed standards of conduct or performance?

Anchor Up
Is it possible that having high personal power and serving as a role model at work can have unintended negative consequences? Why?

Leveraging Your Emotional Intelligence

Emotional intelligence (EI) is most often defined as the ability to perceive, use, understand, manage, and handle emotions. People with high emotional intelligence can recognize their own emotions and those of others, use emotional information to guide thinking and behavior, discern between different feelings and label them appropriately, and adjust emotions to adapt to environments. EI is typically associated with empathy because it involves an individual connecting their personal experiences with those of others.

EI gained popularity with the 1995 best-selling book *Emotional Intelligence*, written by science journalist Daniel Goleman. Goleman defined EI as the array of skills and characteristics that drive leadership performance. Some researchers suggest EI can be learned and strengthened, while others claim it is an inborn characteristic. There are several different theories/models surrounding EI, but they all point toward a few fundamental leadership attributes that underlie high levels of emotional intelligence:

- *Perceiving emotion*: Being able to detect and decipher emotions in faces, pictures, voices, and cultural artifacts as well as recognizing your own emotions
- *Using emotions*: Being able to harness emotions toward problem-solving while leveraging your changing moods to best fit the task at hand
- *Understanding emotions*: Being able to comprehend emotional language and to appreciate complicated relationships among emotions. For example, being sensitive to slight variations between emotions and being able to recognize and describe how emotions evolve over time
- *Managing emotion*: Being able to regulate your emotions and the emotions of others and being able to harness and manage any emotions to achieve intended goals
- *Self-awareness*: Knowing your own strengths and weaknesses, preferences and patterns, and the effect of your behavior on others and organizational outcomes
- *Self-management*: Being able to control or redirect your disruptive emotions and impulses and being able to adapt to changing circumstances
- *Empathy*: Being able and willing to consider other people's feelings, especially when making decisions

So why should you care about building your level of emotional intelligence? A high level of EI will help you to build relationships, reduce team stress, defuse conflict, and improve job satisfaction, which all lead to increased team productivity and retention. It will also enhance your communication and help with your decision-making ability. These are outcomes I think you would want to achieve and that your service expects you to achieve.

Anchor Up
What does humility mean to you? Why is it important to demonstrate humility with your leadership or boss? Your peers? Your subordinates?

There are several online EI tests and assessments you can use to help gauge your level of EI, and I recommend the book *Emotional Intelligence 2.0* (Bradberry and Greaves 2009) as a resource to help you improve in this area of your leadership toolbox.

Finally, when "climbing the ladder of success," empathy is not usually one of the first things that comes to mind as a personal attribute to develop, foster, and prioritize. It is also possible that military culture has discouraged empathy, historically viewing empathetic leaders as gullible, soft, or weak. Some aspects of the military advancement system can also foster a leadership focus on a person's own power and accomplishments instead of encouraging them to empower others. Having empathy and building up your workplace on the foundations of empathetic leadership can enhance your leadership and the mental well-being and success of your team and workplace.

As a leader, it is vital to be able to view situations and responses from the perspective of others—being able to put yourself in the other person's shoes. When someone feels their voice isn't heard, has some advice to make certain processes more efficient and effective, or has their own ideas, those with empathy can then empower them. It demonstrates to your team a sense of care for them, which in turn can shift a non- or underproductive environment, where skills and talents aren't being maximized, to an environment where everyone is inspired to do their best and is encouraged to brainstorm and come up with unique and creative ideas and solutions toward problem-solving. What's beautiful about empathy is that it's not goal oriented—it's people oriented. Empathetic leaders are able to understand the key driving forces and motivations of each team member. As a result, they directly capture the hearts of their people to mold each of them into the best they can become.

Overcoming Derailing Situations

Although not a pleasant topic, it is important to understand that many direct-level and most executive- and strategic-level leaders are subject to being administratively removed from their duty assignment before their planned rotation date. Articles in military periodicals frequently bring to light that capable and proven individuals make mistakes and in extreme cases are relieved from their positions. Holding senior enlisted leaders accountable for failures with a detachment for cause (DFC) or relief for cause (RFC) is one of the most severe administrative measures taken against a member and will have a significant adverse impact on the member's future career, particularly on their promotion, advancement, duty, and special assignments.

It has been said that "absolute power corrupts absolutely." These DFCs or RFCs typically occur when your character or competence come into question and the chain of command loses confidence in your ability to lead or manage in these positions. Not every situation results in the severity of a DFC or RFC; for less impactful failures of leadership, you may simply be removed from your position, given remediation, and then provided an opportunity to recover. However, the need to relieve a member may arise when their performance or conduct dissolves the trust that their leadership and teams have in their unit's morale; adversely impacts unit good order and discipline or mission performance; or negatively impacts the reputation of the command or service. Illegitimate use or abuse of authority breaks down team discipline, impacts team morale, and can lead to disobedience at all levels. Just as you would with your people, your leaders understand that not holding senior enlisted leadership accountable breaks down organizational trust, good order, and discipline, and erodes the reputation of the service and the broader CPO mess.

If you find yourself in a position where you have been formally relieved of your position, you should understand that you can persevere and get back on track. In his article "Don't Give Up the Ship: Leading after Being Crushed" (2023), Navy chief Nicholas Bowlin offers advice to overcome these situations. When faced with a crushing situation, he advises:

1. *Accept feedback.* For feedback to be effective, you must accept it. If you know you don't take critical feedback well, mentally prepare yourself for those hard conversations before they happen, because they will. Self-talk is a great technique to use in this situation. Leaders must have a rapport if they want anyone to accept their criticism. Cultivate that trust now so you're ready to have hard conversations. Bridges aren't built in a day.
2. *Take extreme ownership.* Admit what you did wrong, apologize, and pledge a new direction. You can't move forward until problems are owned. Problems without owners never get attention and therefore won't get resolved. Have the courage to take on hard problems because you can do hard things!
3. *Hold yourself accountable.* Admitting you were wrong is not enough. Seek continuous feedback from the group or person you wronged. Encourage hard questions to be asked and cultivate an environment that facilitates this candor among your team. A mentor providing honest radical candor is invaluable.
4. *Work to re-earn trust.* George Washington's famous quote "Deeds not words" is applicable. Show your people that you care. Fight like hell to win back lost trust. Just understand that when trust is lost, it cannot be taken back and must be given back. You may or may not win everyone back; but at the end of the day, you can sleep knowing you made the best of the situation.
5. *Start with your why.* Don't start with what is wrong or how to fix it; rather, start with why. If you can figure out why you are doing something, the how and the what fall into place.
6. *Share your experiences.* Help someone else avoid or navigate these crushing situations more effectively. Our organizations and their employees suffer if we can't be vulnerable enough to share our experiences.

Many a Chief has found themselves in this position but used the tactics offered above and the guidance of mentors to improve, get their career on track, and even advance to higher pay grades. However, there are some situations that are so egregious that the outcome is an end to your career or advancement prospects. In that case, understand that the world is not ending; there are still plenty of new opportunities for you to succeed on a new path.

Anchor Up

What ethical failure risks are you most susceptible to at this point in your career and why? What controls do you have in place to help you manage the risk and the potentially career-impacting consequences of those failures?

Leading Yourself in Four Domains

The *Petty Officer's Guide* has an extensive section on the importance of developing four domains of resilience in yourself and your teams. This guide does not go that in depth, but it is important for you to take time to reflect on your health in the four domains of resilience you have developed so far—your mental, your physical, your spiritual, and your social—to help ensure a balanced professional and personal life.

As you've come to learn in this guide, you face expectations and demands every day that require you to be resilient in both your professional and personal lives. Research has shown that individuals can strengthen their mental, physical, spiritual, and social "selves" to increase confidence, judgment, problem-solving, coping skills, and focus while reducing stress, depression, and anxiety. Total wellness involves the development and integration of the four domains of mental, spiritual, social, and physical wellness.

Your mental domain includes your ability to use resources and foster emotional, cognitive, and active coping strategies. To reinforce this domain, you can take college courses, read, work to build optimism, laugh, engage in positive thinking, change how you think about negative situations, manage impulses, and build self-esteem and self-confidence.

Many of the skills required of you are, in fact, taught in those off-duty college courses, and you will be a better writer and communicator because you will hone these skills with off-duty college courses. The availability of online courses and credits received from your military experience should make it even more appealing to start your work toward a degree. Investing the time and effort into completing a college degree will develop skills that improve your leadership and management capabilities, increase personal opportunities, and increase the value you bring to your service.

Your physical domain is your ability to adopt and sustain the healthy behaviors needed to enhance health and well-being. The daily challenges of work in the naval service require you to possess a robust level of physical fitness. Navy and Coast Guard jobs are demanding and require you to have physical strength. Long watches also require stamina and physical wellness. Four key areas to focus on to strengthen the body include physical fitness and exercise, proper nutrition, avoiding toxic substances, and restful sleep. Although keeping fit, staying hydrated, and getting a good night's rest are important, you must be prepared to perform on short notice for days on end with little sleep and less than adequate nutrition.

Your social domain captures your ability and willingness to initiate, maintain, and use social resources and connections. Investment in this domain can involve spending time with family, cultivating friendships, and participating in community or command activities. In this guide, family is not limited to a spouse and children but encompasses a larger group that includes significant others, parents, brothers and sisters, and grandparents. Chapter 2 addresses the importance of social networks within the CPO mess; however, relationships away from work are just as important to your success.

The strains on modern military families are great. Families often have two working parents, school and homework, chores, and sports and activities. But additional demands on families include the challenges of overseas duty, intensive operational tempos, or assignment to duty in the Forward Deployed Naval Forces. Without continued family support and efforts at home, you can become distracted—and the readiness of the mission and your people adversely affected. Eventually your time in the Navy will end, and you will have to live with the decisions and priorities you made while on active duty; therefore, it is important that you do not view your family as a distraction. When you come home, they want and deserve your attention. Always be mindful of that and recognize where you are falling short and work to fix it. Take leave when you need to—the command will not stop or fall apart because you took a week of leave. It is imperative to invest time and energy in your family. Children are your investment in the future: take time to love, play with, and educate them. Do not take any day for granted. It can be as simple as periodically saying, "Honey, thanks for all you do" and "I love you." Get family relationships right and your legacy and America will benefit.

Finally, your spiritual domain comprises your ability to interpret meaning in your life, identify a purpose greater than yourself, and make decisions reflecting your personal values. At the core of wellness, spirituality is the driving force behind total well-being. It refers to your value system (ethics, moral compass), your search for meaning and purpose in life and experiences, and your connectedness with others.

Activities involve meditation and prayer, taking college courses or seminars on topics important to you, taking time for values clarification, and participating in the community. Religious ministry programs serve to help strengthen and maintain this domain and are typically available in any of the wide range of deployed or stateside environments in which our people find themselves stationed. There are spiritual skill sets you can develop to build strength in your spiritual domain. These skills include being self-reflective, contemplative, and introspective in order to figure out the kind of life you want to live, demonstrating honesty with yourself and others, and demonstrating kindness, compassion, and empathy for others (goodwill).

Challenging decisions and moral dilemmas are a part of your daily experience. By advancing your spiritual growth, you can be better prepared for whatever life throws you on any given day. You need to make time to tend to your spiritual domain and work to keep it strong and resilient.

Throughout this chapter you've become familiar with advanced tactics, techniques, and tools you can use in a variety of senior enlisted positions to better lead your teams and yourself. It's important to build and maintain physical, mental, emotional, spiritual, and financial fitness. If you find your professional or personal life out of balance, you will be inhibited in your ability to effectively lead and manage to your full potential. You can access a variety of online resources to help remain healthy in this area, including the Navy Medicine's page on resilience found at https://www.med.navy.mil/Navy-and-Marine-Corps-Force-Health-Protection-Command/Population-Health/Health-Promotion-and-Wellness/RESILIENCE/.

Anchor Up
List the activities you could do in each of the four domains of resilience to ensure you are operating at your personal best and achieving the best life balance you can. Compare your list with other members' performance in your mess.

Leadership Courses and Self-Assessment Tools

Leading yourself involves a growth mindset and continued education. There are many in-person and online service leadership courses you will attend, and in some of those you will use personality self-assessment tools to help you gain a better sense of your strengths and liabilities regarding your leadership approaches. Although some of these require an application and vetting, let's look at the opportunities that will be available to you and that you should be aware of and plan to attend.

Leadership Schools and Courses

Your service has invested money, people, and resources to invest in your leadership and management growth. In some cases, failure to attend these educational courses can impact your advancement eligibility.

- *Chief Petty Officer Leader Development Course.* Prepares Navy Chief Petty Officers for increased leadership responsibilities in support of the CNO Navy Leader Development Framework. This course is designed to give the learner an introduction to self-awareness, the naval profession, and naval leadership and ethical decision-making. The curriculum is very closely linked to the Navy Core Values and challenges learners to align their personal values to these values.
- *U.S. Coast Guard CPO Academy.* An innovative curriculum designed to take newly advanced Chief Petty Officers (E-7) in the U.S. Coast Guard and transition them from technical experts to organizational leaders. The CPO Academy experience has been carefully designed to provide students with the skills, knowledge, and attitude to make the transition as smooth and effective as possible.
- *Senior Enlisted Academy (SEA).* A six-week leadership development program for active and reserve E-8/9 personnel from the U.S. Navy,

Air Force, Army, Marine Corps, Coast Guard, National Guard, and Space Force as well as our international service partners. The SEA focuses on management, leadership, national security, and physical fitness.

- *CMC/COB Course.* Hosted by the Navy Leadership and Ethics Center; uses thought-provoking case studies, one-on-one coaching, and other training exercises; prepares the command triad (Master Chiefs/Chiefs of the boat, executive officers, and commanding officers) for leadership success. The programming focuses on developing an effective, integrated command triad as well as preparing command Master Chiefs, Chiefs of the boat, and their spouses for their future roles.
- *USCG Senior Enlisted Leadership Course (SELC).* Focused on creating a pool of highly trained and motivated senior enlisted leaders better prepared for assignment to a Master Chief or Senior Chief Petty Officer billet including select high-profile assignments, such as Command Master Chief and rating force Master Chief. Using the U.S. Coast Guard's Leadership Development Framework, SELC develops critical leadership skills required of Senior Enlisted Leadership positions by addressing human resource and organizational policies, professional communications, the relationships between workforce and senior leadership, and concepts of strategy and organizational change management.
- *Keystone Course.* Hosted by the National Defense University; educates Command Senior Enlisted Leaders (CSELs) currently serving in or slated to serve in a general- or flag officer–level joint headquarters or service headquarters that could be assigned as a joint task force. CSELs will have an opportunity to visit and receive briefings at the National Defense University, the DJS J7 Joint Coalition Warfighting Joint Operation Module in Suffolk, Virginia, and several Combatant Commands and Joint Task Forces. Completion of Joint Professional Military Education Courses I and II are required prior to attending.
- *Navy Senior Leader Seminar.* Provides senior officers (O6/O5), senior civilians (GS-15), and Fleet/Force Command Master Chiefs

with an intensive five-day executive education program that introduces the latest "best practices" in strategic planning, goal setting, strategic communication, effects-based thinking, risk management, financial management, and innovation. The program provides participants with the knowledge and skills required to manage and lead effectively in complex organizations. Learning is enhanced through case studies, small-team exercises, practical applications, seminar-style discussions, peer learning, and faculty presentations.

- *Navy Capitol Hill Workshop.* Provides a first-hand understanding not only of congressional process and procedure but also the "culture" that is the U.S. Congress. Over the four days, participants will hear from—and be afforded the opportunity to ask questions of—members of Congress, congressional staff, academic observers, interest groups' representatives, news media representatives, and executive branch officials, including Navy Office of Legislative Affairs staff. Each four-day workshop is conducted entirely on Capitol Hill. Participants will receive briefings specifically tailored for the Navy on the current status and insider analysis of legislative issues of most interest and importance to officials of the Department of the Navy. Topics range from the issues and politics of the overall Department of Defense authorization and appropriation to the details of specific programs and systems.

Leadership and Management Self-Assessment Tools

A big part of leading yourself is taking time to self-assess your personal strengths and weaknesses so you can remain strong and grow where you need to. During your attendance at the leadership courses listed above, you may take or use one or more personality and trait assessments. Each of them can offer valuable insight into how you engage as a leader and provide the opportunity for improvement.

- *Myers-Briggs Type Indicator ® (MBTI).* The MBTI is based on the influential theory of psychological types that proposes that people experience the world using measured along four dichotomies—Extraversion/Introversion, Sensing/Intuition, Thinking/Feeling, and

Judging/Perceiving—and that one of these from each pair is dominant for a person most of the time. Combinations of these scales produce a four-letter acronym that reflects the dominant score on each factor, resulting in sixteen possible psychological types. The MBTI is thought to be used as an introspective self-report questionnaire indicating differing psychological preferences in how people perceive the world and make decisions. Although interesting and fun to do, the validity of this assessment has been called into question.

- *Hogan Assessment.* This assessment identifies how and why people behave the way they do, how well they will align with an organization, whether they will meet job requirements, and how they will perform. It measures normal personality characteristics, career derailment risks, and core value drivers. Hogan's comprehensive approach to personality assessment provides insights to help hire the right employees, identify and develop talented individuals, and build better leaders.
- *Core Strengths Assessment.* Rather than focusing on what you do, a core strengths assessment helps you understand why you behave the way you do and how you r late to others in normal situations and during conflict. The assessment offers four views of a person, including a Motivational Value System, a Conflict Sequence, a Strengths Por-trait, and an Overdone Strengths Portrait. It helps you understand if you or your people are motivated by people, by performance, or by process.
- *Emotional Intelligence Assessment.* There are a variety of emotional intelligence assessments, but all generally serve to help you measure and improve your level of self-awareness, self-management, social awareness, and relationship management.
- *DISC Assessments.* DISC is an acronym that stands for the four main behavioral styles outlined in the DISC model of personalities. D stands for dominance; I, influence; S, steadiness; and C, conscientiousness. This tool helps you learn which style you gravitate toward most, understand your underlying tendencies and preferences, and adapt your behaviors to interact with others more effectively.

- *Kirton Adaption-Innovation Inventory (KAI)*. The KAI measures your style of problem-solving and creativity (innovative, adaptive, or bridging). It is available both online and as a paper form and is used in the training of managers and key teams as part of the management of change process, in-group training, and individual development as part of the management of diversity to enhance group cohesion and effectiveness, improve leadership techniques, and help with problem-solving and team building.
- *The Johari Window*. This approach, created by psychologists Joseph Luft and Harrington Ingham, is a self-awareness technique designed to help you better understand your relationship with yourself and others. The model portrays graphically the relationships among characteristics we disclose to others and those others see us in. Using this tool can help with communication and understanding and with overall inclusion and equality within the team, and it may also boost interpersonal relationships. The Johari Window is a simple framework that divides personal information into four quadrants: open, hidden, blind, and unknown. The *open* area is that part of your conscious self that includes your attitudes, behavior, motivation, values, and way of life that you are aware of and that are known to others. In this quadrant you are an "open book." In the *hidden* quadrant, your attributes are selected by you but not by any of your peers. These are things either that your peers are unaware of or that are untrue but for your own personal perception of them. Your *blind spot* quadrant is formed with adjectives selected only by your peers. These insights represent what others perceive of you but that you don't see or perceive. This is an area of great opportunity for learning and improvement. Finally, the *unknown* quadrant describes behaviors or motives that no one participating recognizes—either because they do not apply or because of collective ignorance of these traits. When you attend your service's Senior Enlisted Academy, you will participate in this exercise with your classmates. When you are a participant or decide to facilitate a session with a developing or struggling team, the Johari Window exercise can help with team building, conflict resolution, improved communication, and personal/professional development.

Although you may have taken or will take one or more of these in one of your service leadership development courses, I suggest you give each some research and consider taking them all to gain a fuller picture of why you behave and lead the way you do.

Leadership and Management Education Self-Learning Resources

If you feel that your current commitments don't allow time for attendance at a leadership course or you don't meet the eligibility requirements, there are a variety of self-learning resources at your disposal that you can complete on your own time.

First, consider reading as a key component of your mental domain. Several good reads have been cited throughout this guide, but there are also many good titles on your service's reading list. You can learn much and gain great insight on a variety of leadership, management, and naval history topics. Read to improve your rating expertise or to gain knowledge of psychology, sociology, economics, or managerial approaches. Find something that interests you and that is at your level of reading and commit some time daily. Start small and gradually build the amount you read to improve your reading comprehension and stamina. Think critically about what you read and learn to develop thoughtful counterpoints to material and opinions with which you don't necessarily agree. These skills will make you a more effective leader and manager as you progress in your career.

These days there are many online leadership courses that you can access for free. For example, LinkedIn offers a variety of leadership and management improvement courses in their LinkedIn Learning program. LinkedIn Learning has been reviewed and approved by the PMI® Authorized Training Partner Program, and many of their courses qualify for professional development units. You may also have access to service-hosted workshops and seminars.

Knowing Your Resources

Regardless of the strength of your leadership and management skills, you will still come across situations that will require you to seek help. We discussed in chapter 2 that the CPO mess is a primary source of help when you run into problems and lack the experience or resources to get things done. You also have other resources within the lifelines of your command. Although you have personal experience with many aspects of life and with Navy programs, you may find that you just don't have the insight or personal skills to help your people in personal crises. But there are a variety of program managers who can help you with personnel issues that may arise. Key command managers include the following:

- *Command Career Counselor (CCC)*. CCCs help Sailors put their experiences in motion and make wise career decisions. They help Sailors explore and evaluate their education, training, work history, interests, personal traits, and physical capacities and limitations. They work with Sailors in developing skills and assist them in applying for proper job placement. They also arrange aptitude and achievement tests as well as feedback and career guidance. They also provide second career counseling for Sailors who are transitioning or retiring.
- *Drug and Alcohol Program Adviser (DAPA)*. Your DAPA is your command's primary adviser for alcohol and drug matters and can help you navigate the options available to handle alcohol-related incidents (ARIs).
- *Command Managed Equal Opportunity Manager*. This resource functions as a single point of contact for equal opportunity matters within the command. They are a great resource for you in determining available resolution options when your people believe they have been subjected to harassment or prohibited discrimination.
- *Command Financial Specialist (CFS)*. The CFS is the command's principal adviser on policies and matters related to personal financial management (PFM). CFSs are nominated by their commands as special assistants to senior leadership. They receive special training to help with car buying, checking account management, credit and bankruptcy, and financial planning.
- *Chaplains*. Chaplains offer everything from faith and personal advice to much-needed solace. From morning prayers to Sunday mass services to baptisms at sea, your chaplain can support and uplift you and your people during trying times.

- *Casualty Assistance Calls Officer (CACO)*. This is the official command representative who provides information, resources, and assistance to the primary next of kin (PNOK) and secondary next of kin (SNOK) in the event of a casualty. No Chief ever wants to experience the loss of one of their people, and in those situations your CACO is an invaluable resource to help you ensure the families are well taken care of.
- *Educational Services Officer (ESO)*. This is your point of contact for all the Navy's training and education programs. The ESO gives all locally administered tests, fills all orders for correspondence courses, and arranges off-duty education. In short, the ESO is responsible for all the training within and for your unit.
- *Suicide Prevention Coordinator*. This officer is assigned by the commanding officer to maintain a robust suicide prevention program and to help equip people with the knowledge, skills, and resources to proactively navigate stress, support one another, and respond appropriately in the event of a crisis.
- *Sexual Assault Victim Advocates*. These advocates are carefully selected, trained, and credentialed military and DoD civilian personnel who provide support and assistance to victims of sexual assault. They are directly supervised by the sexual assault response coordinator (SARC) and are required to maintain confidentiality of victim communication.
- *Voting Assistance Officers (VAOs)*. These officers work to ensure that military and overseas voters understand their voting rights, how to register to vote absentee, and have access to accurate nonpartisan voting information and assistance.

Your command's collateral duties list should be up-to-date and outline who holds these and any other positions from whom you may need advice, guidance, or assistance. Know who they are and have their email and phone number added to your contacts. You will need their knowledge, experience, and guidance when you least expect it.

You also have resources outside the lifelines of your command, so you should be familiar with what they can offer. Again, there are Chief Petty Officers in a variety of positions around the Navy who are positioned to help you as needed; within a few degrees of separation, you should easily be able to connect to a fellow Chief who can answer your question or connect you to someone who can. Here are some available outside resources:

- *Family Readiness Fleet and Family Support Programs (FFSP).* The goal of these programs is to promote self-reliance and resiliency to strengthen the military and its family members, support mission readiness, assist commanders in planning for and responding to family readiness needs, and facilitate building a strong community network of services through community outreach and partnerships. Fleet and Family Support Centers (FFSC) offer free parenting and life-skill programs, financial programs, deployment support, transition and employment assistance, relocation assistance, counseling and victim assistance, exceptional family member support, information and referral, and many more programs to promote quality of life for military personnel and their families. I highly encourage you to visit https://ffr.cnic.navy.mil/Family-Readiness/Fleet-And-Family-Support-Program/ or the nearest Fleet and Family Support Center to learn more about the vast on-base and community services they offer.
- *Region Legal Service Offices (RLSO).* Your command's legal officer is your commanding officer's resource, but the RLSO is a customer service organization that supports fleet operational readiness by providing high-quality legal services to Sailors and their families. Advice and service regarding the following matters are normally available at legal assistance offices:
  – Wills with and without testamentary trusts
  – General estate planning advice
  – Domestic relations advice, including divorce, legal separation, annulment, custody, and paternity
  – Adoption and name-change advice
  – Immigration and naturalization advice

- Nonsupport and indebtedness, including communication, correspondence, and negotiations with another party or lawyer
    - Consumer fraud and abuse advice, including identity theft
    - Powers of attorney and notary services
    - Basic tax advice and assistance on federal, state, and local taxes
    - Landlord–tenant relations, including tenant advice concerning review of personal leases and communication and correspondence
- *Navy–Marine Corps Relief Society.* This organization provides—in partnership with the Navy and Marine Corps—financial, educational, and other assistance to members of the naval services of the United States, eligible family members, and survivors when in need. Their services are free and confidential and include interest-free loans and grants, postsecondary scholarships, visiting nurses, and budgeting for baby workshops. You can learn more on their website: https://www.nmcrs.org/.
- *Military OneSource.* Both a call center and a website, this resource provides comprehensive information, referral, and assistance on every aspect of military life twenty-four hours a day, seven days a week to all component members of the armed forces, their family members, and survivors. The Military OneSource program is accessible worldwide via toll-free telephone number (800-342-9647) or website (https://www.militaryonesource.mil/). Military OneSource provides service members, their families, and survivors access to confidential nonmedical counseling on a face-to-face basis in the local community, via telephone, or on a secure online chat and video. Moreover, Military OneSource offers financial and tax counseling, specialty consultations (for example, health and wellness coaching, wounded warrior consultations, etc.), educational materials on a variety of topics and formats, mobile solutions, translation of official documents, and simultaneous interpretation in more than 150 languages.
- *Military Health System Nurse Advice Line.* This resource is available to help you and your people navigate their family's health care needs. Here are some of the services they provides:

- Health care advice
- Assistance in determining an appropriate level of care
- Assistance locating a provider or pharmacy
- Same- and next-day appointment scheduling at military hospitals and clinics when advised by a nurse and empaneled to a military treatment facility (MTF)
- Nurses who specialize in pediatric, behavioral health, and obstetric care are available to support your family's needs and can help you and your people with mental health concerns

Several leadership techniques that can be employed to motivate your people and shape the decision-making of your leadership have been used by generations of Navy and USCG Chiefs. Many people wonder which technique works best in a circumstance. Although no guidebook can anticipate every situation you will encounter, continuing to learn new mindsets, techniques, and the underlying principles will help you choose the right tactic to fit the new situations you will find yourself in as you move into positions of increased influence. Naval leadership, influence, and power—getting people and teams to do what you want or need them to do—are what Chiefs are, and have always been, about. Know your power bases, how they are changing, and how to link them to the appropriate influence tactics to ensure positive effect. Continue to seek mentoring and performance feedback from those in the mess who have been there and done that, and you will find that your leadership cutlass stays sharp. And then . . . go out and make a positive impact and difference in your service and the lives of the people on your teams.

Five

Leading Teams and Navigating Change

> Powerful and sustained change requires constant communication, not only throughout the rollout but after the major elements of the plan are in place. The more kinds of communication employed, the more effective they are.
>
> —*strategy consultant DeAnne Aguirre*

The CPO MVGP states that "Chiefs are visible leaders who set the tone. We will know the mission, know our Sailors, and develop them beyond their expectations as a *team* and as individuals." It also expects you to "use experience and technical knowledge to produce a well trained enlisted and officer *team*." Developing and harnessing teams is something you should be fairly adept at by this point. With that said, as you advance, the teams you shape will change, and you will have to manage that change and a host of other organizational changes and adjustments. Policies will change, the people on your teams will change, schedules and missions will change, and social norms will change.

You will influence the wardroom and the broader CPO mess as agents of the change process. As an ISIC CMC or senior enlisted serving in a technical role on a flag staff, you will work with teams of officers, civilians, and senior enlisted on that staff and in subordinate commands to implement and manage change. You will also work to advise your department head, commanding officer, or commander on how well they are developing their department and command teams or on the best ways to incorporate needed change. In this chapter we dive into team development and how to manage those teams through the frequent changes they will experience.

Groups of individuals can be classified into four categories, depending upon the maturity (length of time) and purpose for which they have come together:

- *Aggregates.* Aggregates are simply people who are at the same place at the same time. Think travelers on an airplane. Unless they are part of a preexisting community like a church group or ski club traveling together, the only thing they have in common is that they are booked on the same flight. Each has a different purpose for being on that flight. When you attend a leadership school or college course, you will be joining an aggregate. The only thing you will appear to have in common with other team members is that you all arrived at the same place at the same time for a common purpose.
- *Cohorts.* Members of cohorts have some statistically identifiable characteristics in common. Perhaps you grew up in a small town and attended kindergarten to high school with the same kids. That's an example of a cohort. By having a common memory, cohorts are distinguished from aggregates. Watch the crew of any ship as they return from a long deployment. The crew will make references to or jokes about events that happened during the deployment, comments that, to an outsider, are totally incomprehensible. The mention of a single word or phrase may get everyone laughing as it triggers memories of something that happened weeks or months previously.
- *Groups.* In the technical sense of the word, groups are individuals who come together often for a common purpose or who share a sense of belonging to a specific entity. The success of the group's mission may not require the same level of commitment or interaction by each member, but, if attacked or threatened from the outside, members will quickly identify with the group. Sailors on a large-deck warship may never meet or even have much in common, but let trouble start in a liberty port and an attack on one is seen as an attack on all.

- *Teams.* Teams are composed of individuals with interdependent responsibilities for the success of the mission or task. A group of Sailors or Coasties may be in the crew mess quietly studying for the upcoming advancement exam, but a team of them would be taking turns quizzing each other and developing what-if scenarios for various topics that may appear on the exam. The key word is "interdependence"—the idea that the success of the entire team is influenced by the actions of each member.

You can expect to be called upon to facilitate team development many times in the course of your career. You will start with two dimensions of team effectiveness, the individuals and the task to be performed. You will have some individuals who may seem more interested in personal accomplishment than the success of the team. You will probably have passive "passengers" on your team bus. And the task to be performed can be as simple as conducting a field day or stowing supplies or as complex as flight deck operations on an aircraft carrier or a combat patrol. Regardless, you should know how to coalesce aggregates or groups into teams while recognizing and helping manage the stage of your team's development.

[5-1] A Chief electronics technician, serving as a 3-M supervisor, briefs Sailors on a maintenance check.
U.S. NAVY PHOTO BY MC3 LAURA HOOVER

Stages of Team Development

American psychologist Bruce Tuckman identified five necessary and inevitable stages that all teams go through as they grow, overcome challenges, tackle problems, find solutions, and deliver results (Tuckman 1965). These stages were captured as Forming, Storming, Norming, Performing, and Adjourning. These stages of team development are a framework you can use for analyzing your organizational team's development. Let's quickly review each of the steps.

1. *Forming.* The forming phase occurs when your team meets and learns about its objectives. While team members may feel excited about the work ahead, they're still unfamiliar with each other and the team issues. During this stage, the team or group

- Identifies the task and how the group will accomplish it;
- Exhibits hesitant, insecure participation;
- Defines the ground rules;
- Tests behavioral expectations and ways to handle violations of them;
- Shows suspicion, fear, and anxiety about the new situation;
- Spends time intellectualizing or playing "what-if" games;
- Complains about the organizational environment; and
- Establishes dependent relationships with leaders.

People are usually on their best behavior but focused on themselves at this stage. They tend to be more reserved as they learn more about each other's skills, interests, and backgrounds. This stage is when the leader shares the team goals, scope, timeline, and each member's roles and responsibilities. Because the team is new and just beginning to understand the work ahead, they may not yet know how to cooperate. In the forming stage, leaders must clearly communicate team objectives and expectations to set ground rules and work standards for every team member. To help build relationships among teammates, you can provide socializing opportunities, such as happy hours or team dinners.

2. *Storming.* This phase occurs when the team begins to work out its issues and build trust internally. There is usually low focus on the task and high focus on the process and preliminary task accomplishment. During this predictable stage, your team members may

- Resist the group's influence;
- Compete and become defensive or argumentative;
- Exhibit disunity, increased tension, and jealousy;
- Experience polarization of group members;
- Display interpersonal hostility;
- Become concerned over excessive work; or
- Participate in intergroup conflict.

Team members learn more about each other and disagree about the best way to tackle the project or approach specific challenges, mainly due to differences in personalities and work styles. People can become frustrated with their teammates, leading to clashes and arguments. Because team members are still getting to know each other, they may not fully trust each other's abilities, recognize each other's values, or appreciate their differences. Conflicts, disagreements, and competitions among team members can be frequent during this phase. Leaders should define rules for handling complaints and help team members resolve conflicts as early as possible, as there will likely be more disagreements even after the storming stage. To support their teams in overcoming issues and building trust, leaders can serve as referees to moderate disputes, clarify misunderstandings, and manage competitions.

3. *Norming.* At this point, the light goes on. Team members have resolved most disagreements and personality clashes by this stage to form a culture of cooperation. Sharing a common goal and taking mutual responsibility for the team's success, they recognize one another's strengths, understand each other's roles, and become more comfortable working together. Teammates also accept others as they are and start to socialize more and feel more comfortable asking each other for advice and feedback. During this phase

- Conflicts are avoided or attenuated;
- Cohesion with common goals and spirit is encouraged;
- There is interdependency when performing tasks;
- Trust and communication increase, along with mutual support; and
- There is acceptance of new standards and roles.

While norming is a positive phase, unresolved conflicts from the storming stage can lead to regressions. Additionally, too much focus on being agreeable and avoiding conflicts can reduce team members' willingness to share dissenting opinions, leading to slower progress. In this stage you'll have to stay aware of employee interactions and ensure everyone is communicating respectfully. Encourage productive dissent and a diversity of opinions, and regularly ask for project updates to ensure the team stays on track.

4. *Performing.* Having established a common culture, built productive relationships, and streamlined work processes in the previous stage, team members are now comfortable working together toward their shared goals. Teams and their leaders find

- Emergence of solutions, insights, and collaboration;
- Constructive self-change;
- Group structure emerges as a task tool, not as an issue for debate; and
- Energy is channeled into the task.

People are motivated and effective in this stage as the team reaches peak productivity and becomes autonomous without relying on supervision. Generally, team members are happy working together and appreciative of each other's talents. Teams at the performing stage are typically self-sufficient and highly effective. However, conflicts can still arise to disrupt progress, causing teams to regress to earlier stages. During this phase, you should act as a coach or mentor and offer guidance to ensure the project meets all goals. Pay special attention to group dynamics to prevent your team from reverting to the earlier stages of team development.

5. *Adjourning.* The adjourning phase (also called the mourning phase) occurs when the team has completed the mission or project and breaks up, with some members potentially transferring to new units. Several events may occur:

- Task-maturity level of the group may regress;
- A stated desire to maintain relationships is usually followed by diminishing contact with other team members; and
- Members relinquish identity as a team member.

Team members should feel a sense of accomplishment at the end of a mission, but they may also feel disappointed that the experience is over—especially if they've developed close relationships with their peers. Team members may feel lost once a project finishes, especially if they're resistant to change. During this stage, you and your unit leadership should find opportunities to recognize the team's accomplishments and unite them one last time to celebrate their success together. The adjourning phase is not always applicable because some teams stay together permanently. However, your team may experience a version of the adjourning stage when an especially exciting or labor-intensive project ends or a team member leaves.

Anchor Up

What is the current stage of development in the team you are leading? Are you fulfilling the team manager roles and activities needed? How are you preparing to facilitate the next stage of team formation?

Enhancing Your Teams

Beyond understanding the phase of team development and your role in influencing its evolution, there are other things you can do to help your leadership develop better teams. Research suggests that on average, about 30 percent of an organization is committed to doing a respectable job, 50 percent is merely putting in their time, and 20 percent is counterproductive. You must work to help your department, command, force, fleet, and Navy maintain the commitment of the top 30 percent, develop increased commitment in those simply showing up to work, and reduce the number of team members who are counterproductive. You must work with your leadership teams to develop and nurture elevated levels of morale and esprit de corps that are paramount to getting organizational commitment.

Esprit de corps is one key indicator of the levels of commitment within your organization. It implies enthusiasm, devotion, and zealous regard for the honor of the organization. Esprit de corps is an organizational-wide bond characterized by a high level of trust and loyalty between its members and their command. With thoughtful leadership, this bond inevitably leads to a fiercely proud association. You are challenged with leading and motivating personnel, largely through your use of personal power, to the same intense pride in serving in your commands as has been demonstrated throughout the history of the U.S. Navy and Coast Guard. Esprit de corps can be indicated or measured by the expression of enthusiasm and pride in your team by its members, the reputation of your team among others, your team's resilience under conditions of stress, the attitude of team members toward one another and toward their leaders, and your team members' willingness to help one another.

The achievement of high levels of teamwork and esprit de corps and the commitment that follows requires stable leadership that inspires confidence and, most importantly, the participation of all within the command. This spirit can be developed only if each member recognizes the group's common interest and cooperates toward the common goal, a state that is dependent on the satisfaction everyone gets from being a member of the group. You can enhance team commitment, morale, and esprit de corps by following a few key steps.

1. Envision a preferred future for your teams and commands, setting this picture in the context of your service's overall vision, missions, strategy, and driving forces. You should establish and communicate organizational and team objectives and monitor progress toward objectives; initiate action; and provide structure and systems to achieve goals. Create a shared vision of the organization, promote wide ownership, manage and champion organizational change, and engineer changes in processes and structures to improve organizational goal accomplishment.
2. Select the right people for your team. This isn't always easy in the military since your team members are typically assigned for you. But you do have influence on who leads the maintenance and operational teams in your organization. You will want to consider different backgrounds, skill sets, and work styles. And although it might seem easier to develop a team when everyone is similar, success often requires those who can bring diverse approaches, ideas, and a questioning attitude.

3. Ensure your leaders understand their responsibilities. Successful team development depends on effective leadership. Team leaders must understand what they need to do in each stage of team development and offer the right level of support for the team and each member, such as providing constructive feedback and keeping everyone motivated long term.

4. Strive to provide your team members with the right resources. Work relentlessly to get them the necessary training, supplies, people, technology, information, and other resources so they have the best chance of overcoming obstacles and achieving your goals. Time is also a resource you should value and work to find for your teams. Also, as discussed in the management chapter of the *Petty Officer's Guide*, your team members are more likely to get along and feel less frustration when they have the resources they need to do their jobs. This in turn will maintain or boost morale.

5. Create an environment that supports , and diverse perspectives, approaches, and thinking, fairness, dignity, compassion, creativity. Demonstrate sensitivity to cultural diversity, race, gender, background, experience, and other individual differences in the workplace. Guide and persuade others to see the value of diversity and of building and maintaining a healthy working environment.

6. Maintain a general attitude of approval of the team, and understand that demonstrating distrust in the chain of command results in distrust in their personnel. Communicate widely and often; let the team know what is expected of them by explaining formal directives or by using clear verbal instruction, and keep them informed of and connected to the mission. Teams usually work better when they understand where their work fits into the big picture and the duties, assets, and systems they are responsible for. Leaders need the perspective and ability to balance the tension between short- and longer-term strategic actions, between daily tasks and tactical concerns, along with strategic possibilities and actions that impact the long-term viability of the organization. As an SEL, you should learn to evaluate what your command teams are doing to step back, think about their vision, and clarify their strategy. You should

also offer advice and guidance on what new skills your leadership team should be developing, relationships they should build, and information and trends they should be aware of.
7. Let the team know you support them as they perform their duties to the best of their abilities. Keep the team informed of progress they are making, of whether the work is good or bad, and of changes that will impact their personal lives and futures; and let them know about advancement, education, and retention policies while giving useful guidance to personnel.
8. Avoid allowing yourself to be perverted into a pursuit of some form of hyper-sterile team environment. No one is interested in a workplace so politically correct that good-natured fun, whimsy, and creative humor are all out of bounds. Strive to preserve the balance that includes a time and place for good-natured kidding and humor that doesn't threaten or offend anyone. That may sound easy, but it's not. It is a challenge you should take on with continued vigilance and a full knowledge of what's at stake for organizational reputation and morale.
9. Delegate authority, with corresponding responsibility, as far down in the organization as the competence exists. The *Petty Officer's Guide* offers ample guidance and self-assessment tools on the art of delegation.

How well you and your organization develop and manage your teams is a critical contributor to or detractor from your unit's culture and its reputation. Your team's attitude is a dependable measure of morale, and high morale and commitment are present only in those teams that have discipline and efficiency. Experienced senior enlisted can walk on board a cutter or station and, in a very brief time, gauge the level of commitment, compliance, or resistance aboard. Organizations have personalities—you can sense it as soon as you cross the quarterdeck or meet with staff. As we have discussed, team and commitment building are not easy tasks, and you influence many of the conditions that impact the level of morale in a unit. In your role, you can represent the existing team attitude to leadership and suggest how to best shape it. The chain of command must be used up and down.

Open and candid input from the crew should be encouraged, and the crew should know their recommendations are considered through transparency from the command. Your job is to make those working for you feel valued.

Much of the work of developing and managing a positive command climate revolves around building a sense of trust between the command, department, and section leadership and the crew. Soliciting frank feedback, conducting critical self-assessments, making adjustments when required, and letting people know you are acting and that they are heard are all ways to maintain or improve the climate, morale, and cohesiveness of a unit that underpin the trust required for teams to operate most effectively.

Building high-performing Navy and Coast Guard teams is challenging considering how often team members come and go and especially as team members learn to work alongside people with different work styles. However, with your leadership and support, your team's performance can be increased by following the advice offered in this section.

[5-2] U.S. Coast Guardsmen assigned to a Maritime Security Response Team conduct hook-and-ladder climbing drills during a training exercise.
U.S. ARMY PHOTO BY SSG ARNELL ORD

Navigating Change

By now you've had your experience with change—new leadership, new people, new mission, new port visit, new uniform policy, and so on. You should know that change is inevitable. You must also understand that you have a role in the change-management process and will help your leadership team introduce, navigate, and manage major changes. Change management is the process businesses and organizations such as the Navy use to implement changes by developing and delivering effective change strategies. It includes identifying and reviewing reasons for change, implementing changes, and helping your teams adapt to these changes. Common situations include implementing new technology, leadership, or management turnover; change in work culture; policy changes or adjustment; and emergency situations.

Types of Change

There are four general types of change you can experience or may have to initiate or manage:

1. *Anticipatory*. Anticipatory change is when an organization makes changes in response to something expected to happen. For example, environmental concerns or new trends the organization wants to capitalize on can cause stakeholders to anticipate the need for change.
2. *Reactive*. Reactive change happens in response to an event that impacts the business. This could be new technical requirements, regulations, or changes to deal with an unexpected situation . . . think the COVID-19 pandemic.
3. *Incremental*. Incremental change is a series of changes, usually at a micro level, that adds up to wider overall changes. Examples include implementing a reward system, introducing new flexible working policies, or changing office hours.
4. *Strategic*. Strategic changes are made at and filtered down from a higher level, impacting the whole organization. An example of this is a change in leadership or organizational structure.

The Change-Management Process

Regardless of the type of change you may be introducing or helping manage, the change-management process is achieved through five steps. As you read through these steps, take note of where they align with the general management functions of planning, organizing, directing, and controlling. Also, take some time to compare these steps with some recent changes you have seen or personally implemented, and evaluate how well the process went and what could have been done better.

1. *Preparing for change.* This step involves understanding the necessary changes and preparing staff members and stakeholders for what's to come. It's an important part of the process, ensuring the change manager supports staff through any concerns and manages resistance by communicating the process and getting buy-in from employees.
2. *Creating a vision for change.* This stage is about creating the strategy to reach transformation once stakeholders have agreed to a change. Those involved set goals, delegating key performance indicators (KPIs) and tasks to the relevant parties. The change-management team makes plans to account for possible problems and helps everyone understand their role in managing processes at each level.
3. *Implementing changes.* This step puts the change plans into action. Excellent management and communication are key here; to make sure everything runs smoothly, change managers need to make sure everyone is doing their duties and employees are still happy and empowered.
4. *Embedding and solidifying changes.* Once the changes have been made, it's vital to make sure the transformation is in place so that staff members don't slip back into old ways. This step ensures that systems are in place to train staff and clarify new structures, workflows, and rewards.
5. *Reviewing and analyzing.* The final stage of the process is important to make sure changes continue and are beneficial. Change managers review what worked and what didn't work, and they make adjustments accordingly.

Change Management and Agency

Change-management roles and responsibilities vary depending on your role in the organization and the change that's being implemented. As a Chief, you are expected to serve as a change manager or agent regardless of your position or attitude toward the change. Your leadership expects you to fulfill one or more of the following roles:

- Communicating and liaising with leadership and your teams to drive the project forward
- Consulting with your leadership and teams to manage resistance
- Overseeing and helping manage the change strategy and the required timeline for the change
- Creating and distributing training and educational materials that aim to embed change into the organization
- Helping the wardroom and CPO mess implement change and navigate resistance
- Helping manage the change process to ensure the process meets its objectives
- Monitoring change and coordinating any activities to support the process
- Delivering feedback and after-action reports to help direct any future change initiatives

Furthermore, effective change management requires you to harness your leadership, management, and communication skills. You may also find yourself using your negotiation, organizational, process improvement, and time management skills. At this level, challenges simply can't be solved within any one function alone, so your commander and staff must leverage leadership to impact organizational outcomes across boundaries. You must be able to help understand and manage organizational politics, form alliances, and build collaborative relationships. Collaborating across organizational boundaries means spanning vertical, horizontal, demographic, cultural, and geographic differences and is a key part of your SEL role. If you know how to use your influence well, your actions and activities can and will have an impact across the whole organization. Are you ready and able to operate across an entire command structure?

The Coast Guard has a set of twenty-eight leadership core competencies that fall into one of four categories. One of those categories is "leading performance and change." Each service recognizes that its members constantly face challenges in mission operations. They also know that to meet these challenges, their leaders must apply performance competencies to their daily duties. Having these competencies enables each leader—and their service—to perform to the utmost in any situation. These competencies that any USCG or Navy Chief should develop to help enable their change management and agency skills include the following:

- *Customer Focus.* Service leaders should know who their customers are and make every possible effort to learn their customers' needs and hear their customers' voices. Understand the importance of measuring and monitoring the degree to which your customers' needs are met or exceeded and continually strive to improve that, and understand the distinction between "customer" and "boss," acting accordingly to balance competing demands.
- *Management and Process Improvement.* You should be able to plan, organize, and prioritize realistic tasks and responsibilities for yourself and your people. Use goals, milestones, and control mechanisms for projects, and seek, anticipate, and meet customers' needs—both internal and external. To achieve quality results, monitor and evaluate progress and outcomes produced by current processes, ensure continuous improvement through periodic assessment, and commit to improving policies, process, and overall quality. Effectively manage time and resources to successfully accomplish goals.
- *Decision-Making and Problem Solving.* You should identify and analyze problems; use facts, input from others, and sound reasoning to reach conclusions; explore various alternative solutions; distinguish between relevant and irrelevant information; perceive the impact and implications of decisions; and commit to action, even in uncertain situations, to accomplish organizational goals. Evaluate risk levels, create risk-control alternatives, and implement risk controls. Isolate high-important issues, analyze pertinent information, involve others in decisions that affect you, generate promising solutions, and consistently render judgments with lasting, positive impact.

- *Conflict Management.* You should facilitate open communication of controversial issues while maintaining relationships and teamwork. Effectively use collaboration as a style of managing contention; confront conflict positively and constructively to minimize impact to self, others, and the organization; and reduce conflict and build relationships and teams by specifying clear goals, roles, and processes.
- *Creativity and Innovation.* You should develop new insights into situations and apply innovative solutions to make unit and functional improvements. Create a work environment that encourages creative thinking and innovation. Take reasonable risks and learn from the inevitable mistakes that accompany prudent risk-taking—and apply this same thinking to those who work for you, encouraging innovation and helping your people apply the lessons learned. Design and implement new or cutting-edge programs and processes.

Team Reactions to Change

Everyone reacts to change differently. Ken Blanchard (2020) explained different reactions in his article "7 Common Reactions to Change and How to Respond to Them." Common reactions and attitudes include

- Feeling awkward, ill at ease, and self-conscious;
- Focusing on what people have to give up;
- Feeling alone, even if everyone else is going through the same change;
- Feeling that you are able to handle only so much change;
- Frustration at people being at different levels of readiness for change;
- Concern about having enough resources; and
- Annoyance at people wanting to revert to their old behavior.

As a change agent, you should look for these reactions and attitudes and be ready to address them. Much can be mitigated with frequent and authentic communication about the change and giving your people a chance to express their concerns and frustration with the pending changes.

Another theory of cognition by which one could identify a person's favored approach to problem solving and change was developed by Michael Kirton and is called the Kirton Adaption-Innovation Inventory (KAI). Kirton suggests that all individuals lie on a creativity continuum between high adaptation and high innovation. Those with high adaptation prefer to find solutions using established systems, whereas those with high innovation prefer to go beyond the current norms to find new and untested answers to problems.

There are some clear and obvious differences between individuals at either end of Kirton's continuum, but all of these perspectives are important to understand and leverage in decision-making and organizational change. Individuals at both ends of the continuum offer value to the change process but in different ways, and both perspectives are required to solve complex problems.

Innovators would prefer to be challenged by very different problems than adapters, and they would approach things with very different perspectives and solutions. Innovators tend to be forward-thinking brainstormers, unwilling to accept the status quo. They want to break the mold and find new and untested solutions.

Adapters have a preference for well-established organizational structures, systems, and processes. They tend to excel in finding ways to complete everyday tasks and overcome predictable challenges. Adapters are the agents of stability and progress, often found in managerial or defined leadership roles; innovators are agents of change and reactiveness, often found in visionary leadership positions.

There are also *bridgers*, who tend to blend the attributes of adapters and innovators. With an understanding and identification of these cognitive styles, you can see how you could best match them to roles and projects that suit their particular cognitive style and skill sets while leveraging these styles and skills to encourage collaboration and creatively solve problems. Identifying these team members can help make the team more informed, intelligent, and help mitigate emotional decisions.

You'll also have to assess your attitude—are you supporting the change, neutral to the change, or resisting the change, and why? As a change agent, it's important to understand your attitude toward change. As a senior enlisted, you have felt frustration with—and have had to absorb your team's frustration with—policies that are not within your scope of control but that impact your teams and people. You also know that organizational priorities change frequently, requiring you to adjust plans and resources. You must learn to manage this pressure to give your team more of a sense of control.

MCPON Mike Stevens used to champion "controlling what you own" as a line of effort under his "Zeroing in on Excellence" approach. He encouraged focusing on the things you can influence and not being distracted by the things you cannot. He encouraged a renewed focus on primary duties above all else, not allowing non-mission-collateral tasks to interfere, and not burdening your people with useless and redundant training or meetings without stated objectives. His approach also has an emphasis on accountability or owning what you control and the outcomes that your leadership and management approaches have delivered, both good and bad.

I think this is a great mindset to adopt when broad organizational change is happening and you're feeling frustrated. If you take time to reflect on the many things you can control in the span of a workday (the accomplishment of maintenance, improving the living conditions in your spaces, helping solve personal problems, planning and executing effective crew training events,

[5-3] MCPON Mike Stevens championed "controlling what you own" as a line of effort under his "Zeroing in on Excellence" approach. He encouraged focusing on the things you can influence and not being distracted by those things you cannot.
U.S. NAVAL INSTITUTE PHOTO ARCHIVE

etc.), you will find that your focus on these broader frustrations will diminish. Take time today to determine whether the pressure you feel is authentic or generated from your own sense of importance and urgency. Managing these feelings can help reduce your levels of stress and help ensure your attitude stays positive.

Final Thoughts

Achieving change is hard. People get comfortable. We get familiar. Soon we get stagnant and perhaps a bit defensive of the roles we play, our knowledge of the job, and the "as is" we understand and support. Absent complaints or outcry from the public or customers, only a new set of eyes on a problem, informed not by the history of how things have always been done but on the negative impacts that current processes have on outcomes, will be what predicates change. But changing the minds of those with decision-making authority, or those who control the flow of information, can be a herculean task when the solution requires some effort to adapt on their end. Resistance to change is strong with those who happily work short days in ignorance and indifference.

Progression toward meaningful change in such situations comes with some predictable behavioral responses. First, the change agents—the individuals or group having identified the problem and having a vision for a new "to be"—use good followership skills and work to inform decision makers and information gatekeepers. Favorable solutions demand work by all stakeholders, and change involves disagreement, which can naturally yield defensive postures, arguments, or subtle credibility sabotage efforts such as the insidious use of the "Reply All" function in email.

Leaders who are made aware of the disagreement and contention may make some effort to resolve it. They may ask both sides to explain their stance or direct both to communicate through established channels in the management scheme or chain of command. Aware such bureaucracy will never yield change, the change agents may prematurely abandon their interest, passion, and energy for the needed change. But, particularly in public service, they learn they cannot sustain inaction as their internal drive to serve won't allow it. When normal approaches to achieving a solution become disruptive, those desiring and working to influence change use versatility and shift to attacking the problem from unconventional angles with large wins or even minor improvements, which collectively can yield broader desired outcomes. Want to use new angles to attack the process? Consider these options:

- Highlight the lack of outcomes in required reports and in regular correspondence.
- Draft needed revisions to all existing and related policies and then route them for review through every available channel.
- Inform, garner the support of, or develop coalitions in the organization with others who may be experiencing a similar issue.
- Use your writing skills and submit articles to internal and external professional publications or blogs.
- In every line of effort, seize any opportunity to discredit the knowledge and abilities of those responsible. Shame is a peerless motivator. Understand how to professionally "push back" throughout the assault on the "as is."

Change is hard. It requires commitment and time. Some days we suit up and crash into the line just to be knocked back. Other days, we crash in and gain a few inches. On yet others, we crash in, break through, or figure out how to go around—and score a touchdown. Sturdy sustainment of influence tactics using all available communication channels will gain you ground with the right audience through one of the angles you've taken, and change will result.

Finally, because change is such a frequent and impactful process, you should continue to build your knowledge of the process and hone the skills required for you to be an effective change agent. This topic may be touched upon in your service leadership/management development courses, but there are also many professional change-management certificates available, including ACMP Certified Change Management Professional (CCMP), MSI Change Management Specialist (CMS), and CMI Accredited Change Manager–Foundation/Specialist. I encourage you to research to help develop your expertise and proficiency in the area of change management.

Six

Increasing Your Range of Communication

You encourage open and frank dialog, listen to Sailors, and energize the communication flow up and down the chain of command. This will increase unit efficiency, mission readiness, and mutual respect.

—*from the CPO Mission, Vision, and Guiding Principles*

With a suite of well-developed power bases, proficiency with influence tactics, and established interpersonal communication skills, you must now learn to become adept at organizational communication and at helping your leadership teams select and use the channel(s) of communication that best allow them to inspire, inform, or manage change or disruptions. As a junior leader, you frequently communicated one-on-one and with small groups. The *Petty Officer's Guide* covers the basics of communication, and you should continue to reflect on and improve your fundamental communication skills using the checklist in the "Communication Fundamentals Self-Assessment" text box (see Text Box 6-1). Regardless of your time in service, you can and should always improve in any of these areas. I have seen many "senior" Chief Petty Officers who are unable to handle a fundamental brief, struggle to provide an effective and engaging training session, or are intimidated by the prospect of a public speaking role.

You will continue to engage your deck-plate audiences, but as a CPO, SCPO, or MCPO, you must now start to think about how to harness more

6-1 COMMUNICATION FUNDAMENTALS SELF-ASSESSMENT

- I take time to consider by target audience when shaping my message.
- I take time to consider my own attitude, bias, and motives before communicating.
- I think about the best venue to communicate what I want to say.
- I consider any "noise" (physical, psychological, cultural) that can impede my message delivery and work to mitigate it.
- I know and adapt nonverbal cues, the tone of my voice, and my choice of words to my audience.
- I listen actively and with an open mind.
- I take time to practice and improve my communication skills and seek opportunities to put them to use.

strategic channels of communication to help shape broader organizational objectives and to reach larger, more dispersed audiences. Further, you will help senior officers communicate and shape their messages, advise them on the best channels of communication to use, and provide feedback on how their target audiences are receiving the message. You must start thinking about communication differently, with a focus on how you can use all the channels of communication available to you.

Communication has only become more complicated as the channels and platforms available to reach specific and larger audiences are ever increasing. Anyone can post on Facebook, X, or Threads, and anyone can make a YouTube video, so the risk of misinformation has increased exponentially. This translates to a great need for coordination and consistency of messaging across platforms to limit confusion and ensure dissemination to the intended audience. Despite the challenges, these advances are proving overwhelmingly useful for education, marketing, advocacy, fundraising, and a host of other ventures. Another challenge is the complex logistics of sharing information—often across time zones, organizations, service cultures, and operations—and leading teams from a distance. Effectively communicating your CO's or commander's vision and goals while inspiring trust is another.

Encouraging open communication and discussion among your teams is a huge part of what you should be doing daily. Building a climate of candor and respect for differences is critical for ensuring individuals and teams feel supported, motivated, and fully engaged in the success of the business. You and your leadership teams should be able to communicate your team's mission and your CO's or commander's vision while articulating complex ideas. You must have the ability to express your ideas clearly through what you say and write, and you should be able to effectively communicate with geographically dispersed teams to share important information, give feedback, and address concerns.

Many in the CPO mess have sound insight, opinions, and recommendations on how things are getting done and how they could be better, but often these comments are only communicated verbally and within the confines of the mess. When your writing ability is lacking, your ability to influence is diminished. Ideas that are written down have a much longer lifespan than those that are merely spoken. Memorandums, letters, performance evaluations, message traffic, emails, point papers, and even social media posts influence organizational decisions, particularly those made well above an individual unit or cutter. Writing is a key vehicle of influence and cannot be avoided. Like most things, the more you write, the better you will become at it. You have several resources to strengthen and guide your writing, including *The Naval Institute Guide to Naval Writing* (Shenk 2011) and the *Coast Guard Correspondence Manual* (2024). Skillful writing requires confidence, practice, and resources—the more you do it, the better you will be. However, effective influence requires the use of and proficiency in all forms of communication—speaking, writing, listening, and reading.

The Power of Information

A complementary power base to expert power is information power. People's ability to leverage information to shape behavior and attitudes has dramatically increased. In your service, so many policies are in effect and so much information is available that it's next to impossible for you to have all the answers immediately ready. And that's OK if you know where to get the information. Sources of information include meetings, articles, personal records, networks and professional organizations, and face-to-face discussions. Today the Internet and a wealth of social media sites provide your people immediate access to volumes of information that was once held tightly in the hands of a few leaders. Instructions can be found with a simple Google search, YouTube videos offer "how to" instructions on anything your people would want to do, and closed-group Facebook pages provide access to the information and advice of large peer networks. With all this information available, you must know how to use this power base to stay relevant.

Chiefs are known for their powerful base of information. You should ensure that you know how and where to quickly get the answers you need. Access to information online is a modern convenience and enabler. Search engine tools are readily available, and a search box is included in most applications. No longer must you keep tabbed binders of instructions and policies on the shelves in your office. To maintain an information advantage, in many instances you need only to know and bookmark the key instructions, manuals, and websites that have the information you need. Remember to familiarize yourself with "Frequently Asked Questions" (FAQs) and leverage "Live Chat" support functions where available, as these could potentially cut down your research time. It's also beneficial to pick up the phone and call a source or subject matter expert directly for the information that you or your people desire. Furthermore, you should be well informed of online periodicals, newsletters, and social media channels that can provide insight into strategic and operational-level decisions being made that impact your people, resources, and schedules. The online resources available to you are too numerous to list in this guide, but with some thought, you can have a well-developed catalog of instructions, manuals, and websites to help keep you informed. We recommend that you develop this catalog of resources as you will undoubtedly have to reference them throughout your career. Coupled with your connection power developed through the CPO mess and with other senior enlisted leaders, your access to information from the highest levels of the organization and your ability to disseminate it are greatly amplified. The challenge then becomes what to do with all of it. As has often been quoted, "information is power," and this power is typically used in several ways to shape behavior and attitudes.

First, you can share information. Today it is very easy to send a link or share a post over social media that has insights on policy, management, or leadership. This is information you should strive to communicate to your people because it puts a great amount of decision-making in their hands. Today's Navy and Coast Guard are experiencing a period of tremendous change. Our mission sets are changing, and many of the policies designed to recruit, retain, educate, train, and distribute our people are under review or have changed. Many of the policies have a direct impact on the quality of work or quality of life of your people and can cause anxiety, so you should strive to get them answers so they can understand the what, when, where, and why behind the policies and make their own informed decisions.

Information can also be withheld to shape behavior. For example, many underway patrols have been extended when the unit's schedule unexpectedly changed. Depending upon the circumstances, the CO may elect to withhold

[6-1] Former CNO ADM Jonathan Greenert talks about the status of the Navy during an all-hands call with the Office of Naval Intelligence and Navy Cyber Warfare Development Group commands.
U.S. NAVY PHOTO BY MC1 PETER D. LAWLOR/RELEASED

communicating those changes until a more appropriate time to ensure the unpopular news does not take your team's focus off the mission. In a more sinister example, a person with access to unique information may hold it to make themselves the "go-to" person for answers and to gain leverage over their people. Or in more extreme cases, they may even provide misinformation to alter the behavior of their people. Leaders and managers who elect to withhold or distort information are risking the trust and support of their people. Considering how readily available information has become, in many cases your people have access to the same information resources you do, so if you try to shape behavior with misinformation, you may find your personal power base severely eroded as your people quickly lose trust in you.

Information power can be used for leading up as well. For example, you may have access to information your supervisor needs or would benefit from when making plans or decisions. You may be brought into working groups or be asked to provide briefs to senior audiences on a particular issue as a subject matter expert or accomplished performer. This puts you in a position of power to influence policy or mission outcomes, so take these opportunities seriously. Reflect on why you are providing, withholding, or changing the information you have access to, and always provide input that best serves the command and the mission regardless of your personal feelings about it. Do not misuse your information power to exaggerate your accomplishments, cover up your mistakes, or misrepresent situations to gain access to more resources.

Other tactics of information power include using information to shape opinions and raise issues, pairing information with rewards to get others to help share messages that support your objectives, or using coercive power to deter people with information that could serve to counter your objectives or expose your personal power shortfalls. You may be in a rating that gives you access to personal information about people in your command. This information is often sensitive and subject to rules and controls on its distribution. Or you may have access to classified or sensitive information that, if not properly controlled, could risk operational advantages or national security.

One of the CPO guiding principles expects you to be an agent of active communication. In this capacity, you serve several critical functions in the flow of information. You monitor and seek current information from many sources. As a disseminator of information, you transmit this information to others, both inside and outside the organization. Make sure that the sources of information you use are credible, and take time to consider any potential bias associated with the source. Work to be well versed in the sources of information, and honestly and candidly communicate to your teams and your leadership. If you do, you will see that you have significant power to use information to resolve problems that arise within and across the domains you influence.

Broadening Your Personal Communication Skills

With well-developed power bases and knowledge of influence tactics, you must be able to select the vehicle of communication that best allows you to wield its influence. Effective influence requires effective communication, and that, in turn, requires consideration of things such as your communication skills and objectives, the makeup and attitude of your audience, the channels of communication available to you, any feedback you receive, and noise that may distract from your message. Without consideration of each of these elements, effective communication is hindered and your influence will suffer.

As a Chief you serve as a vital link of communication between the enlisted "working class" and the officer "professional class." Both groups have their unique beliefs and attitudes shaped by their unique upbringing and experience. You have the experience and exposure to, and attributes of, both classes, which enables you to understand both perspectives and convey the concerns and priorities each has to the other. To capably do this, you must take time to think clearly about what you are trying to communicate. This skill, also known as cognition, requires that you first understand what you are trying to say and accomplish. You must also consider the audience: no two audiences are identical, and they bring different depths of knowledge and understanding, so you must be careful when using jargon and abbreviations. Finally, you must transmit in a way that ensures listeners will fully understand the message. This requires the use of frequent pauses for emphasis and reflection and a chance for the receiver to ask questions or seek additional information. Again, prior to speaking to an audience, you must take time to reflect on how they will receive your message especially when it challenges their mental models of the "as is" and what they consider "right." It's acceptable (and even productive) to challenge these, but be mindful of the attitude of the receiver and use your emotional intelligence to gauge if you're pushing your message too hard.

Other communication channels include face-to-face communications, visual communications like the choreographed signals on a noisy flight deck, presentations, and written and social media. Each communications channel has its own rules and procedures, and you are expected to be proficient in using them all to increase the success of your influence tactics. In addition, there are many skills you must have and hone to effectively influence others, including decision-making, writing, speaking, and understanding strategy. As you advance, you must learn and develop new skills and attributes such as emotional intelligence along with managing teams, coaching, and mentoring—all of these require strong communication skills. And at the highest positions within your service and DoD, you must have a handle on change management and strategic communication. You should also be learning to use modern tools of digital communication to host meetings over geographical distances.

Written Communications

You have learned many things as you have advanced in your career. You have realized that replacement parts don't appear magically—someone has to order them. Flight or life-saving operations don't happen automatically—someone has to plan and organize them. Awards and evaluations don't just write themselves—someone has to write them. Budgets aren't randomly distributed—requirements must be developed and approved. And guest speakers don't have a consultant to write their speeches—they do that work on their own. Whatever happens in your service usually happens first on paper.

You should know by now that as you advance, you are faced with steadily increasing administrative responsibilities. As a Chief Petty Officer, your ability to quickly read and comprehend complex documents is vital and becomes even more important as you assume greater levels of responsibility and maturity. And your writing skills can often be the difference between success and failure. There are performance evaluations, official messages, important emails for reports, and point papers that will influence command

and policy decisions. Writing is a huge skill that you want to be able to harness in your leadership toolkit. Unfortunately, many Chiefs don't refine this skill and, in turn, their people are put at a disadvantage.

As a Chief Petty Officer, you'll usually be concerned with, and should have proficiency with, seven common forms of written communication:

- Messages and email
- Standard Navy letters
- Point papers
- Memoranda
- Casualty reports (CASREPS)
- Enlisted evaluations
- Citations, commendations, and awards

This guide won't go into details on each of these, and they're not solely the job of your administration department to know and compose, but you have access to and should be familiar with several guides, including the *Petty Officer's Guide*, that exist to help you write these and other correspondence effectively:

- *The Naval Institute Guide to Naval Writing*. Written by a naval officer who taught English at two service academies, this is the third edition of the premier guide to professional writing for the naval services. The book is widely used by officers, enlisted men and women, and civilians in both the Navy and Marine Corps. The author provides sound, practical advice on all common naval writing assignments. The third edition adds a new chapter on writing emails, and updates to the whole book account for the way naval writing is done in today's computer age.
- *Department of the Navy (Coast Guard) Correspondence Manual*, SECNAVINST 5216.5/COMDTINST M5216.4 (as amended). These manuals are arguably the most readable naval instructions ever written. The tone, quality, and responsiveness of correspondence is important. Your service's image and effectiveness are impaired if correspondence is sloppy, difficult to understand, unresponsive,

cold, impersonal, or incomplete. These manuals provide standards and procedures that apply to managing and preparing correspondence. They offer guidance on writing endorsements and point papers and offer practical advice on how to improve your writing.

- *Navy Eval Instruction*, BUPERS 1610.10 (as amended) / *Enlistments, Evaluations, and Advancements*, COMDTINST M1000.2 (as amended). These guides have chapters and appendixes that offer targeted guidance and language for writing enlisted evaluations.
- *Navy and Marine Corps Awards Manual*, SECNAV M-1650 (as amended) / *Coast Guard Military Medals and Awards Manual*, COMDTINST M1650.25 (as amended). Both of these references offer format and style guidance for drafting official awards and include examples.

Communication requires an intelligent sender, a receptive audience, a clear channel, a well-crafted message, freedom from noise, and provisions for adequate feedback. All of this requires you to continuously improve your writing skills. This is not as hard as you would believe, and you don't have to wait to attend the Senior Enlisted Academy or take a college course

[6-2] MCPOCG Jason Vanderhaden speaks during the Master Chief Petty Officer of the Coast Guard Change of Watch ceremony. U.S. COAST GUARD PHOTO BY LADONNA DAVIS

(although formal courses can be quite helpful). As a Chief Petty Officer, many of your seniors will personally observe your performance, but many more will know and judge you by the way you write.

Effective Listening

Surprisingly the complex skill of effective listening is something that is rarely taught. After all, we have two ears and only one mouth for a reason—surely nature intended us to be effective listeners. By now you should understand and embrace that one of your most important skills and tasks is to be an active listener. You are expected to listen when your division officer or department head is passing the word, and you are expected to listen with great interest and attention when counseling and coaching your people. Active listening is an expression of how to listen to someone else and, ultimately, the ability to put oneself in the other person's shoes. Unfortunately, although the fundamental attributes of listening appear to be common sense, all too often they seem to get lost in the heat of "battle."

The *Petty Officer's Guide* offers more in-depth guidance on active listening. You should know that when you listen, face the speaker, maintain eye contact to the degree you feel comfortable, minimize internal distractions, respond appropriately to show you understand, and focus solely on what the speaker is saying. Try to keep an open mind and avoid being defensive to the extent possible, which is much harder to do than many think. Take time to solicit feedback on and reflect on how well you are exercising your active listening skills.

Verbal and Nonverbal Communication

You should make a habit of giving frequent feedback to subordinates and division officers on their day-to-day performance and of working this communication into daily routines. Feedback can be verbal or nonverbal communication offered to a person or group that provides information as to how their behavior or message is affecting them. Words, gestures, posture, or the absence of expected reactions are all forms of feedback. Effective feedback considers the needs of both the giver and receiver. Giving effective feedback pays big dividends for you and your organization over the long run. Feedback is immediately useful if directed toward behavior the receiver can control and if delivered at the earliest opportunity. Telling a leading petty officer (LPO), "Overall, I was happy with the work you did on this project, but I noticed some areas to improve on," is better than saying nothing and then losing your temper the next time that person makes the same mistake. Although you are not required to give justification for your orders, you should explain your reasons to your Sailors when time permits. Sailors who understand the reasons for an order not only appreciate that you took time to explain it but are much more likely to carry it out enthusiastically and thoroughly.

> *Anchor Up*
>
> In your current position, what are the top three barriers to your influence objectives? Why? What can you do to reduce or remove the barriers? What resources do you have available to help?

To help juniors develop their own decision-making skills, sometimes it is clever to tell what you want done without specifying exactly how you want it done, particularly when interacting with and developing your LPOs. At the same time, make it a point to be clear about exactly what results you expect from your people's efforts. Once you become familiar with the individual personalities and abilities of your people, and they in turn become familiar with your expectations, you can then use verbal shorthand that reduces overly explicit detail in orders.

Then there are those times when you will be communicating with your leadership. Day-to-day interactions are easy . . . it gets tougher when things aren't going so well. Most senior officers, department heads, and division officers take a dim view of a Chief who begins every conversation with a lengthy preface, particularly when they recognize a pattern: a preface in the form of a series of excuses that leads up to the ultimate bad news. Putting the bad news first (what we call the bottom line up front, or BLUF) can help prevent the buildup of anxiety in the officers you want to influence as they wait to find out what you are trying to say. Putting the bad news first often makes them more willing to hear you out without interruption. When the news is exceedingly bad, however, as in a report of an accident involving members of the crew, your seniors appreciate hearing early reassurances about casualties or damage.

But you should avoid bringing your boss a problem without suggesting an appropriate solution to address or correct it. You must know when to make exceptions to this rule and when to delay providing supervisory reports in order to take immediate corrective actions needed to save a life or the ship. In such cases, you should make a timely report and then return with an update and solution as soon as reasonably possible under the circumstances. This kind of interaction with the boss can be challenging for new chiefs if they have not had a demanding LPO experience. The approach of simply reporting the situation and awaiting instruction will not work once an individual is the Chief. Regardless of the position you find yourself in, your ability to make timely reports with strong, well-thought-out recommendations is key to enhancing your personal reputation. You should also train your division officer on how to make these kinds of reports and recommendations.

Speaking Skills

More people report a fear of public speaking than report fears of heights, tight spaces, spiders, or other things that "bug" us. For some, the ability to speak comfortably in public may be a gift requiring little practice to master; but for most of us it is a skill that demands many years of practice and experience. Although it is doubtful you will ever have to become a skilled orator, as you move into positions of increased influence, you will speak at a number of activities where your ability to speak clearly and forcefully will be a valued and required asset. You will speak to small groups and teams during briefs and debriefs, you may be detailed as an instructor or perhaps selected to facilitate a working group, and you may find yourself offering your perspective in front of a group of flag officers.

At this point you should be capable of giving a rousing or inspirational speech, and you must be adept at speaking with groups and presenting a well-organized and informative talk designed for an audience. The *Petty Officer's Guide* offers much more guidance and advice on strengthening your verbal communication skills.

Anchor Up
How effectively do you use all vehicles of active communication (oral and written) to achieve your influence objectives in your current position? What can you do to improve your speaking, listening, and writing skills? What resources do you have available to do so?

Holding Effective Meetings

You have participated (and will continue to participate) in work groups, task forces, planning teams, or in other settings where participants will shape opinion and policy and will work to influence outcomes. You will be called on regularly to solve problems well outside your rating, problems that you lack training or experience to deal with. You can be assigned to lead or participate in finding solutions. To help the group succeed, you will need to rely on the help of others, and the normal venue to do this is in meetings.

[6-3] The commander of the *John C. Stennis* Carrier Strike Group (CSG-3) holds an online meeting with the families of Sailors deployed aboard the aircraft carrier. U.S. NAVY PHOTO BY PO3 WILL TYNDALL

Holding meetings is easy, but holding effective and efficient meetings can be a challenge and can be more art than science. Still, there are guidelines to consider when using this venue of influence.

- Clearly identify the purpose of the meeting and ensure the agenda supports that purpose. We have all been to that recurring meeting: it tends to develop a lot of discussion but fails to develop a solution or fails to improve a management process or project. Before scheduling a meeting, make sure you know your objectives and communicate them in advance so participants can come prepared to contribute. Shape the length of the meeting to the objectives, allowing adequate—but not too much—time for each portion.
- Read and understand the psychology behind meeting dynamics. Know the personalities of those on your team and consider how they may impact or distract from your meeting dynamics. For example, if one of the team members has a bad habit of interrupting the flow of the brief, set guidelines up front, noting that questions and discussion will be entertained at the end of the brief. There is an art to managing a team, and effectively "herding cats" comes with experience and preparation.
- Focus on key issues, which aligns with the first point. Many times meeting agendas and discussions skirt the tough issues that often get talked about in the mess or outside of the meeting. The leader of the meeting must work to ensure that these discussions come out because they often are the root issues that must be resolved.
- Stick to timelines. Time is a precious and valuable resource. It is not a luxury. Arrive on time and ensure that briefers and other attendees arrive on time as well. The mantra that the "chief is never late, just detained elsewhere" is a false argument. It represents a belief that the chief's time is more important than anyone else's. And once the meeting begins, stick to the agenda.
- Consider the full range of potential meeting venues. Not everything requires a formal meeting in the conference room. Options include video teleconferencing, phone calls, and formal and informal lunches and dinners. Select the venue based on the desired outcome

and consider where you can gain efficiency. An informal "brown bag" lunch meeting might allow you to exchange or solicit the information you need while providing an opportunity to strengthen networks.
- Consider clustering your meetings to increase efficiency. You may have several different meetings that require the same people to attend. You can help them better manage their time by holding those meetings on the same morning. You will better manage your time and gain their appreciation. And reserve days with no meetings. This break provides space within your personal schedule to reflect on discussions from meetings you had that week and to read and write about topics important to you.
- Locate and prepare a space conducive to the successful wielding of influence. This may not be as easy as it sounds because space, especially onboard ships, is always at a premium. The physical conditions of a meeting space, however, will have an impact on the success and effectiveness of the meeting. There are options for configuring spaces to maximum effect, depending on the situation and audience.

[6-4] Coast Guard Force Readiness Command holds a board of advisers meeting to discuss issues aimed at ensuring that best practices and policies are in place to guarantee mission success.
U.S. COAST GUARD PHOTO BY CWO JOHN EDWARDS

Strategic Communication

Strategic communication is the process and art of linking communication efforts with an agenda or plan. Strategic communication is a framework of the best or right message, the right channels for distribution, the right audience, and supportive or actionable feedback. As a Chief you can expect to be and should seek to be involved in your organization's strategic messaging.

Strategic communication plans can be developed at all levels of the chain of command. For example, you can help a new department head or CO communicate their vision and philosophy, or you can help senior flag officers and their staff implement policy that will create broad culture change. This is not "off the cuff" speaking and engagement; it is engagement with a purpose. At this point in your career, you have been the target of strategic communication efforts, and you have seen when they have succeeded and when they have failed. You will influence the success or failure of those strategic communication plans and efforts. As a senior enlisted leader, you bring great value to any strategic communication plan. You will serve as a vital link of communication between the enlisted "working class" and the officer "professional class," but your "reach" will grow. Regardless of the audience, you should know the plan and help your leadership teams manage it. To capably do this, there are several things you can do.

First, you should ask, "do we have a strategic communication and engagement plan?" In many cases you will find that one does not exist, and if it does, it is off track. In smaller level organizations, the "plan" is probably just jotted down by your department head or CO. They have a general sense of their goals and what they want to communicate, and the crew is small enough that they can execute without a detailed and organized written plan. At higher levels of the organization, the plan is typically owned by the public affairs officer (PAO) or an officer assigned to develop and execute a strategic communication plan for the command. Find out who owns the plan and review it. If one does not exist, address that with the team.

As you review the plan, take time to see if it meets the requirements for an effective strategic communication plan. Here are some good questions to ask:

- What behavior or effects are we looking to achieve with this plan?
- Are we using all the right channels to communicate the message?

- Does the plan include all the right audiences and the best people to deliver tailored messages to them?
- How do we measure the effectiveness of the plan?
- What is my role in this plan?
- How will we measure our plan's effectiveness?

This approach to communication requires that everyone knows what they are trying to say and accomplish—the right message, who it needs to be delivered to, and how it should be delivered. No two audiences are identical. Each brings different attitudes, backgrounds, depths of knowledge, and understanding, so any strategic communication efforts should be mindful of who is best suited to deliver the message. This also requires responding to questions from, and offering feedback to, the audience. Sometimes the target audience rejects the message outright if it contradicts or challenges their values and beliefs or if decoding takes more effort than the information is worth to them. Questions from the audience are often an indication of the depth of their understanding. How the message is delivered may include large venues for face-to-face communications such as an all-hands, newsletter or journal articles, and social media campaigns on channels such as Facebook, Instagram, YouTube, or LinkedIn. Each communication channel has its own rules and procedures, and the more proficient you and your organization are at using them, the greater the success of the strategic communication plan becomes.

The ways the strategic communication plan influences the effectiveness and efficiency of your organization depends on many variables. "Noise" describes the factors that individually or collectively work against leadership goals and that interfere with the effective exchange of information. For example, generational differences can yield different values, beliefs, attitudes, and priorities that may run counter to your influence objectives and that must be considered when selecting tactics or channels of communication. The emotional state of the sender or receiver as well as any prejudices or biases can prevent the information from being received as intended. And teams that are geographically dispersed will have distance that serves as a barrier to messaging. You must be aware of the noise, gauge the impacts, and help your team and your command adjust to its effects.

If you are serving as an SEL, you should work with the staff and give deliberate thought to and discuss how you are or could be integrated into strategic engagement and communication efforts. Rather than basing your engagement on the direction to "go do what SELs do," take time to reflect on how your boss can best leverage your engagement in ways commensurate with their own scope of responsibility, authority, and accountability. Proactively engage to help your commander and staff determine how to best use you to your full potential to further organizational objectives. You may also have a role in your service senior enlisted leader's communication plan, so you will have to consider how to integrate that message as well. As an SEL, you should not be off on your own agenda; rather, your engagements should be well thought out and complement organizational strategic communication and key leader engagement plans and objectives. Although you and your commander may often have to execute "unit circulation" alone, your messages must be aligned and should be guided by a well-thought-out communication plan.

Communication as a Tool to Manage Team Climate, Trust, and Cohesiveness

Your teams have high expectations of you. They expect proactive and clear communication, challenging work assignments, managerial competence, professional performance feedback, opportunities for growth and advancement, and effective training. They also expect to be treated with dignity and respect and expect leadership interest in their quality of work and quality of life. The *Petty Officer's Guide* offers ample guidance and advice on how to achieve these things, and by this point in your career you should be proficient in them and be a positive and effective mentor and coach.

One of the most important responsibilities you have is to help manage the division, department, or command climate. At the highest levels, you will work to influence the organizational culture and climate. If neglected, the morale and effectiveness of a unit can decline, which, if not corrected, can lead to destructive outcomes. Frequent, transparent, and authentic communication underpins a positive command climate and culture and is key to a successful team. Leaders who fail to implement dynamic, two-way communication mechanisms will not see their units perform to their full potential. Sometimes just providing avenues for the crew to be heard at regular intervals and then providing timely and candid feedback is enough. The answers will not always be popular, but the fact that your crew is heard shows you care and are interested in their well-being. There are a wealth of communication tools, tactics, and techniques at your disposal that can be effective for helping shape and maintain a positive work climate.

Formal and Informal Surveys and Metrics

Command climate assessments are required and are guided by instruction. And although they may be administratively burdensome, they can offer some great insight if executed properly. Ensure that they are conducted and that the results are fed back to the command. Too many times the surveys are completed, but the crew is never provided feedback that you heard what they took time to say. Others are less formal. For example, check the leave balance of your crew. Members with greater than sixty or ninety days of earned leave may indicate they have a desire to be involved and perform the mission but could also indicate a poor work–life balance. Health and fitness data, the number of crewmembers eligible for advancement or on "A" school wait lists, the number of crewmembers who have completed resident courses or are working toward advanced qualifications, the number of crew requesting extensions, or the insights you gain from out-briefs with transferring and temporarily assigned personnel will all help tell you a story of your command culture and climate. These tools and feedback sessions will also offer your commanding officer the opportunity to clear up misunderstandings or make policy adjustments.

If you are an ISIC SEL, you have a role to help the units within your sphere of influence. You should take time to ask how thorough command climate assessments are and keep tabs on whether someone on your staff reviews written comments. You should also engage in trend analysis to determine whether the climates in your subordinate commands are improving or declining, and use that to engage with coaching for the leadership at those commands.

CMC/CSEL Calls

CMC/CSEL calls can be a very effective tool for pulsing command climate. I recommend you do these at the division level. More candid feedback will come out if divisional leaders are not invited and when you host these sessions in divisional spaces. I recommend that you use a free-association technique to generate discussion. For example, rather than simply asking what's wrong, prompt the group and ask, "What comes to mind when I say, 'command safety,' 'MWR,' or 'chow'?" Once a crew member comments, use that to see if there is consensus on an issue or if that view is just an outlier. Take notes on the concerns and provide the command with feedback on what was discussed and what you think requires action. It's good practice to include division leadership and the department head and department LCPO on what came out of the meeting. This tactic can be easily translated to and used by department- and division-level leaders. As you move up the chain of command, you will conduct these kinds of sessions in bigger venues such as "all-hands calls," but you can still engage in smaller settings like the ones described above.

CO's Calls

Each pay grade in a unit typically has its own concerns and maturity level, so by breaking these sessions up, you can get a great command-wide perspective on issues. Using information gathered from CSEL calls provides content to base these meetings on. Cutter schedules, upcoming inspections, and command philosophy are all good topics of discussion, and they also provide opportunities for your people to ask questions and provide timely feedback. When conducted at frequent intervals and coupled with other avenues of communication, this proactive approach to managing climate provides a constant relief valve for the stressors that build up in a command and prevents angst that results when effective avenues for communication are absent or lacking. Once again, you should encourage your department heads and division officers to conduct these sessions as well.

Attend Board and Council Meetings

There are a variety of board meetings that your people are members of that you should attend. For example, on ships there is usually a menu advisory board that meets, and most units have an MWR committee meeting to discuss and plan events. Safety boards and councils offer insight into the strengths and weaknesses of safety culture. In many cases you don't have to speak; your presence shows you care. You are there to listen and learn about what is working well and what needs adjusting and then work to help make things better.

CMC for a Day

During my first CMC tour I decided to invite a crew member to shadow me over the course of the day when we were underway. This person was selected by their department, and being a squared-away person wasn't a criterion. We would meet at the CPO mess for breakfast and then that Sailor would attend all my daily meetings, meals, walk-arounds, and work out with me. We would finish up in my office after eight o'clock reports, and I would get feedback on what the crew member learned about the command and the CMC position. It was very eye-opening for them, gave them a great deal of face time with command leaders, and it gave us both an opportunity to learn a great deal of things about each other and our perspectives. The Sailor would then go on to talk to their peers about insights regarding the command that may not have been getting effectively communicated, so that helped spur improved information flow and awareness.

Getting Around

You should make time daily to talk to your people and other stakeholders to evaluate the effectiveness of evolutions and the philosophy behind current strategies and policies and to learn the inside thinking—do not try to connect the dots yourself. Walk the decks of your ship and talk to watchstanders, those eating a meal, or those in their divisional spaces. If you are in a squadron, foreign object damage (FOD) walkdowns are a good time to engage in a conversation. You should meet with leadership and your teams as a group and individually, and formally and informally, to debrief planned and unplanned evolutions so you can gain a sense of alignment with expected outcomes and improve processes or identify new hazards that may accompany the evolution. Ask questions like, "How is a possible cause prevented or its effects minimized?" Take time to observe the actions of your organization. Watching what your people do and the way they behave while doing it can provide great insight into organizational culture. Take time to walk around and just talk to the crew about how things are. You'll be amazed at how much info you can get from your people if you just give them the opportunity to let you know. This is a great tool and technique to demonstrate your personal power and build trust.

Your service has invested in policy, education, and resources designed to strengthen command climate and culture. Initiatives such as the sponsorship program, command indoctrination program, ombudsman program, career development program, Command Drug and Alcohol Representative (CDAR) program, and the Equal Opportunity (EO) program are important not just because they provide valuable information and resources to personnel and their families but because they demonstrate that we care about our crews. Ultimately, they demonstrate the competence and character of your service as an organization, which helps our credibility and builds trust within our people. A strong working knowledge of these programs is a key component of institutional expertise. You have many opportunities to promote these programs, including morning quarters or stand-up meetings, command indoctrination programs, general military training (GMT) sessions, and one-on-one discussions and mentoring sessions.

Much of the work of developing and managing a positive command climate revolves around building a sense of trust between the command, department, or division leadership and the crew, and it all starts with open communication. Soliciting frank feedback, conducting critical self-assessments, making adjustments when required, and letting people know that you are taking action and that they are heard are all ways to maintain or improve the climate, morale, and cohesiveness of your unit, which underpin the trust required for teams to operate most effectively.

Finally, Navy and USCG families make tremendous sacrifices, and there are programs and resources in place to help them cope with the stress related to separations and the uncertainty associated with service requirements. Your command leadership must foster an environment that makes families a part of your team and helps them become resilient and prepared to navigate the challenges of military service. Family readiness is not managed in isolation. You are supported in this effort by ombudsmen, family resource groups, and Fleet and Family Support Centers. You can help by ensuring families are knowledgeable about challenges they can expect, are familiar with the resources available to them, and develop the skills necessary to function and thrive in the face of challenge and uncertainty. Consistent information flow to families is the single most important element in maintaining family readiness. A family that feels connected to the command has a positive influence on the servicemember and your command's climate.

Having and harnessing effective communication skills and plans are key to getting the mission accomplished and keeping unit morale high. They will also enable you and your command teams to create context, inspire hope, demonstrate your authenticity and transparency, connect with your people intellectually and emotionally, and give you confidence. You have a signi-ficant role in clearly communicating standards to your people while consistently keeping the chain of command informed with facts and your perspective. Go out and put these skills to use to make a positive difference in your teams!

Seven

Organizational Management Processes and Your Influence on Them

> Most managers would rather focus on lofty policy matters. But when the details are ignored, the project fails. No infusion of policy or lofty ideals can then correct the situation.
>
> —ADM Hyman Rickover

As a Chief you wear many hats. Some of your roles are obvious: leader and mentor to young men and women who have chosen naval service. But equally important is your role as manager; the objectives, actions, and activities of any organization must be directed and managed. Although you possess leadership competence, you must also possess keen management skills such as decision-making, problem solving, personal planning, time management, and effective communication. It is a rare Chief who does not find herself with limited resources—there are never enough people, parts, tools, time, or opportunity to do the job quite the way it should be done.

A 1990 Navy Education and Training (NAVEDTRA) manual titled *Management Fundamentals: A Guide for Senior and Master Chief Petty Officers* captured many key management principles and practices still relevant to the effective and efficient operation of maintenance and watch teams today (Gamer 1990). These concepts can be used by those below the Senior and Master Chief pay grades; some core content from this publication is included in this chapter, but each of these management "fundamentals" is presented more in depth in the *Petty Officer's Guide*.

7-1 SELF-ASSESSMENT:
MANAGERIAL ATTRIBUTES OF U.S. NAVY CHIEFS

- I work to resolve conflicts in scheduling and priorities so that my people are not left to choose their own schedules and priorities.
- I ensure my people have access to—and use—all the references they need to do their various jobs correctly.
- I walk through all my spaces frequently and regularly to check for cleanliness, preservation, and stowage.
- I look in on work in progress; my people are not surprised by it. I require my people to show me the maintenance and operational procedures.
- I check up after work is done to make sure it has been done properly, the equipment is correctly restored, and the work area and tools have been stowed.
- I offer praise on the spot when I find my people doing good work.
- I provide closer supervision and more careful planning of tasks that are hazardous or unfamiliar to my people.
- I lead pre-evolution briefs and take the opportunity during the appropriate debrief meetings to share lessons learned from recent issues.
- I objectively audit programs I am responsible for, taking advantage of check sheets and past inspection reports to find potential problems.
- I actively manage the manning of my division, looking ahead to replace personnel losses.
- I actively look for ways to improve existing programs instead of settling for "That's the way we've always done it."

Management Fundamentals

Management can be defined as the process of getting projects, work, or tasks done that are required for achieving the goals of an organization in an efficient and effective manner. Efficiency is the amount of effort or resources used to produce a specific output and asks the question "Are we doing things right?" Effectiveness is the degree to which the organization achieves its stated objective and asks, "Are we doing the right things?" Typically, being efficient is not as important as being effective—doing the wrong things well doesn't benefit you, your people, or the command. As a senior enlisted leader, you will manage or help manage personnel (manning, training, qualifications, projected rotation dates, etc.), maintenance, supply inventories, information, and special projects. Your unit and team succeeds by completing the mission or the demands placed upon it by the chain of command. Investing time, resources, and strong organizational and personal managerial skills toward the successful completion of the required tasks on time will preclude investing time and resources toward other objectives.

Although you have developed some level of management capability and proficiency, it is important for you to remember as you progress up the chain of command that the complexity of maintenance and of other projects requiring sound management skills increases. You must reflect on how your management skills are maturing or need to improve or where you can help impact the success of broader organizational management goals. Whether you serve as a division chief, department LCPO, or senior enlisted leader, developing and honing the appropriate level of management acumen will help you enhance your unit's mission readiness and climate.

From a management perspective, your role as a CPO is that of senior technical supervisor with primary responsibilities for supervising and training enlisted personnel in system and subsystem maintenance, repair, and operation. When advanced to SCPO (or selected for limited duty officer [LDO] or chief warrant officer [CWO]), you will provide the command with a higher level of technical and managerial expertise and impact than that expected at the E-7 level. And as an MCPO you can expect to help manage the development, implementation, and execution of broader organizational policies and processes within the occupational field, across the warfare community, or across the fleet or Navy. As a senior enlisted leader, you may be assigned to several project management–type billets, such as 3-M assistant, maintenance Master Chief, rating force Master Chief, or community manager.

Like civilian projects, day-to-day military operations, preventive and corrective maintenance, and policy development and management have specific objectives, defined timelines, and resource limitations, and they require effective management. You will manage projects ranging from helping plan high-level military operations to transitioning a ship out of an availability back into an operational posture to managing a large maintenance project or one of your command's collateral duty programs. Furthermore, your CPO mess should be using active communication and collaboration to manage the successful completion of significant command milestones and objectives such as inspection and survey (INSURV), shipyard availabilities, and other unit- or operational-level training requirements that certify warfighting readiness.

The basic management functions—planning, organizing, directing, and controlling—are interdependent; removal of one function renders the entire management process ineffective. By now you have managed maintenance,

[7-1] U.S. Navy Chief supervises Sailors as they load ammunition into a close-in weapon system aboard a guided-missile destroyer.
U.S. NAVY PHOTO BY MC2 DONALD R. WHITE JR./RELEASED

operations, and personnel assignments and training. You may have even managed a major command collateral program. You should understand that the objectives, actions, and activities of any organization must be directed and managed, and although you possess some amount of leadership competence, you must also possess keen management skills. These skills include planning and organizing, decision-making, problem solving, inspectmanship, time management, and effective communication.

Anchor Up
Which of the four management functions are you (and your mess or organization) strongest at? Why? Which one is your weakest? Why? What can you do to improve in that management area? What resources are available to help you?

Although you possess some amount of management capability and proficiency, it's important for you to remember that as you progress up the chain of command, the complexity of maintenance and other projects requiring sound management skills increases, so you must reflect on how your management skills are maturing and recognize areas requiring improvement. And as you move into positions working on ISIC staffs or on training and assessment teams, you will use your management experience to help those organizations ensure that their units are properly manned, trained, and equipped—your management focus will shift toward organizational and project management.

Managing Bigger Projects

Although you probably don't have any formal project management training or responsibilities, you may be assigned to a unit in a variety of maintenance postures, or you may be involved with mission planning. Or you may find yourself in a position such as a command or assistant 3-M coordinator, maintenance Master Chief, operations Chief, or executive petty officer, so there will be new processes, functions, and planning tools that you will have to become familiar with, qualify on, and enhance your skills in. Regardless of the specific management role you are filling, you will find that there are four elements to consider when managing projects:

- *Resources.* Resources include people, equipment, materials, software, hardware, and more. Technically, anything that provides effort or must be used during a project can be deemed a resource.
- *Time.* Time will have a huge impact on every aspect of your project from start to finish. You must keep a close eye on time in the form of deadlines, task durations, milestone achievements, project progress, dependencies, and much more.
- *Budget.* If there's one thing more important to your project than time or resources, it's the money available. A project budget impacts every aspect of a project's completion, from paying manpower to the cost of supplies or travel. The budget ensures or disrupts the availability of those resources available to you and, in turn, the time it takes to complete the project.
- *Scope.* Scope is one of those things that can be difficult to determine. It involves many different factors, including project requirements, project goals, and project size (size and scope are not necessarily mutually exclusive). Although the scope of the project may be the most fluid of the four elements, it can have serious impact and will affect the other elements. For example, the more complex a ship's availability, the more resources, time, and money it will require. Additionally, a ship may only have a short amount of time for a given maintenance availability, so the scope of the project must be shaped accordingly.

Project management is the set of functions that helps you and your organization achieve your goals and objectives. It involves a series of processes, methods, and tools to initiate, plan, execute, control, and close a project. Effective project management requires a comprehensive understanding of the four key elements of project management: scope, time, cost, and quality. As a senior enlisted leader, you may be involved in complex maintenance and project management, so you should be aware of the four elements, help your leadership evaluate where they are working well or not so well, and provide recommendations on how to adjust. If any of these elements are not managed, maintenance schedules can be extended and operational schedules impacted. In turn, negative impacts to team quality of work and life are sure to follow, and you will find yourself working to help your leadership mitigate those negative impacts.

- *Scope Management.* Scope management is the process of defining, documenting, and controlling the scope of a project. This involves identifying the project's deliverables, requirements, objectives, and goals. Doing so can ensure that your project stays on track and meets stakeholders' expectations. To manage scope effectively, there is usually a scope statement outlining the project's boundaries, goals, and objectives. This statement is reviewed and approved by a variety of stakeholders to ensure that everyone has a clear understanding and agrees on the goals and outcomes of the project.
- *Time Management.* Time management involves planning, scheduling, and controlling the time needed to complete a project. Ensuring that the project is completed on time and within budget is essential. To manage time effectively, a project schedule is created that outlines the tasks and milestones and their estimated durations. One common tool used to create a project schedule is called a Gantt chart. You have probably seen or used one. It shows each task's start and end dates, the dependencies between tasks, and the critical path, which is the sequence of tasks that must be completed on time to ensure the project's success.
- *Cost Management.* Unfortunately, this is an aspect you probably won't be able to control, but you should be aware of it. It involves estimating, budgeting, and controlling the costs associated with a project. To manage costs effectively, a project budget is created and approved to outline the estimated costs for each task and milestone. This cost management plan outlines the cost estimation methods, the budgeting process, and the controls used to monitor and control costs. Additionally, project managers track and report actual costs to ensure they stay within the budget.
- *Quality Management.* This element involves ensuring that the project meets the required quality standards. It's essential to deliver a

high-quality product that meets the safety and operational standards expected. To manage quality effectively, project managers define quality standards, create a quality management plan, and implement quality control processes. Organizations typically use a quality management system (QMS)—the set of policies, procedures, and processes that ensure the project meets the required quality standards.

Managerial Roles, Attributes, and Skills

Regardless of your level of management experience, there are key management skills and areas of competence that you should continue to hone and evaluate in yourself, your subordinate managers, and your leadership teams and that can significantly contribute to the successful planning, execution, and assessment of military operations and readiness.

- *Leadership Skills.* Successful managers are strong leaders who inspire and motivate their teams to achieve project success through a variety of operating environments and challenges. You must lead by example, communicate a clear vision for the project (whether you own it or not), and inspire your team members to work together toward a common goal. You will also have to make difficult decisions, delegate tasks effectively, and hold team members accountable for their performance. Guidance on accomplishing these things is covered in the *Petty Officer's Guide.*
- *Communication Skills.* Effective communication is essential to project success, and in your managerial role you must communicate effectively with a wide range of internal and external stakeholders, including team members, leadership, and contractors. You should clearly articulate project goals and expectations, provide feedback and guidance to team members, and address any conflicts or issues that arise throughout the project life cycle.
- *Time Management Skills.* One of the most critical skills that successful project managers possess is managing time effectively. This involves setting clear timelines and milestones, prioritizing tasks, and ensuring that team members work efficiently and effectively.

Effective time management also requires identifying and addressing any potential roadblocks or delays that may arise throughout the project.

- *Risk Management Skills.* You and your teams must be able to identify and manage project risks effectively, including anticipating potential problems and developing contingency plans to address them if they do arise. It also involves mitigating risks by identifying and addressing potential issues before they become major problems. Chapter 8 provides more insight and guidance on this topic.
- *Problem-Solving Skills.* Projects usually encounter unforeseen hurdles, so problem solving is a critical skill you should have to identify and address any issues that arise throughout the project life cycle. This involves thinking creatively and analytically to develop and offer solutions to complex problems. It also involves working collaboratively with team members to identify and address any issues that may arise.
- *Organizational Skills.* Complex operations require you to be highly organized and able to manage multiple tasks and projects simultaneously. You must be able to prioritize tasks, manage personnel and material resources, and ensure that all project deliverables are completed on time and to standards. You should also understand how organizations such as shipyards organize and track progress.
- *Stewardship.* Stewardship is an ethical value that encompasses the responsible planning and management of resources. You are entrusted by the American people to maintain the platforms and people entrusted to your care. Leaders such as you, as well as organizations, have a role as stewards in service, from taking responsibility for forming working relationships to drive transformative change to being a catalyst of advocacy, shared responsibility, and collective action to address resource shortfalls and needed policy change.
- *Attention to Detail.* Drilled into you from the time you went to boot camp is the concept that mission success often hinges on the small details, so you and your teams must be able to pay attention to the small details that can make or break a project. This includes identifying potential issues or roadblocks early on and addressing or communicating them to your leadership proactively to ensure project success.

- *Adaptability.* You and your teams must be able to adapt quickly to changing circumstances and pivot quickly as required and adjust the project plan as needed to ensure project success.
- *Stakeholder Management.* Your role here is to help team members, clients, vendors, and other stakeholders involved in the project perform to their best. This involves communicating effectively with stakeholders, building relationships, and managing expectations to ensure that all stakeholders are satisfied with the project outcomes.
- *Technical Competence.* While soft skills are critical to project success, senior enlisted managers must also possess technical skills related to their industry, platform, or rating. This includes understanding the technical aspects of the mission or project and knowing and being able to manage technical resources to ensure project success effectively.
- *Inspectmanship.* A pending inspection often brings out the worst in a chain of command. Formalities, reports, formations, and interruptions are common elements of any inspection and cause unnecessary anxiety, perhaps because we are not always inspection ready. Working up to an inspection implies that a unit does not already work at the anticipated inspection-ready level or does not have strong self-assessment and training capability. You should know and be able to ensure that your platforms, systems, people, and administration are in a 100 percent state of readiness—that your unit is capable and prepared to handle any tasking. Chiefs who achieve this avoid the frenzy that comes with preparing for an inspection and understand that the inspection or assessment is an opportunity to improve and make them better rather than an evolution that ensures they are meeting minimum standards.

Whether you are directly managing a project or working on a flag staff in an advisory capacity, you will manage projects and resources, meet deadlines, complete milestones, brief stakeholders, and ultimately accept responsibility for the success or failure of those tasks. Over your career, your increasing positions of authority and responsibility have armed you with the skill sets to help with your organization's project management goals. You can get those skills formally recognized into certifications that translate into civilian positions. The Project Management Institute's (PMI) Project Management Professional (PMP) is an advanced skill level credential offered through Navy COOL (Credentialing Opportunities On-Line) for professionals who lead and direct projects. PMPs demonstrate strong interpersonal skills, the ability to lead, and an understanding of technical processes and the business environment. Candidates must meet a combination of education, experience, and training requirements and pass a written exam. Despite its civilian sector origins, this certification is relevant and valuable for military leaders at all levels. Its comprehensive approach to project management can arm you with the skills critical for the successful execution of military operations and maintenance and can give you a leg up in your post-career job prospects.

Areas of Organizational Management Competence

As you move into positions higher in your chain of command, your role and impact on management processes will change. You will need to learn and understand broader processes and realize that a multitude of stakeholders are planning, organizing, directing, and controlling policy and resources. As frustrating as this may be, gaining knowledge of these areas and processes is something you should do to become a much more effective senior enlisted leader. Unfortunately, many senior enlisted find themselves in positions on a flag staff with limited or inadequate knowledge of the processes and governance structures that impact the quality of work and life of their people. Taking time *now* to learn more about how your service manages policy, people, and other resources is a time investment well spent. Although this guide can't cover all these areas in depth, there are several areas that you should work now to learn more about.

Strategic Thinking

You are usually so focused on your day-to-day tasks that you continue to focus on being tactical—concentrating on completing a certain thing without ever learning the purpose behind it—instead of learning to be strategic. Being strategic means being able to see the bigger picture, learning the reasons behind certain processes and tasks, and working smarter. As you move into higher positions, your thinking needs to shift. Far too often leaders who move into new positions revert back to the thinking and behavioral patterns of their prior positions. And although some of that can be useful, your leadership expects you to evolve with the scope of the position.

Financial Management

Many senior enlisted leaders don't understand or only loosely understand that many of the challenges with resourcing (manning, supplies, maintenance, etc.) shortfalls in the fleet are linked to budget. There is only so much money allotted to the Department of the Navy and Coast Guard, and hard decisions must be made concerning where to allot funding among competing priorities . . . people, current readiness, and future readiness. The budget can enable or disable organizational lines of effort and force readiness, so it is extremely important that you learn how the budget is planned and executed, where the competing priorities are, and how you can have a voice in the process in the interest of your people.

The planning, programming, budgeting, and execution (PPBE) process is used across the DoD to allocate resources to provide the capabilities deemed necessary to accomplish missions. As an SEL, you should be aware of the nature and timing of each of the events in the PPBE process since you may be called upon to provide critical information or advice that could be important to program funding and success.

The PPBE process is "calendar driven" and aligns with the fundamental management process you have learned. During the process, the secretary of defense establishes policies, strategy, and prioritized goals for the department, which are subsequently used to guide resource allocation decisions that balance the guidance with fiscal constraints. The PPBE process consists of four distinct but overlapping phases of planning, programming, budgeting, and execution.

Your service's budget and financial management systems are analogous to a nervous system. You must demonstrate broad understanding of the principles of financial management and marketing expertise necessary to advise on appropriate funding levels for your areas of responsibility. You should know enough to help your leadership teams prepare, justify, and administer the budget for the unit or program; use cost–benefit thinking to set priorities; and monitor expenditures in support of programs and policies. You should also seek and identify cost-effective approaches and manage procurement and contracting appropriately.

Force Generation and Deployment

Your service has an operational framework and readiness generations model that often consists of phases (basic, integrated, or advanced maintenance and sustainment, etc.) designed to optimize the return on training and maintenance investments, to maintain personnel quality of service, and to ensure units and forces are certified in defined, progressive levels of employable and deployable capability. In the Navy, this is called the Operational Fleet Response Plan (OFRP), which outlines the time from the beginning of a maintenance phase to the beginning of the next maintenance phase. The length of the cycle will be established for each service's force element to meet designed mission goals demanded by the combatant commander. These readiness generation models aim to achieve predictable force generation cycles, a consistent chain of command, the right personnel with the right training at the right unit and billet, and a stable and predictable maintenance plan.

Each phase of the cycle brings its own challenges to fleet units and your people that you should be aware of when conducting fleet circulation so you can bring specific feedback points back to the appropriate stakeholders. It is recommended that you review *OPNAV INSTRUCTION 3000.15A Optimized Fleet Response Plan* to gain more knowledge and insight on the goals and flow of the OFRP.

Manpower Management

Manpower management is the process your service uses to get the right person to the right place to support the mission of your unit. From learning to interpret and use an enlisted duty verification report (EDVR); to knowing why, when, and how to send enlisted manning inquiry reports (EMIR) to report significant manning issues that directly impact operational readiness; to understanding why and how the Navy recruits, prioritizes manning assignments across the fleet, and sets high-year tenure (HYT) limits, there is much you should learn about manpower and manning processes and management. There are many aspects of your service's manpower planning that you will be involved with in some way, but this guide can't go into the all the complexities. To gain more comprehensive knowledge and understanding of the manpower and manning process, take time to read through OPNAVINST 1000.16 (series) *Navy Total Force Manpower Policies and Procedures* and a Center for Naval Analysis (CNA) paper titled *Navy Manpower Planning* (Rodney 2017).

Training and Education

Your service has an organization that designs, develops, and administers voluntary education programs and career development policies and programs; administers technical training and the enlisted advancement program; and provides resources management services to assigned activities. As a Chief, you should have a solid understanding of the cradle-to-grave process of the education and advancement of personnel assigned to your rating. And when you move into higher positions such as force or rating Master Chief, you will have to understand even broader processes and the people and organizations who shape them.

Supply and Material Management

Another area of management you should understand is how your service manages supplies, services, and quality-of-life support to the force. Your service has an organization that manages supply chains that deliver material for Navy aircraft, surface ships, submarines, and their associated weapons systems. In the Navy, Naval Supply Systems Command (NAVSUP) executes a wide range of base operating and waterfront logistics support services, coordinating material deliveries, contracting for supplies and services, and providing material management and warehousing services. In the USCG, there are different logistics centers that serve this management function.

Shore Installation Management

Commander, Navy Installations Command (CNIC), headquartered at the Washington Navy Yard in Washington, DC, is responsible for worldwide U.S. Navy shore installation management as the Navy's shore integrator, designing and developing integrated solutions for sustainment and development of Navy shore infrastructure. CNIC is responsible for the operations, maintenance, and quality-of-life programs across 10 regions, 69 installations, and 123 Naval Operations Support Centers. Navy housing, Fleet and Family Support Centers, and child and youth programs are all part of their portfolio. By this point in your career, you should be familiar with these programs and understand the resources that are offered to help shape individual and family quality of life.

At some point you may find yourself assigned as a base or region master chief or working on a region or installation staff. Although the staff and leadership structures are similar to fleet staff, there are differences and terms you should take time to learn. If selected as a base CMC, you will attend the Senior Shore Leadership Course (SSLC), which helps prepare senior shore installation leaders to more effectively lead and manage assigned resources to provide cost-wise shore services and support to the fleet, fighter, and families. During this course, students will receive ten days of CNIC-focused education and training in functional areas typically encountered with shore installation management (SIM). Topics of presentations, seminars, case studies, and professional readings include strategic business planning, budgeting, manpower and human resources, labor and employee relations, workforce development, communications, operations, fire and emergency services, public relations/media training, family services, legal, NEX, DECA, safety, funeral services/CACO, facilities, energy conservation, inspector general, environmental, and several mentor sessions.

Risk Management

Another area of organizational management competency is the management of the hazards and risks associated with ratings, platforms, and life at sea as well as the management of your service's risk management model. Mishaps cost your service on several levels. At the strategic level, severe mishaps can impact organizational reputation or budget priorities. Mishaps at the operational level can result in missions lost and financial costs incurred. And at the unit levels, deployment schedules can be changed and the loss of a life or lives can have deep emotional and psychological implications for unit morale. This guide goes into much more depth on this topic in chapter 8.

Although the management functions and areas of competence can be applied to any organization, the management processes within which these functions are used are unique to each organization and each organization's objectives. This is true even within your service. For example, the way surface ship and submarine maintenance are managed differs from how aviation and shore maintenance is managed. Although the ship's maintenance and material management (3-M) program and Naval Aviation Maintenance Program (NAMP) involve planning, organizing, directing, and controlling, each has its own unique differences such as the management tools that each uses, which you should have mastery over by this point in your career. With that said, you should continue to learn more about those specific maintenance programs from a broader perspective since you can expect to serve on a maintenance or safety assessment team at some point.

The Flag Staff

Most of your career to date has been spent at units at the tactical level, and by now you should be an expert in that level of organizational structure. But at some point you may find yourself assigned to work in a senior enlisted position on a service or DoD staff where major policies, processes, and culture are shaped and managed. Transitioning to working on a flag staff takes time. You will notice the pace slows down from what you are used to and your autonomy increases. More advice and guidance are offered in the sections below that cover the specific roles of the SEL working on a flag staff.

Staffs are organized and operate differently from the ship, squadron, or shore unit you have been assigned to in the past, and you will need to understand who does what so you can best integrate into your staff quickly and effectively. A staff exists for one purpose: to assist the commander in carrying out the functions of command for which he or she is responsible. These include operational functions and supporting functions. Operational functions are the missions assigned to the command: making decisions, evaluating intelligence, and formulating plans for executing missions. Supporting functions provide for the welfare of assigned personnel, for training, for personnel management, and for supply and allocation of resources. They also fulfill higher-level management functions.

Staffs are absolutely essential for the smooth functioning of a military organization. No commander acting alone, no matter how versatile and intelligent, can hope to gather and collate all the information available, make a reasoned and correct decision, organize assigned personnel and forces, and then issue detailed orders for the execution of the decision. A staff is the organization that exists to assist the commander in all these functions.

Because military operations are increasingly employed in joint or federal interagency settings under reactive or contingency circumstances, staff composition and organization have adapted accordingly. In practice, depending on their function, staffs may be organized differently from the notional staff organization described in this chapter. Staffs vary widely in size, from the handful of officers and dozen enlisted personnel on the staff of a destroyer squadron commander to the hundreds of personnel assisting the chairman of the Joint Chiefs of Staff (JCS). A staff may have a largely administrative function if assigned to a commander in the administrative chain of command, or an operational function if assigned to an operational commander, or both if assigned to a commander who has a role in both chains of command.

The magnitude of these functions will vary with the commander's mission. For example, in a role on an administrative commander staff such as a type commander (TYCOM), you would be concerned mainly with support to the fleet: personnel administration, basic-phase training, and maintenance and repair of ships and aircraft. These support tasks form the basis for operational functions. If you are assigned to a role on an operational commander staff, you would be more concerned with advanced training for combat and with planning, supervising, and evaluating the execution of combat operations and those impacts on the personnel assigned to that operational component. In some cases your commander will wear multiple "hats," and you will find yourself working to shape administrative and operational aspects of readiness. Regardless of the mission and size of a staff organization, some basic functions are common to all staffs.

Flag Staff Organization, Positions, and Functions

Staffs are assigned to flag officers or other senior officers who are in command of a group of subordinate commands. A commander who is not a flag officer normally has the title commodore. A staff's organization will depend on its mission and size. While staffs are generally organized by standard operational functions for consistency and to facilitate external liaison with other organizations and patterned after the joint staff, there are many variations on the pattern described below. In addition, as threats and technology evolve, staff organizations change to optimize their effectiveness. As an SEL, you will need to understand that although you have great access to your commander or commodore, there are other staff officers who enjoy that same, if not more, access. You are highly advised to meet these other staff officers and develop positive relationships with them as soon as possible once assigned to a position on a flag or general officer staff. Although the division heads, sometimes called assistant chiefs of staff or deputy chiefs of staff, are all on the same level organizationally, they may be of widely disparate ranks. The chain of staff authority extends from the commander to the chief of staff (or chief staff officer) and on down through each division but does not cross from one division to another.

- *Chief of Staff.* The chief of staff (COS) is the senior officer on an admiral's staff. Instead of a chief of staff, the officer assigned to coordinate the activities of a commodore's staff is called a chief staff officer (CSO). The COS functions much as an XO does. He or she keeps the commander informed of the condition and situation of the command, subordinate commands, and other commands in the theater of operations; advises the commander on administrative matters; supervises administrative work; and coordinates staff activities. The COS signs routine correspondence for the commander, except those concerning policy or legal action, and acts for the commander on issues for which the commander's policy is known, such as requests for repairs and maintenance, endorsements of routine correspondence, and orders to subordinate officers other than flag officers. The admiral's COS may exercise nonjudicial-punishment authority for the admiral, if the admiral delegates this authority.
- *Flag Secretary.* The flag secretary is a personal aide who, on many staffs, acts as assistant COS for administration. He or she is responsible for routing, filing, and managing incoming and outgoing

correspondence and message traffic; managing the commander's directives and instructions; administering the flag office; and supervising the preparation of evaluations and fitness reports.

- *Flag Lieutenant.* The personal aide to a flag officer, the flag lieutenant looks out for such matters as honors, presentations of awards, official calls, uniforms, entertainment, invitations, and liaisons with other organizations. He or she schedules the commander's calls; maintains the commander's schedule; arranges transportation; and keeps the COS, staff duty officer, officer of the deck of the flagship, and other interested persons advised as to the commander's prospective movements.
- *Principal Assistants and Deputies.* Assignments and titles of staff division heads depend in large measure on the mission of the staff. Administrative staff have different primary functions than do operational staff, and their organization reflects that difference. Although no staff will have an assistant or deputy COS in every one of the positions described below, the following numbering system is fairly standard throughout the Navy.
    - *N1/CG-1, Administration and Personnel.* The officer heading the administration division is often also the flag secretary. In addition to the duties already discussed for the flag secretary, the N1 advises the commander on the formulation of command administrative policies and handles all administrative matters for assigned staff personnel. The N1 also supervises training for enlisted staff members.
    - *N2/CG-2, Intelligence.* The head of the intelligence division formulates and implements policies pertaining to combat intelligence, counterintelligence, information operations, and public information. The intelligence officer also keeps the commander and staff informed as to the capabilities of present and potential enemies by the collection, evaluation, interpretation, and dissemination of information regarding the enemy, hydrography, terrain, and weather. Through liaison with subordinate, parallel, and higher commands, and by using all existing sources of intelligence, including aviation, satellite, and submarine visual and

photographic reconnaissance, the N2 strives to maintain accurate and current intelligence on all actual and potential enemies. The Navy staff was recently reorganized to combine N2 and N6 as well as other information capabilities into a single organization (N2/N6) under the Deputy Chief of Naval Operations for information dominance.

- *N3/CG-3, Operations.* The operations division is the primary executive element of the staff. The operations officer is responsible for the functions that relate to organization and command: training, preparing and issuing directives for combat operations and training exercises, and managing related reports. The N3 also prepares operation orders, prepares the command employment schedule, issues the necessary movement orders, keeps track of the location and movement of ships and units assigned to the command, and advises the commander on the assignment of ships and other units to task groups to perform specific tasks. On the Navy staff, N3s and N5s are combined as N3/N5, Deputy Chief of Naval Operations for information, plans, and strategy.
- *N4/CG-4, Logistics.* The logistics division is responsible for advising the commander on all matters relating to logistics and material. Logistics is essential to strategy and the execution of operations and is emphasized throughout the planning process. The assistant chief of staff for logistics prepares studies for proposed operations and the logistics annex for all operational orders and plans. The N4 also maintains full liaison with subordinate, parallel, and senior commands.
- *N5/CG-5, Plans.* This officer prepares and develops operation plans, monitors force levels and structure, and makes plans to carry out all assigned missions of the commander under peacetime, limited-war, or general-war conditions. As previously described, on the OPNAV staff, N3 and N5s are combined into a single division.
- *N6/CG-6, Communications.* This officer is responsible for providing adequate, rapid communication within the command and with other commands, and operation of the message center.

Normally, cyberwarfare falls under the N6 umbrella, as do information warfare activities that don't fall within the purview of N2. As previously described, on the OPNAV staff, N2 and N6 are combined.
  – *N7/CG-7, Readiness and Training.* This officer conducts readiness inspections, reviews inspection reports, and oversees training of individuals, ships, units, and special task organizations.
  – *N8/CG-8, Resources and Assessment.* This officer is the commander's representative in the development of primary mission assessment and procurement.
- *Other Staff Officers.* In addition to the positions described above, staffs may include a chaplain, medical officer, staff judge advocate general (JAG) officer, PAO, meteorologist, and other specialists. These officers are typically assigned three-digit numerical codes beginning with the number 01.

Also, if you are assigned to a joint or sister service staff, you will find the positions are fairly consistent, with the change being the letter assigned to the staff code. For example, in the Army it would be G1, and the Air Force would use A1 instead of N1. And if you are assigned to a joint staff, you would see the position assigned by a J code instead of an N code.

Civilians on the Staff

The DoD employs 95,000 civilian employees worldwide in approximately 675 different occupations between the Army, Navy, Air Force, Marine Corps, and other DoD agencies. The Coast Guard also provides nonmilitary employment opportunities. At some point you will work with civilian employees and contractors, or may have already, so I'll touch on those relationships a bit here.

- *Senior Executives.* The Senior Executive Service (SES) consists of executive positions, including managerial, supervisory, and policy positions classified above General Schedule (GS) grade 15 or equivalent positions in most executive branch agencies of the federal government. The SES is a corps of men and women who administer

public programs at the highest levels of federal government using well-honed executive skills and broad perspectives of government and public service. Positions are primarily managerial and supervisory and serve just below top presidential appointees, forming a vital link between these appointees and the rest of the federal workforce. SES members are considered flag equivalents. You can expect to see them in positions on major flag staff as executive directors or directors of staff codes. They have a tremendous amount of experience and insight into the mind of the commander and their predecessors, so if you are in a position of trying to figure out how a given policy was developed and went right or wrong, take some time to meet with them and you will learn much.
- *General Service Employees.* The General Schedule (GS) is the predominant pay scale within the U.S. civil service. The GS includes the majority of white collar personnel (professional, technical, administrative, and clerical) positions. Although your fellow Chiefs have signi-ficant resource capability, there are key GS personnel you will want to develop relationships with who can greatly help with situations involving your people. Many are retired Chiefs and are willing and able to lend a hand when needed or offer insight on issues that may arise.

Relationships among Staff and Flagship Personnel

At some point you may be assigned as a carrier air wing, destroyer squadron (DESRON), or numbered fleet CMC (affectionately referred to as "ship riders"), so it's important to understand the roles and lanes of the staff and crew leadership. Or you may be a CMC of an aircraft carrier or big-deck amphibious ship, so you will want to develop a productive relationship among the crew and embarked units. Officers and senior enlisted leaders serving in a flagship or on the staff of an embarked commander are involved daily in relationships between members of the staff and flagship crew.

A flagship crew plays a dual role. The CO is always responsible for the safety of the ship and its performance, but the CO and the ship are answerable to the embarked commander. While underway, the flagship maneuvers as directed by the signals from the officer in tactical command (OTC).

When the embarked commander is the OTC, he or she may verbally direct the flagship to maneuver, in which case the flagship must notify other ships in the company. The embarked commander takes over responsibility for the operation of all communications of the flagship, absorbing into his or her organization the members of the flagship communication unit. This unit is then responsible to the flagship for all communications.

Staff officers and flag SELs embarked in a ship must always be careful to respect the flagship's unity of command. When making requests to the ship in the name of the admiral, staff officers should always make requests directly to the CO or XO, and preface them with "The admiral desires that you . . . ." All officers and enlisted personnel who serve in a ship, except for the commander, are subject to the authority of the CO and to his or her discipline and punishment. Staff officers have no authority of their own; all of their authority comes from the admiral.

Also, shore leave and liberty for staff members should conform as closely as possible to that of the flagship and the CMCs of the ship, and embarked staff should work closely in policy development. The embarked unit leadership should encourage ownership and participation in daily routines. Flag watch, quarter, and station bills should be kept up-to-date, and flag personnel, unless excused by proper authority, should promptly observe calls to general drills. Staff compartments, lockers, berthing, and messing areas should be kept in a condition on par with or better than that of similar ship facilities. Again, the collaboration of the Command Master Chiefs is a crucial element in making this happen.

Decision-Making and Your Role in It

Now that you have a better understanding of how the flag staff is organized, functions, and your role in it, let's take time to think about how you can best impact organizational decisions. As a Chief you will play an entrepreneurial role in initiating change and being proactive. You will also serve as a peacekeeper working to resolve conflicts among subordinates, peers, or departments. You should know that wisdom, level-headedness, and the ability to compromise go a long way toward getting things done in your command. Furthermore, you serve as a resource allocator, making or helping to make decisions to allocate people, time, equipment, budget, and other resources needed to attain desired outcomes. And as you have come to learn, only rarely is all the desired information at hand to make the best and most informed decision. Like tools, parts, and people, we could all always use just a little bit more information, but the important thing is being able to make the decision with the information you have at hand, with team input, and with your personal experience.

You also should understand that so many decisions are made daily that they must be prioritized. You will have to determine whether a decision is strategic—it will impact the broad direction of the organization; important but not time dependent; or not important or time dependent. Knowing the context of the decision helps determine how much time you or your leadership should spend on it. For example, because strategic decisions can have significant impacts on the efficiency and climate of your organization, they require more thought and time. Decisions that may be less important require a different level of thought; those routine decisions can often be delegated to others, made on the spot, or made with the guidance of a checklist. On the other hand, strategic and important decisions may require collaboration or consultation, so time must be allotted for meetings and discussions.

There are widely differing decision-making styles. Some people are problem avoiders who ignore information that points to a problem; others are problem solvers who attack problems as they arise. Others are problem seekers who actively investigate problem areas before difficulties arise. By now you should know your individual style, but you should start to evaluate leaders and bosses with widely differing decision-making styles and the impact their decision-making styles are having on team efficiency and effectiveness. Some leaders solicit team input, but they don't react so well when it's offered, which hinders future input. You should strive to be a problem seeker in the decision-making process; in this role, walk around and observe. See where things are going well or where things could be dangerous or could present problems later. You should be working with your leadership team to gather information, consider alternatives, and help them act decisively when needed.

As you do this, try to be aware of and review the performance metrics of your organization's success in achieving goals (performance, fiscal, material, etc.) and how they use the results of audits, certifications, and inspections to measure time, cost, and quality. There are many computer-based controlling tools available to you, but getting out from behind the screen and hitting the deck plates is still, by far, the best form of managerial control you can practice.

Anchor Up
What is your decision-making style? Does it serve to aid or hinder your current leadership position and the objectives of your organization?

As you move into positions of greater influence, you will make and be involved in the decisions to develop and shape policy, allocate resources, and resolve conflicts that impact large parts of your organization. You will advise your commander and staff one-on-one and in group settings, and you will participate on a variety of advisory and decision-making boards and panels. Decision-making power presents a huge opportunity, but with it comes risk that you and your organization must manage. Your value in contributing to the decision-making process of your leadership and organizations cannot be understated. You should take time to develop relationships with the key staff who can provide you with meeting schedules, read-ahead materials, and background information. Insist on being involved and invited.

You must learn to integrate yourself into your organizational governance—the process of establishing policies and continuously monitoring of their proper implementation by members of the governing body of an organization. This is where the decisions are made, the results gauged, and adjustments made. When assigned to a unit or staff, you must take time to learn the governance drumbeat, which includes things like stand-up meetings, operational and intel briefs, initial proposal meetings, boards and councils, and other bodies of information exchange and decision-making. It is not about where you sit in the process; it is the fact that you are in the room for the discussion that informs the decision-making. Some COs and commanders actively solicit your input. Others won't, but that does not mean they don't want or value your input. You are in the room for a reason. Offer your feedback, insights, and perspectives.

Organizational Management Processes 183

[7-2] Flag briefing at Coast Guard Headquarters
U.S. COAST GUARD PHOTO BY PO1 TIMOTHY TAMARGO

You will also have to learn to balance the time spent "up and out" on travel with the time spent in the HQ in working and focus groups and in staff governance. Although fleet circulation serves a purpose, SELs who dedicate too much time on the road will be at risk of irrelevance in headquarters policy discussions. Time with your boss and staff is critical. As a senior enlisted leader, you will enjoy direct access to your department head, CO, or commander. Plan time with them and their deputies into your weekly schedule, value it, and be prepared to use it to further shape organizational decisions. Be efficient with your travel. The "privileged autonomy" you enjoy is exactly that, a privilege. Which are the locations where you can visit two, three, or more relatively collocated bases or units with one trip? Can you link information-gathering travel with ceremonial opportunities? Work with the senior enlisted leaders in those areas to develop a schedule of events that will accomplish your goals and support the needs and wants of the local leadership. Work to gather information from your SEL networks and your site visits and bring it back to your leadership team and staff to help assess whether the organization is "on course," "off course" but can adjust, or a new course needs to be plotted. Help them consider alternatives and encourage them to act decisively when the situation dictates.

You should draft and share a trip report. These reports and recommendations should be formal and well written. They are not just for the commander. Make sure to include the deputy, executive director, and any applicable staff directorates on the "To" line. Explain why you traveled, whom you met with, and what you observed, and complement this information with personal stories that humanize and strengthen the report.

Anchor Up
As a technical and policy "expert," many will ask you for your advice, recommendations, and solutions. Occasionally you will be faced with an issue you have no answer for. What do you do when placed in this situation?

Your activities and the decisions you influence will also involve process improvement, also known as business process improvement, which is the ongoing practice of finding ways to make existing processes faster, more accurate, more efficient, and more reliable. The benefits of process improvement can include improved productivity, improved mission agility, efficiency in workflows, operational excellence, and better quality of work and life experiences. From training and education, manning, pay and benefits, technical aspects, or fixing communication problems, there is a process behind everything your service does. From tactical to strategic levels of management and leadership, you have a role in and should encourage process improvement.

You should work to gauge how well your boss and team are open-minded and the level to which they allow fear of being judged to close their options. Challenge you and your staffs' beliefs about what they consider "right" and "wrong," and ensure that they are seeking input from the widest audience of stakeholders possible. Your boss and organization will no doubt face multimillion dollar and life-and-death decision-making. There will be winners and losers, and decisions will be second guessed, but they will have to make decisions on the best info available.

7-2 DECISION-MAKING INSIGHTS

- Good decision-making is crucial at any level of leadership, but it changes as one moves up in organizations.
- Experience, education, and wisdom are key factors in making intelligent decisions.
- Understanding the desired outcomes and measuring the effectiveness of decisions are important aspects of decision-making.
- Factors such as risk tolerance, normalized deviance, and external pressures can influence decision-making.
- Tough and realistic training as well as continuous learning can help improve decision-making skills.
- External factors such as drug and alcohol use, external noise, and personal pressures can also influence decision-making.
- Knowing your people and being able to identify when external pressures are affecting their decision-making is crucial for a leader.
- The art of leadership involves intuition, empathy, and understanding the strengths and weaknesses of your team members.
- Understanding organizational decision-making processes and working effectively with teams is essential for senior enlisted leaders.
- Developing decision-making skills requires curiosity, lifelong learning, and the ability to challenge the status quo.
- Managing the emotional burden of decision-making involves being fair and consistent, maintaining accountability, and seeking challenges to grow as a leader.

Managing Command Culture and Climate

Far too often the words "culture" and "climate" are used interchangeably, but they are distinctly different. "Culture" can be formally defined as "the social behavior and norms found in human societies," but it's often captured as "what people do around here." "Climate" could be formally explained as "the prevailing trend of public opinion or of another aspect of public life," but it could be explained more easily as "how people feel to be around here" or the feelings they have about you, your boss, or your overall organization. When put in this context, the difference should become apparent. Culture and climate can be shaped from the macro and micro levels. For example, the Navy at large has a culture, but each warfighting community, command, department, and division has a culture as well that the CPO mess has a direct impact on shaping. How you shape culture and climate at each level brings its own challenges.

One of the most important responsibilities CPOs, SCPOs, and MCPOs have is to help get a pulse on and manage organizational climate from the division to service level. If neglected, morale and effectiveness can decline and, if not corrected, can lead to destructive outcomes. Climate is one measure of the culture that you are positioned to influence. It is a shared perception among members about what is expected of them, how they will be treated, and what professional and personal opportunities will be made available to them. One of the most important determinants of an organization's culture and climate is the behavior of its leaders. The team must believe their leaders have their best professional and personal interests in mind when they make decisions and must be able to explain when they must make decisions that will result in negative impacts to the organization.

Organizational culture and climate are developed and managed from the top down—the command leadership owns it. The tone must be set every day, and it starts with communicating a command philosophy. Laying a foundation for a positive command attitude and high levels of commitment begins with a well-thought-out command philosophy. This is the OIC or commander's public strategy for organizational success. It will communicate the values and beliefs that underlie the culture they strive to develop in their unit or organization. Posted and readily available to the crew for reference, an ideal command philosophy provides insight into the style, priorities, and expectations of the command. Most importantly, the philosophy serves to inspire the crew to excel, to exceed all expectations, with a clear understanding that the command exists to support and serve them so the mission can be accomplished. Be sure to model and point out elements of the command philosophy often.

Fostering a positive organizational climate requires a proactive approach and relies on a recipe of trust, teamwork, and frequent and effective communication. Leadership teams that fail to implement dynamic two-way communication mechanisms will not see their units perform to their full potential. Sometimes just providing avenues for the crew to be heard at regular intervals and then providing timely and candid feedback is enough. The answers will not always be popular, but the fact that your crew is heard shows you care and are interested in their well-being. There are a wealth of tools, tactics, and techniques at your leadership team's (division, department, and command levels) disposal that you should work to implement and execute to help shape and maintain a positive work climate.

Taking care of the crew means attending to their personal, physical, mental, and spiritual needs—and to a great extent their families' needs as well.

[7-3] Fleet Master Chief takes a photo with Sailors aboard an amphibious dock-landing ship.
U.S. NAVY PHOTO BY MC3 JONATHAN CLAY/RELEASED

7-3 MORALE AND COMMITMENT ARE HIGH IN UNITS WHERE YOUR PEOPLE BELIEVE . . .

- Their service and rating is an honorable and desirable career.
- Policies and practices are reasonable and sound.
- Training is thorough and good. If a Sailor is asked to do a job and does it well, the feeling of accomplishment improves morale and commitment.
- The job is appropriate to the team's abilities and interests.
- All work receives proper recognition and reward.
- People are receiving consistent and impartial treatment.
- Living conditions are as good as circumstances permit.
- The team's health, family, and personal problems are being cared for.
- Free time and opportunity for recreation are provided as much as possible.
- They are accepted and valued as an important member of a first-class unit. You are the link in the chain of command that can make or break a team effort.

It also means training and educating the crew for the demands and challenges of their individual jobs and the unit's missions. In its fullest sense, crew development means going beyond the immediate requirements of the job and mission to helping them grow in their careers, thereby preparing them for advancement/promotion, greater responsibility, and most especially current and future leadership of their own crews. A good leader leads; a great leader develops other leaders!

Leaders with poor management competence and focus can have detrimental impacts on team climate and mission readiness/performance. Conversely, those with great planning and organizational skills who have poor leadership skills won't recognize the full potential of their people toward achieving goals and objectives. If you are a poor manager or can't help your team and leadership plan, prepare, direct, control, communicate, or make effective decisions, you risk creating team frustration that can result in significant negative impacts on warfighting readiness or organizational climate. These undesirable outcomes can arise from the unavailability of resources, wasted time, or lack of job satisfaction.

Ultimately, poor management focus and performance can impact team retention and personal behaviors in ways that increase the probability of destructive behaviors. Don't be the Chief who lacks strong management skills and leaves their teams feeling that their time is being wasted and frustrated by the lack of efficiency they expect and seek. These feelings can be avoided or minimized by developing and leveraging strong managerial skills at all levels of the chain of command.

Effective planning, organization, and trying to help your unit stick with the plan as much as possible will help you and the people on your team. Strong personal and organizational self-assessment skills, frequent formal and informal inspections, strict execution of maintenance and operations, a long-range plan, and organization-wide focus on formality, forceful back-up, procedural compliance, and an ever-developing level of knowledge will ensure that your teams and platforms are set up for mission success.

Eight

Helping Your Organizations Manage Risk

> Losing colleagues, having them sustain injuries or being threatened with harm, affects us all.
>
> —MCPOCG *Steven W. Cantrell*

By now you understand that serving in the Navy or Coast Guard can be dangerous. You are part of a high-reliability organization—one that operates in complex, high-risk domains for extended periods without serious accidents or catastrophic failures. Risk management must be implemented throughout the chain of command because it is what allows these dangerous activities to take place successfully without harm or damage. By this point, you should also be familiar with the principles of risk management and have used these principles during day-to-day on- and off-duty operations. The *Petty Officer's Guide* and your service training and education cover operational risk management more in-depth, but it is now time to for you to understand broader risk management systems, processes, and theories that help shape organizational risk management culture and success.

Mishaps cost organizations at all levels, and understanding these outcomes, which are the result of a decision or series of decisions, is important. Favorable outcomes occur when desired effects are achieved without damage to equipment, harm to personnel, or loss of life. At the strategic level, severe mishaps can impact organizational reputation and impact budget

8-1 THE *EASTWIND* COLLISION:
THE LOSS OF A CHIEFS' MESS

On 19 January 1949, the Coast Guard cutter *Eastwind*, a 270-foot icebreaker bound for the Chesapeake Bay from Boston, was steaming at fourteen knots off the New Jersey Coast when her radar operator reported the tanker *Gulfstream* nine miles off her starboard bow. Subsequent reports made it clear that the two ships were on collision courses, and the tanker's bearing remained constant as its range decreased.

On entering fog, the *Eastwind* neither slowed nor sounded fog signals. Radar contact was lost as the vessels closed, and neither sighted the other's running lights until they were close aboard. The vessels turned away almost simultaneously, but the distance was too close and the tanker's bow smashed into the *Eastwind* just abaft her bridge. Fire broke out in both ships. Luckily the fire in the *Gulfstream* was confined to the forepeak and never reached her tanks. The fire in the *Eastwind* spread rapidly, however, engulfing the CPOs' quarters, radio room, and the bridge, killing eleven men and seriously burning twenty-one others. Two of the merchant vessels that answered the *Gulfstream*'s distress signal embarked the *Eastwind*'s injured men for transport to the Staten Island Marine Hospital, where two more died. The buoy tenders *Gentian* and *Sassafras* helped extinguish the *Eastwind*'s fires and then towed the badly damaged icebreaker to New York, stern first. The *Eastwind* returned to service eighteen months later.

priorities. At the operational level, missions can fail, and financial and human costs can be incurred. And at the unit level, watch bills or leave plans can be impacted, unit morale can diminish, and individuals may suffer long-lasting physical and psychological effects. The human toll associated with these incidents is one of the most difficult burdens any leader must bear.

Pause for a moment and consider how many daily decisions are being made at all levels of the Navy or Coast Guard. Most, if not all, of the decisions involve the management of risk. The nature of the work performed by the service exposes its people to a range of hazards with potentially fatal outcomes. Throughout your career you have been involved in mitigating these hazards and accepting risk by making decisions largely at the individual and team levels. Now you must consider that high-level leadership also makes risk-based decisions. Understand that organizational "hazards" can be introduced as a result of high-level decisions, and these can have significant impacts down to the unit level. For example, decisions may result in shortfalls to manpower, training and education, or assets and supplies, or may introduce pressure, whether deliberately or inadvertently, on lower-level leaders. Risk tolerance—the amount of risk a person or organization is willing to tolerate—and the factors influencing it must now be considered from the context of organizational risk versus personal risk decision-making. As a senior enlisted leader, you should understand how organizational hazards are introduced, help identify them when they arise, and help mitigate the effect they have on lower-level decision-making and readiness.

Anchor Up
Do you know all the risks, hazards, and potentially life-threatening outcomes your people and team are susceptible to in all the maintenance and operational processes your organization is responsible for?

To be a valuable contributor to a high-reliability organization, you must build your knowledge of safety management systems and safety leadership—applying influence to manage the hazards and risks associated with your service, operational environment, rating, or platform to help prevent mishaps. In this chapter, I explain key risk management concepts and show how you can tailor your power bases and influence tactics specifically toward mishap prevention. We move beyond tactical-level and operational-focused risk management and spur you to think more about organizational risk management, safety culture concepts, and how hazards and risks are managed at the operational and strategic levels.

The Management of Safety

The intent of risk *management* is not to eliminate risk but to operate effectively while avoiding harmful outcomes. Formally, the Navy and USCG each have a safety management system (SMS) comprising four areas or "pillars": safety policy, risk management, safety assurance, and safety promotion. This framework is designed to help shape decision-making processes and support service objectives at all levels. The objective of an SMS is to achieve the preservation of human and material resources and enhance operational readiness by identifying hazards and mitigating risks through leadership, the establishment and enforcement of high standards for conduct and performance, regular safety awareness training, and implementation of risk management tools. The building blocks of a safety management system consist of written policies, procedures, and plans coupled with attitudes and practices that enable the former to succeed. You must buy into safety and model your behavior so that others do the same.

Safety management systems are relatively new, formal, top-down, professional approaches to managing organizational hazards and risks. Prior to the 1990s, the approach to safety was focused on individual programs for specific hazards. As organizations improved their knowledge and began to see value in integrating separate programs into a more holistic framework,

[8-1] Federal firefighters and a helicopter from Helicopter Sea Combat Squadron 3 combat a fire on board the amphibious assault ship USS *Bonhomme Richard* (LHD-6) in San Diego, July 2020. U.S. NAVY PHOTO BY MC1 OMAR POWELL

there was a shift to the systems approach. By coupling policies, training, and promotion into a safety management model, leadership can now better leverage the tools they have to reduce mishap rates and, in turn, enhance mission effectiveness. Let's explore each of the components of a management system a bit further.

Pillar I: Safety Policy

Policy is the first component of any safety management system and serves to achieve many objectives: It establishes leadership commitment to safety performance and clear objectives and commitment to manage it, provides transparency in the management of safety, ensures accountability, and facilitates cross-organizational communication and cooperation. It starts with formally and informally asking questions such as, "Is safety policy clearly articulated?," "Do my people understand why specific policies exist?," and "Do my people feel that the command is personally committed to their safety?"

There are many policies that govern your service's commitment to safety, outline risk management practices, and define methods, processes, and structures to support safety requirements. Safety policy is more than just written instructions; it is a means to capture leadership's values, beliefs, and attitudes toward safety, and the behaviors that are expected on and off duty. It also provides the *where* and *how*, which helps focus these behaviors toward specific and measurable goals. When the collective behaviors of an organization reflect the values, beliefs, and attitudes expressed in safety policies, a positive culture results.

You should strive to capture safety as a value versus a program, and demonstrate commitment to it. Although Navy and USCG units inherently take risk in a knowing and calculated fashion, the policy component provides the written commitment and guidance necessary to do this successfully. You and the larger organization communicate commitment to safety through leader behaviors. Your behaviors demonstrate that you mean what you say, and your actions reinforce that you care about the words in policy. There are many things you can and should do to help ensure a strong safety policy component.

8-2 CPO ACTIVITIES TO STRENGTHEN SAFETY POLICY

- Review your organization's current policy and be involved in future revisions.
- Become familiar with higher echelon safety policy and philosophy and evaluate how well your command aligns with it. Provide feedback when appropriate.
- Communicate the values, beliefs, and attitudes of organizational safety policy to your teams as you walk around or conduct calls.
- Evaluate and solicit feedback on safety policy. Is it clearly articulated? Do your teams and people understand why specific policies exist? Do they feel leadership is personally committed to their safety? What is the safety climate?
- Observe organizational behaviors or metrics to help gauge the current state of safety leadership.
- Gauge the level to which the CPO mess internalizes safety as a value and embodies service and command safety policy.

Through strong, well-thought-out vision and policy, your leadership sets the foundation for a strong safety culture. Your leadership in helping to shape and facilitate these policies will promote positive behaviors and continued success. And when your people see that you and other leaders are acting in their best interest, a positive safety climate will develop.

Anchor Up
What is your commander's, CO's, or OIC's philosophy on risk management? Do you effectively translate it to your teams? Do your words and actions reinforce or degrade your unit's safety policy and desired culture?

Pillar II: Risk Management

Effective risk management and good decision-making are crucial to executing the mission. Risk management is inseparable from operational excellence and mission accomplishment. Your service manages risk to ensure that the right people, the right resources, and the right processes are available to accomplish missions effectively, efficiently, and successfully. Most risks that affect operational readiness can be broadly categorized as risk to mission or risk to forces. Risk to mission is anything that could potentially put the mission in jeopardy. Risks to forces are those hazards that pose a threat to people on or off duty. In both cases, the harm those unmitigated risks could do ranges from grave national security implications to reduced morale and negative impacts on work–life balance due to equipment, platforms, or personnel lost or degraded through mishaps.

The risk management process involves identifying hazards, assessing the degree of risk for each hazard (severity and probability), making risk decisions, implementing controls, and supervising. The nature of naval missions requires the risk management process to be tremendously flexible. Your organization will have to make tough, complex decisions, sometimes under pressure and with limited time.

Every person has a role to play in managing organizational and operational risk. For example, junior personnel manage risk while they are doing tasks. Leaders use the risk management process to plan unit operations or make organizational decisions. These roles require different skill sets and knowledge. You must be able to recognize when organizational hazards are introduced and help mitigate the effect they are having on lower-level decision-making, operations, and readiness.

You can help by attending decision-making briefs where discussions of risk happen. You can help interpret metrics at governance meetings. You can pass on the insight gained through unit engagements to help identify where shortcuts or resistance to safety practices, termed "normalized deviance," have taken root. And you can help identify where subordinate leaders are inappropriately assuming risk, or when they are making risk decisions at the inappropriate level. In your position of responsibility, you are one of only a few people who can candidly bring these conditions to the attention

8-3 CPO ACTIVITIES TO STRENGTHEN UNIT RISK MANAGEMENT

- Help ensure that organizational policy communicates the expectations for on- and off-duty risk management.
- Review instructions and attend operational briefs to help gauge the effectiveness of the risk management process.
- Know the safety officer or manager in your organization and develop a working relationship.
- Inform leadership and staff of hazards identified by the risk management process that cannot be controlled at the unit level (e.g., resourcing and training shortfalls).
- Help gauge organizational risk management behaviors through walk arounds and metric reviews.
- Ensure that organizational indoctrination programs provide risk management training.
- Provide advice on how leaders can effectively conduct risk management stand-downs.
- Inculcate the importance of risk management in your CPO mess.
- Develop a strong questioning attitude in your people and teach them to ask often: What could go wrong? What is different today?

of senior decision makers. You also have the perspective and access to have conversations with subordinate leadership teams who may be succumbing to factors impacting their risk tolerance. You are now another "control" of organizational risk and a key identifier of organizational hazards; therefore, your experience and access to organizational leadership is valuable.

Your service has learned from prior mishaps and has done a respectable job at identifying and educating on hazards and training you on risk mitigation techniques. It strives to ensure that our people understand the outcomes that can result from failure to use hazard controls, but it must continue to educate and pass on the corporate memory of mishaps. With that said, effort must continue to do these things while identifying new hazards due to new missions or evolving technologies.

Pillar III: Safety Assurance

This pillar serves as a management controlling function to ensure that policy and risk management are effective. This pillar helps leadership evaluate the continued effectiveness of implemented risk control strategies and processes while supporting the identification of new or unmitigated hazards. It is designed to help your organization meet or exceed safety goals and objectives through the collection, analysis, and assessment of data concerning the command's performance.

Safety assurance is closely linked to risk management. The information and learning gained from it feeds the other components of the safety management system to strengthen its effectiveness. Safety assurance helps to ensure that discrepancies are documented, solutions are implemented, and corrective actions are recorded for future learning. Safety assurance can be viewed from the context of activities designed to gain confidence that the risk controls established by the risk management process continue to be effective. Examples of these organizational tools and activities include hazard-reporting systems and processes, mishap and safety investigations, safety reports, safety investigation boards, and safety inspections and assessments.

The Department of the Navy with U.S. Marine Corps (USMC) employed several mishap reporting systems, including the Web Enabled Safety System (WESS); Enterprise Safety Application Management System (ESAMS); and ESAMS' Injury Illness Tracker (INJTRACK). Safety issues are formally tracked in the Coast Guard Safety Information System (CG-SIS) and managed by the Coast Guard Health, Safety, and Work Life Service Center.

Anchor Up

How well does your unit capture and communicate near-misses and best practices? Are there communication venues available that allow you and your people to bring these issues up in a non-attributional way?

8-4 CPO ACTIVITIES TO STRENGTHEN UNIT SAFETY ASSURANCE

- Participate in higher-level governance and boards, command safety councils, and committees; and help evaluate your team's effectiveness at identifying new or unmitigated hazards.
- Observe and provide advice on organizational safety audit effectiveness and solicit feedback on unmitigated hazards.
- Observe behaviors to determine the current state of safety culture in your organization.
- Supervise evolutions to identify where your people are taking too much risk by not following procedures, failing to use proper personal protective equipment (PPE), or falling victim to a lack of experience.
- Reflect on your own behavior and observe lower-level leaders to ensure they are not exemplifying poor behaviors and are performing effectively as safety leaders.
- Encourage near-miss, or high potential, reporting and hazard identification and observe evolution debriefs to help gauge how well unmitigated, newly identified hazards are captured and fed back into instruction, procedure, and policy.
- Attend organizational safety councils, boards, and committees to evaluate their effectiveness and to offer experience and insight.
- Observe and provide advice on organizational safety audits and inspections.
- Ensure that enlisted professional and leadership education includes information on safety assurance processes.

You likely have knowledge of and experience with these activities at the unit level. As you promote and serve in positions of higher authority, you will have to take time to learn the safety assurance activities that you could and should be involved in for those jobs. Rather than being an executor of those processes, you will become an asset to shaping them and providing your unique input. But to be involved, you must first know what activities exist.

Although there is no absolute metric that captures your organization's safety posture, there are four general approaches to safety assurance:

- *Reactive.* The reactive approach deals with responding to incidents or accidents after they have occurred; it is most useful when dealing with technological failures or unusual events. Its effectiveness is based on the quality of investigation processes, reported incidents, and learning from accidents.
- *Proactive.* The proactive approach seeks to identify safety risks before an incident through the analysis of organizational activities. It is based on the notion that system failures can be minimized by identifying safety risks within a system before it fails and then taking necessary action to mitigate the risk. Tools used are reporting systems, safety audits or assessments, culture workshops, and other awareness programs.
- *Predictive.* The predictive approach uses prediction based on performance data and captures system performance as it happens in normal operations to identify potential future problems. It requires the continuous capture of routine operational data in real time.
- *Iterative.* The iterative approach integrates both reactive and proactive safety initiatives and tools. With this approach safety is enabled through the integration of reactive, proactive, and predictive safety data capture systems, mitigation strategies, and mitigation methods.

Pillar IV: Safety Promotion

Through the use of education and training with frequent communication of safety information, this pillar strives to enhance unit performance. It involves promoting a positive safety culture, visible involvement, personnel education and training, and strategic communication. Safety promotion activities can include formal safety training, posters, magazines, newsletters, social media posts, venues for your employees to raise safety concerns without fear of retribution, safety stand-downs, and safety award programs.

Your service's leadership influences the tone of the risk management culture and climate through policy and vision, the risk management process, and professionalism, but your organization must use the tools of safety promotion to help communicate these values, beliefs, and attitudes to all members of the service. Safety promotion should touch key milestones in a person's career, from command indoctrination to rating training and leadership development courses to periodic leadership messages and briefs. The promotion pillar helps communicate "the way we do things around here" to every person in your service. Let us look at how the two major components of promotion—safety training and safety communication—are related.

Safety training. People must be trained and competent to perform their responsibilities and their roles within the safety management system. Training must meet the needs of the organization. Most required safety training is incorporated into training pipelines and personnel qualification standards (PQS). How much and what type of safety training each person

[8-2] Members from a Coast Guard Air Station conduct helicopter rescue training. U.S. COAST GUARD PHOTO BY PO3 CLASS BRIAN MCCRUM

gets should be tailored to their role. For example, a young petty officer's training and education would be tailored to the hazards related to the maintenance or operations they would perform. But an MCPO working at the flag or headquarters level should be educated and focused on organizational safety concepts like those found in this chapter.

Safety training and education provides another way to shape the risk decision-making process. For people involved in operations and maintenance, it provides the opportunity for them to understand and appreciate material and operational hazards, mishap reporting procedures, potential outcomes, emergency procedures, the limitations of technology, and the risks of complacency. It also informs them of how they can and should be involved in the broader risk management system and encourages them to provide feedback. For leaders, command indoctrination and stand-downs provide the opportunity to explain leadership roles in and commitment to safety culture, unique risks and hazards, and the importance of compliance with procedures and policies.

Safety communication is the tool your organization uses for two-way communication to ensure your people are fully informed about and understand your safety management system. At a minimum, safety communication should strive to convey critical safety information, ensure that all staff are aware of the risk management process, and explain why safety procedures have been introduced or changed. There is a wide array of safety communication tools your organization should use, including bulletins, newsletters, safety notices, posters, social media sites, seminars, workshops, awards programs, and periodic refresher training. Regular discussion about the reasons for incidents and near-misses will foster a learning and reporting culture.

You should promote safety as a core value with practices that support a positive safety culture, including promoting management involvement, personnel competency and training, and communication.

Sometimes the most important concepts to understand about leadership and management are the ones we take for granted. The safety management system model is applied in a variety of ways. It can be applied to your service at large; toward more specific risk management areas such as fall protection, cutter operations, and flight operations; or toward individual off-duty activities.

8-5 CPO ACTIVITIES TO STRENGTHEN UNIT SAFETY PROMOTION

- Observe the frequency and effectiveness of safety-related communication and recommend methods to improve it.
- Share safety-related communication such as bulletins and newsletters with your teams and require them to read them.
- Incorporate safety and risk management messages into your communications.
- Review rating and leadership training and education for safety topics of relevance and recommend areas of improvement.
- Help shape the frequency and conduct of safety-related stand-downs.
- Know and attend the safety councils, committees, and boards and socialize the outcomes of those meetings to applicable stakeholders.
- Learn about and socialize to force the variety of safety award programs available.

Anchor Up
How well are you performing activities that support and strengthen your organization's safety management system?

Safety Climate and Culture

The safety management system is a key component of organizational success, but it must be influenced by organizational leaders to succeed. Leaders throughout your service, from the MCPON/MCPOCG to supervisors of small teams, play a key role in the development and maintenance of a safe climate and culture. "Safety climate" refers to the shared perceptions among the people of a team or organization about their leaders' commitment to safety, measures they take to communicate safety principles, and adherence to safety standards and procedures—what your people *feel* about safety. "Safety culture" is the collection of safety-related behaviors at a unit—what your people are actually *doing* regarding safety. The outcomes of a strong safety culture include leadership and each member of the organization valuing and prioritizing personnel safety; individual and group commitment to a personal responsibility for safety; a willingness to actively learn, adapt, and modify individual and organizational behavior based on lessons learned from mistakes and mishaps; and high levels of organizational and individual accountability for safety performance.

There has been substantial research showing that organizational culture is a tangible force that influences decision-making and actions at all levels. Chapter 2 of *Changing the Workplace Safety Culture* (McKinnon 2013) provides a great overview of the evolution of these cultures. Through time, what has been prevalent is the existence of a "blame the worker" approach toward causal analysis of mishaps. However, recent approaches have tried to shed light on leadership and process influences as significant contributing factors.

In 1931 W. H. Heinrich published *Industrial Accident Prevention* in which he proposed that unsafe acts accounted for 88 percent of accidents, while unsafe conditions accounted for only 10 percent. This approach put the root cause of accidents primarily on the worker, reinforcing the "blame the worker" response to mishaps and doing very little to fully evaluate system process and leadership influences. In the past we dealt primarily with symptoms, not causes.

Later in the 1970s James Reason focused his research toward human error and the way people and organizational processes contribute to the breakdown of complex, well-defended technologies such as commercial aviation, nuclear power generation, and financial services. His error classification and models of system breakdown are widely used today in these domains and others, particularly by accident investigators. Reason developed the Accident Causal Chain, or the "Swiss cheese" model (Reason 1997). In this model an organization's defenses against failure are modeled as a series of barriers, or slices of cheese. The holes in the slices represent weaknesses in individual parts of the system and are continually varying in size and position across each slice. The system produces failure and a mis-

CPO ACTIVITIES AND FUNCTIONS TO IMPROVE SAFETY CULTURE

- Encourage near-miss reporting and evaluate reporting processes and audits for effectiveness.
- Encourage minor injury reporting and sailor involvement/ownership for safety.
- Be involved with incident/accident investigations and lessons-learned development.
- Follow and model safety rules.
- Train and communicate about recent mishaps, hazards, and safety improvement efforts.
- Recognize and report hazards.
- Provide corrective feedback and praise.

hap occurs when a hole in a slice momentarily aligns with others, permitting—in Reason's words—a "trajectory of accident opportunity" so that a hazard passes through the barriers of control in all slices, leading to failure. The model includes active failures, which are the unsafe acts that can be directly linked to an accident such as pilot error, and latent failures, which include organizational influences, supervisory deficiencies, and preconditions for unsafe acts that may lay dormant for days, weeks, or months until they contribute to the accident.

Reason (1997) also did significant work in the area of safety culture, proposing that the culture of an organization is fundamentally composed of five critical subcultures:

- *Informed culture.* Those who manage and operate the system have current knowledge about the human, technical, and organizational factors that determine the safety of the system as a whole.
- *Reporting culture.* Personnel know how to report all hazards and violations.

- *Just culture.* There is no fear of retribution for reporting hazards and near-misses.
- *Flexible culture.* The organization is able to quickly respond to needed change.
- *Learning culture.* The organization has the willingness and ability to reflect on the state of safety, to learn, and to use this information to educate its people and implement major reform when needed.

When all five of these subcultures are developed, the result is a broad and effective safety culture that is greater than the sum of the parts.

In 2001 Patrick Hudson expanded on Reason's work, noting that safety culture is seen as a way to ensure high levels of performance in organizations. The organization can control all activities, enforce strict rules, and enact broad and prescriptive procedures for all activities. Opposite of this approach, an organization can opt to promote an organizational culture in which all people are personally involved and engaged. He found that the strength of organizational culture can be gauged on a spectrum of care and involvement. On one end of the spectrum, there is *pathological* culture, represented by organizations in which there is little trust, leaders do not care about safety, and leadership sees accidents as the cost of doing business and solely blames workers as the fault of all mishaps. In the center of the spectrum are organizations with *calculative* culture, in which leaders control all operations, enforce strict rules, and enact broad and very prescriptive procedures for all activities. And at the far end, organizations can evolve to promote a *generative* culture, where all members are personally involved and engaged. Generative cultures are frequently cited as the norm for military operations; however, this culture must be nurtured to avoid erosion. Generative cultures possess the attributes that underlie the success of the high-reliability organizations we discussed at the beginning of the chapter, including a preoccupation with failure, a reluctance to simplify, a sensitivity to operation, a recognition of leadership as a partner in risk management, and a demonstration that leadership knows, cares about, and shares lessons learned with other parts of the larger organization.

As the levels of information flow, trust and accountability increase, as does the strength of the safety culture. Within the Navy and USCG, all these cultures can exist, determined heavily by the potential cost of outcome and leadership that supports or resists them. It takes good leadership and your knowledge and involvement to nurture and cultivate the desired climate and culture within your unit. As you advance within your service, you must be able to help assess the safety climate and understand, gauge the strength of, and help shape organizational safety culture.

Anchor Up
How would you characterize the safety culture at your unit? Which safety leadership activities do you routinely do to shape a positive and proactive safety culture?

Helping Organizations Manage Risk Tolerance

Risk tolerance is the amount of risk a person or organization is willing to tolerate. As a Chief with the potential to influence the highest levels of the organization, you must now consider factors influencing tolerance from the context of organizational risk versus personal risk. Even with hazards identified and understood, the opportunity for a poor decision still exists and is shaped by the risk tolerance and factors that increase or decrease this tolerance (Paraventi 2015). Rather than focusing only on how individuals tolerate risk, you must now view risk tolerance from the perspective of how leaders and staff make decisions to accept or reject risk, or how processes influence broader organizational risk tolerance. As discussed in the *Petty Officer's Guide*, several factors influence this decision-making:

- Overestimating capability and experience
- Familiarity with the task resulting in complacency
- Underestimating the seriousness of the outcome
- Voluntary actions and being in control
- Personal experience with an outcome
- Cost of noncompliance
- Overconfidence in equipment
- Overconfidence in PPE and rescue
- Potential profit or gain (fiscal, emotional, physical)
- Role models accepting risk

Anchor Up
Review the factors that impact risk tolerance and risk decision-making. What factors are your teams susceptible to at this point? What could you be doing to help ensure your people and teams are making good decisions?

Normalized Deviance

The book *Challenger Launch Decision* identifies three key faults that led to the space shuttle *Challenger* disaster: competing projects and resource scarcity, regulatory ineffectiveness, and organizational factors, specifically, a failure in the organizational and professional culture (Vaughan 1997). These faults yielded *normalized deviance*, instances of groupthink, and compliance issues. Normalization of deviance occurs when people become so used to procedural or cultural norms being violated that they no longer recognize these variances and the potentially negative impacts to their personal or team safety. Research of normalized deviance in the health-care industry and others reveals that deviations or rule violations are rarely motivated by malice or greed but often result from personnel feeling intense performance pressures. Navy and Coast Guard units routinely operate under such pressure and are vulnerable to the risks of normalized deviance. Be aware of the concept and be able to identify when it has taken root in the tactical, operational, or strategic levels. Normalized deviance happens for several reasons:

- *The rules are perceived as stupid and inefficient.* In this case, people will develop shortcuts and workarounds when the rule, regulation, or standard seems irrational or inefficient.
- *Knowledge is imperfect and uneven.* People know the rules exist but fail to appreciate their purpose.
- *The work itself, along with new technology, can disrupt work behaviors or rule compliance.* New technologies and personnel can force people to devise novel responses to new challenges.
- *Rule-breaking is intended for the good of others.* Justification of deviation is when the rule or standard is perceived to be counterproductive.

- *The rules don't apply to me / you can trust me.* When people believe they are not tempted to engage in the behavior the rule is supposed to deter, it is perceived as superfluous.
- *Workers are afraid to speak up.* The likelihood that rule violations will become normalized increases if witnesses or those in the know refuse to intervene.
- *Leadership withholding or diluting findings on system problems.* A supervisor or leader may be abundantly aware of standard or rule violations but be fearful that if their supervisors knew about them, the person and unit would look bad to organizational leadership. Furthermore, efforts to correct standards violations might be perceived as too time-consuming and as threatening to cause short-term productivity losses.

There have been recent examples of normalized deviance, some contributing to cataclysmic outcomes, and they continue to demonstrate how broader program policy requirements can impact behavior, specifically risk tolerance. You have a responsibility to reflect on how your leadership and broader organizational factors and processes affect your people and then to act with their best interests in mind. Regardless of your current position, you can and should learn to directly identify the indicators of normalized deviance and bring it to the attention of leadership. Understanding concepts such as risk tolerance and normalized deviance helps you guide your organizations and teams to make better management decisions while working to avoid putting them in situations where they can make poor risk decisions that have catastrophic outcomes.

As much as you can help improve safety culture, you also can inadvertently encourage at-risk behavior by failing to praise safe practices, ignoring at-risk behaviors, overemphasizing production and operational necessity, or modeling risk behaviors. Your attitude will directly impact the behaviors and practices that your people will "buy in" to.

Anchor Up
What pressures are impacting the risk tolerance of your organization? Where is normalized deviance taking root? What have you done to bring these pressures to the attention of leadership?

Managing Team Stress

Stress affects everyone—service members, spouses, and children. Some amount of stress is healthy for each of us; it provides focus, drive, that sense of urgency that allows us to meet our commitments and responsibilities. However, too much unmanaged stress can be counterproductive and even harmful to our health. A career in the armed services brings unique stressors that, if not properly managed, can become dangerous to your mental and physical well-being and could result in a range of unfavorable outcomes, such as alcohol abuse, domestic violence, or suicide. Unhealthy Chiefs are unable to do their part contributing to the command's mission, so they have a personal responsibility to manage the stress in their lives. Perhaps the most important things you need to understand are your personal limits regarding stress and the stress continuum.

We all handle stress differently because our genetics have wired us to respond to stressors in diverse ways. Some of us thrive on the thrill of risky, life-threatening activities while others simply don't do so well dealing with crises at all. Unfortunately, some probably didn't understand how to effectively manage stress prior to choosing their Navy or Coast Guard career path or rating. Many learn that this can cause issues down the road. For example, those who were "low-stress" personalities prior to joining the Navy or Coast Guard find themselves in a high-stress rating or billet. It's crucial that you take time to evaluate your ability to handle stress and recognize the associated warning signs when you are starting to move into the more dangerous areas of the stress continuum. The stress continuum is a color-coded map that helps you identify behaviors that might arise from serving in combat, in dangerous peacekeeping missions, or the highly charged day-to-day work that is required of today's military personnel. While its primary use is for individual service members, the continuum also is a valuable tool to track behaviors of military families and commands. The spectrum ranges from the Green Zone (indicating you are ready to go) to the Red Zone (indicating you are suffering from stress-related illness). You should be familiar with this tool and teach your crews to do the same.

You should work to recognize and manage the factors that increase stress levels. How well do you cope with deployments or the stress of being assigned overseas? How effective are your anger coping mechanisms? Are you getting enough sleep, and is your nutrition adequate? Do you understand the effects your alcohol consumption has on your stress levels? These are all questions to reflect on when evaluating your current readiness to handle stress. Also take time to consider how well you are building up your resilience to stress. Resilience can best be understood as a type of response to intense stress. Resilience means "bouncing" or "returning to form," or your capacity to withstand, recover, grow, and function competently in the face of stress, adversity, and changing demands. You are personally responsible for your own mental and physical health, and taking time to evaluate your strengths and weaknesses concerning stress is a key part of that.

Due to the nature of maritime operations, the CPO mess has not traditionally had a reputation as a "touchy-feely" body of leadership. Chiefs have been characterized as overweight, cigarette smoking, beer drinking, no-nonsense leaders who had little concern for their crew's feelings or their own personal well-being. In prior decades, attitudes concerning family health were represented by the mantra, "Your family wasn't issued in your seabag." With time, however, attitudes change, and modern chiefs now value the total wellness of themselves and their Sailors.

Managing Team Fatigue and Endurance

I remember being assigned to a six on, six off watchstanding cycle as a young Sailor. In addition to my watches, I had divisional and departmental training responsibilities to fulfill and the demands of the ship's schedule as well. Needless to say, I was tired and suffered from a variety of negative emotional and physical impacts. The worst part was that my leadership seemed unaware and unable or unwilling to help manage these impacts. Fatigue is a critical consideration for any watchstander. Decades of scientific research and maritime safety studies have shown that fatigue has a negative impact on decision-making and the way the human body and mind perform, especially under stress. The human need for sleep is a physiologically driven event that dominates our daily activities and is central to our ability to perform both physical and cognitive tasks.

The quantity and quality of sleep is a significant factor in determining how well humans function within a system. Most adult humans require an average of eight hours of sleep per day; when this sleep requirement is not met, performance can suffer dramatically. The human circadian rhythm is a human's natural daily cycle—roughly twenty-four hours in duration—and governs things such as hormone release and alertness. Performance degradations frequently result from disruption of circadian rhythms from jet lag or shift work. Any traveler transiting time zones, particularly traveling east, will testify to the cognitive challenges posed by jet lag. Watch standers are likely to experience the same type of challenges, especially in a rotation that disrupts the body's normal circadian cycle, if sleep periods are too short or if the quality of sleep is poor.

The literature on shift work is rife with examples of diminished performance and health risks associated with working night-shift and swing-shift schedules. Some aspects of performance are more susceptible to sleep deprivation than others. Given that sleepiness causes increased eye blinks, longer eye closure durations, even brief bursts of sleep called "microsleep," it is understandable that tasks depending on visual input are particularly sensitive to sleep disruption. Studies have demonstrated that individuals whose jobs require them to perform vigilance tasks (e.g., monitoring visual displays with little or no external visual stimulation) tend to miss subtle pattern changes. This vigilance decrement has major implications for the DoD, given that individuals standing watch in combat information, fire-control, and sonar stations may be required to monitor visual or auditory displays for extended periods of time. It can also affect other watchstanders, such as on the bridge of a ship or monitoring an engineering display.

The bottom line is that sleep is a biological imperative, and a vital requirement for life, often defined as "the rest and recovery from the wear and tear of wakefulness." In addition to its impact on real-time performance, a lack of sleep can have detrimental health effects long after an individual has left the service. Just as shipboard equipment requires periodic maintenance to operate in peak condition and meet its expected service life, the human body must have sufficient sleep to function properly, especially in an arduous shipboard environment. Fatigue is often listed as a causal or contributing factor by the National Transportation Safety Board in maritime accidents. Recently, the U.S. Navy has implemented measures to reduce fatigue that center around three guiding principles:

[8-3] Quartermaster 2nd class stands lookout watch aboard an aircraft carrier as it departs its home port for routine operations. U.S. NAVY PHOTO BY MC3 BRITTNEY CAMACHO-PIETRI

- *Use a circadian watch rotation.* The first guiding principle is the use of the circadian-based watch rotation that leverages the human body's natural circadian rhythm, based on a twenty-four-hour day, to build a watch schedule. In general, any combination of watch durations that adds up to twenty-four will support this process. Some examples are: four on, eight off; three on, nine off; or six on, eighteen off. Numerous studies have shown that watchstanders are more alert when using fixed, circadian watch rotations and that reaction times and decision-making are improved compared to rotating watch bills. Ships may choose a static watch bill where everyone stands the same watch all the time or may rotate on a periodic basis. In general, three weeks is the ideal duration of a shift, and the preferred rotation direction is forward (add one hour to the evening and night watches to shift the rotation). This process requires detailed planning, a qualification path to the desired number of watch sections, and frequent review to develop the required watch rotation. Designating fixed watch teams early and setting qualification goals well prior to deployment is one way to ensure

- *Build a stable ship's routine around the watch rotation.* The second guiding principle of a good watch rotation is a supporting schedule. Work with your department heads and executive officer to build a daily routine that supports protected sleep at specified times for those individuals expected to stand watch at night. This can include such measures as restricting announcements during morning and evening hours, adjusting meal hours to accommodate the chosen watch rotation, and focusing the bulk of training, meetings, and drills during the heart of the day—for example, between 0900 and 1500. Most ships conduct a daily operations / intelligence brief; doing this in the late afternoon instead of after dinner can allow the watch team to attend the brief and maintain situational awareness while still executing their assigned watch and sleep rotations.
- *Focus on alert watchstanders.* The final guiding principle is to focus on alert watchstanders; review the schedule periodically and watch for violations of protected sleep; conduct individual risk assessments based on rest prior to an event, and plan ahead for upcoming evolutions to either ensure that watch standers and participants are rested or, if that is not possible, allow time after the event to catch up. Certainly, operational commitments and unforeseen emergencies will arise; maintaining a "sleep reservoir" by using a circadian watch rotation and supporting schedule will result in more resilient crew members who are more likely to perform better under stressful conditions.

Finally, it goes without saying that drugs are dangerous for you and your people's physical well-being in the short and long term. But drugs aren't the only toxic substances that have negative impacts on team readiness. Abuse or misuse of alcohol, prescription medications, or energy drinks can all have caustic impacts on your team's health.

These guiding principles work together to produce well-rested watch standers, giving them better situational awareness during routine operations and increased resilience in case of an emergency. This process can improve watch team performance, reduce fatigue, improve morale and productivity, and decrease the risk of a mishap. Best practices and lessons can be found and shared, and a *Crew Endurance Handbook* downloaded, at http://my.nps.edu/web/crewendurance.

Anchor Up
Recall and share three situations in which your leadership made a difference in safety and team effectiveness.

The concepts presented in this chapter are important, and they should help you begin to think differently about risk management, read more in-depth about it, and understand factors that can impact individual, unit-level, and service-wide decision-making and culture. As you have learned, the academic research and general attitudes toward safety have changed and continue to evolve. Viewing the risk management process and your involvement in it from these new perspectives requires your willingness to learn and reflect. If you are engaged and care about the health of your service, you will take the time to learn how to best influence a safety culture that is in the best interest of your people.

Nine

Preparing for and Growing into New Leadership Positions

And it was there that I realized that a squared-away command master chief could do so much good if they were proactive and so much harm if they were just satisfied to claim a parking space on the pier, follow the CO around during zone inspections, and perform a few recurring ceremonial duties. So I decided then that I'd try to go the command master chief route, to see what I could do for sailors and for their families.

—MCPON *John Hagan*

As you become more senior, you will have opportunities to serve in positions on larger vessels; at the sector, region, force, fleet, or headquarters (HQ) level; or in key roles within your rating or community of work, and your scope of influence will increase accordingly. Therefore, you must learn to adjust your influence targets and style. The most successful CPOs, SCPOs, and MCPOs can increasingly empower their subordinates as the sphere of their influence increases. This requires savvy communication skills and an understanding that you will now lead through others. It also requires you to consider how your general and specific responsibilities and authorities have changed, who your new influence targets are, how your power bases have expanded or contracted, and how you can wield influence tactics differently for these new audiences.

As your audience grows and the potential impacts of your position expand, you must start to think about influence differently—to think of it from the perspective of systems, processes, and culture. As you move into positions further up in the service hierarchy, your specific authorities may be less defined, but your impact through influence increases significantly. It is now less about what you want to achieve with a small team and more about how you help your command and the larger organization achieve its goals.

This chapter offers guidance on the opportunities available to you and how to best prepare for them. Before you think about becoming the MCPON, MCPOCG, warrant officer, or limited duty officer, you should focus on your advancement to the next pay grade, succeed in that pay grade, and then identify and prepare for the positions that are available. This chapter highlights the career paths available to you and offers insight on how to best prepare for them.

Adapting to New Influence Positions and Challenges

Knowing and harnessing your power bases and influence tactics is one thing, but understanding how to effectively use them is another. Before you can begin to effectively leverage power bases and use influence tactics, some relationship fundamentals related to power and influence must be understood. This requires you to reflect on how you are applying or can expect to apply your power and influence to a variety of situations you could encounter in new positions (how to wield influence over geographical distances, for example).

Again, as you move into positions of increased influence, from direct to executive to strategic levels of leadership, you must start to understand how organizations wield power and use this model to understand which staff directorate owns that power base. For example, the United States has national power bases reflected in their diplomatic, information, military, economic, finance, intelligence, and law enforcement powers that are used to achieve strategic ends. Flag and general officer headquarters and directorates function in a similar way with their own power that they use to achieve their strategic goals. On these teams, you will spend more time influencing senior officers, their staff, and subordinate commands and teams (often physically dispersed) rather than people and teams on the deck plates, and you'll have to consider how to leverage your own and your organization's power bases and influence tactics in new settings and situations such as shipyard environments or new missions.

As you advance or assume positions of higher authority, you must consider how your influence is changing, how your power bases have expanded, what organizational power you have access to, and how to wield influence tactics for a new set of influence targets. For example, as a divisional Chief, you will spend much time with your leading petty officers, division officers, department's leading Chief, fellow division Chiefs in your department, and your divisional Sailors and Coasties. As a departmental leading Chief Petty Officer, you will work closely with your department head, division chief petty officers, fellow department LCPOs, and your SEL, but you will spend less daily face time with a team of Sailors. And when selected as an SEL, you will spend more time influencing unit success through engagements with your commanding and executive officers, department heads, department leading Chief Petty Officers, and influential program managers such as the command managed equal opportunity (CMEO) manager and the command career counselor. If selected to serve on a flag staff, you will advise the commander and other staff officers and work with your CMC team.

Anchor Up

In your current position, what are the top three barriers to your influence objectives? Why? What can you do to reduce or remove the barriers? What resources do you have available to help?

With a position of increased influence at the highest levels of the DoD and your service, you will be able to achieve many things. However, if you want to be able to generate team buy-in and elevate the attitude of your organization toward high levels of commitment, you must back your positional power base with solid bases of personal and organizational expertise and personal power.

Also, as you move into positions of authority or influence as command or assignment to a command or program staff, you will help with organizational management success. To do this, you must build upon your fundamental knowledge of management functions and personal management competence. You must also understand that organizational competence is held by many people who are assigned key responsibilities. For example, your service's personnel office is the commander's expert for matters on personnel management, and the comptroller serves as the expert for financial management. Although you may not be assigned to these directorates or have the depth of competence in these staff functions, you must build some degree of knowledge in those areas so you can help with decision-making and organizational efficiency and effectiveness.

Although we cannot go into depth on each, the following list provides a sample of areas you should spend time reading about and gaining familiarity with to best contribute to staff and HQ efforts:

- Planning, programming, and budgeting
- Acquisition and appropriation processes
- Manpower and manning
- Organizational behavior
- Change management
- Safety management systems and safety culture
- Systems and process management
- Advanced service and joint military education
- Strategic communication

As with all new positions of power, taking these steps away from the deck plate and growing into them will take time and learning beyond what this chapter has offered. You should seek the guidance and advice of those who have served successfully in these positions.

You may think of leadership as an individual effort; although you use power and influence, your leadership teams and their staffs have power bases too. For example, the personal and expert power of your command is reflected in its organizational reputation. Is your unit the "go to" for tough missions, or does it have the reputation of the unit people avoid? Does it have a favorable command climate? Consider how the comptroller on a flag staff, which is responsible for budgeting and financial management, works from a significant base of ecological power that can enable or constrain the readiness and performance of multiple subordinate units. Or your public affairs officer, who wields information power that can shape local, national, and even global perceptions of your unit, people, or their service. When developed and used well, these organizational power bases will help signal the character and competence of your organization and hopefully strengthen its reputation and credibility. As you move into executive and strategic levels of leadership, you must think about how you can integrate into and harness your organization's power bases to help your leadership teams attain their goals.

In concert with developing the knowledge, skills, and abilities to wield power and influence power structures, you should also take time to consider potential obstacles to your influence and the changes that result from being assigned to new positions. Now that you are aware you are a key agent of influence, you should also recognize that other people and situations are influencing your team's priorities, processes, and people. Learn those who can make your leadership efforts easier or more difficult. Furthermore, although you have positional and connection power unique to your role, remember that your subordinates and peers are also using their power and influence that accompanies their positions to meet the demands of their work. While giving them room to grow, you should take time to watch and coach them on their leadership approaches and impact. You should also have transparent discussions on how you can work to avoid disruptions from leadership boundaries. This is especially important in the delegating stage of leadership. The best leaders learn to use *all* their power bases and apply them as each situation demands; there are no assembly line–produced leaders. Your personality, experience, and audience will affect how you lead, and just because others do things differently doesn't mean they are any less effective. What has made you successful to date is probably the model of leadership you want to continue to use, but you can always learn new tactics from others.

How you use power and influence as a divisional Chief will be different from how you use it as a Master Chief working on a flag staff. You will attend service leadership schools that will help you navigate these changes, but you should also seek coaching and feedback from others who have "been there and done that" and who can help you gauge the depth of your power bases; offer insight on how things change as you move up the chain of command; and gauge the impact you have on people, the mission, and your potential for service in future roles. And if that feedback reveals weaknesses or lack of knowledge, accept it and strive to improve.

Senior Enlisted Career Paths

Once you advance to SCPO, you will find yourself confronted with the choice of two enlisted career paths. The first will be focused on in-rate technical management and rating community health. This path can culminate in enlisted or officer positions such as department head, officer in charge (OIC), rating community manager, or rating force Master Chief (RFMC). The second path is a track focused on organizational management and leadership, which leads to selection and assignment in command senior enlisted positions leading to the MCPON's or MCPOCG's office or even the senior enlisted adviser to the chairman of the Joint Chiefs of Staff (SEAC). Although the knowledge, skills, and abilities may be similar for both tracks in some areas, competency changes depending on the path you commit to. Although there are educational requirements, experience, and career milestones unique to each path, your focus should be on acquiring the knowledge and skill sets that best enable your success in the given path. The following descriptions of positions you may fill serve to inform and illustrate how positions can be as impactful as pay grade. I divide these roles into three categories—direct, executive/command, and organizational/flag levels of leadership.

Direct-Level Leadership and Management Positions

Chiefs assigned to the department or team level within a command practice direct leadership. These direct leadership positions could come in the form of primary or collateral duties. In the Navy you will serve as a division or department leading Chief Petty or as a department-level collateral duty manager. In the Coast Guard you can serve in direct positions such as department head, food service officers, training petty officer, or surfmen trainer. At this level you work with division or department-level leaders (division officers, department heads, leading petty officers, division/department collateral duty managers) to manage the matériel, personnel, and operational readiness of your part of the overall mission.

As the top technical experts within the department, you are expected to plan, monitor, and supervise assigned or needed work. Senior and master chiefs assigned to LCPO or department head will similarly provide direct leadership, but through subordinate Chief Petty Officers. In general, the policies and practices you influence will be limited in scope to the division, team, or department level, although the work you are responsible for performing is what your organization's overall success ultimately hinges on. As a direct-level leader, you should know those assigned to you on a fairly personal level as you work alongside each other and experience challenges and successes together daily.

Executive/Command Leader Positions

Chiefs assigned to executive/command-level positions practice executive leadership. In these positions, your influence will be absolute but largely confined to your specific command, although your performance will significantly contribute to overall organizational performance. Some of these billets are typically reserved for commissioned officers but may be filled by senior enlisted in their absence. In the Navy these positions include Command Master and Senior Chiefs and command-level collateral duty managers such as drug and alcohol program adviser (DAPA), CMEO manager, or command training coordinator. One unique opportunity for USCG senior enlisted in some ratings is to serve in positions collectively known as the command cadre. These positions include engineering petty officer, executive petty officer, and OIC.

Executive leaders generally work through key personnel assigned to head unit departments or sections and focus on the climate of the command as a whole rather than routine personal interactions with everyone they lead. Your service places its highest expectations and trust in the ability and judgment of those selected for these command-level positions. Selection for these positions is the result of superior performance, dedicated study, experience, and demonstrated leadership. While demanding, command-level leadership is one of the highest privileges and most rewarding opportunities, allowing you to help shape the quality of work and life of the people assigned to your command.

There are many expectations for command leadership positions. You are expected to lead by example, ensure the unit is operationally ready to perform all assigned missions, and understand and promote service and national strategic objectives. You will ensure that your crew, squadron, or team is prepared to serve in full measure by shaping good morale, maximizing readiness and training, ensuring health and physical fitness, cultivating family support, ensuring fair and equitable treatment, and maintaining good order and discipline. You will strive to provide for the smooth, efficient, and productive administration of your unit.

Command positions are not about those serving in these assignments; they are about the unit and the crew. Remember—you are in the inspiration business. Organizational success rests on the leadership and example set by the command triad or cadre, and that group must embody the service's core values and instill the same in the crew as they strive to meet service and national objectives. The crew will not trust or follow a command that fails to hold itself accountable. As leaders, the command triad or cadre must work through their crew to complete assigned missions, ensuring they are always ready. To achieve success, the entire cadre must perpetuate the enduring principles of proficiency in craft, proficiency in leadership, and disciplined initiative, setting the example and expecting the same from the crew. Command is an art. It requires a combination of leadership, moral courage, ethics, judgment, and awareness. Its gravity must be reflected on, and clear expectations established for, both personal conduct and the conduct of the crew.

Organizational/Flag Leader Positions

Chapter 1 highlights a brief history of the evolution of the senior enlisted positions that evolved, expanded, and were formalized over time and are now collectively identified as command senior enlisted leaders (CSEL), to include Command Master Chiefs, Command Senior Chiefs in the Navy, and gold and silver badge Command Chiefs in the USCG. Senior and Master Chiefs assigned as CSELs or to HQ positions such as RFMC practice strategic leadership and wield influence to shape community-wide and long-term organizational priorities and resource allocations. They have direct access to service leaders who are empowered to make decisions that impact the whole organization, or at least large swaths of it. Because they are engaged in issues that affect so many, their daily interactions are centered on the high-ranking service leader or principal they advise and any associated staff. These strategic leaders also frequently interact with large groups as they solicit feedback or disseminate information in order to better advise their principal of current trends and conditions. With that said, some direct and command-level positions blur the lines between two or more levels. For example, in the USCG, "A" School Chiefs practice a brand of executive leadership over any students undergoing training, and their personal preferences are reflected in the manner training is carried out at the school. But these school Chiefs also lead strategically, anticipating changing technology, service needs, and national priorities to craft curricula for future courses involving in their rating.

CSELs ensure and enhance naval warfighting readiness by providing leadership and mentorship to the Navy and advice to commanders and COs in partnership with deputy commanders, chiefs of staff, or executive officers (XO). Their duties include the dissemination and promotion of command policy and matters that support mission accomplishment. They also uphold and enforce the highest standards of professionalism and integrity while enhancing active communication at all levels of command throughout the Department of the Navy and Coast Guard.

CSELs report directly to their respective commander or CO, advising and providing input on matters affecting operational mission success, operational readiness, manning, and training of all their people, as well as providing input to the formulation, implementation, and execution of policies concerning the culture of excellence to include the morale, welfare, job satisfaction, discipline, and support to families. They advise commanders and COs on the formulation and implementation of changes in policy affecting the command(s). Furthermore, they provide solicited and unsolicited advice and recommendations to the chain of command as well as to their respective ISIC CSEL (see chapter 2 for more insight on this relationship). Some specific SEL lines of effort include the following:

- Establishing and maintaining the conditions that ensure their unit is fully prepared for warfighting while enabling a culture of excellence that includes a productive and positive command climate;

- Developing a CPO mess climate that serves to develop and maintain the highest levels of matériel and warfighting readiness, professional excellence, and esprit de corps;
- Possessing a detailed understanding of the different phases of their force generation and deployment cycles and their role in ensuring its success (see chapter 7);
- Instilling a culture of excellence throughout their command and sharing responsibility for successful training, certifications, and assignments;
- Promoting and ensuring that official ceremonies, such as retirements, frocking ceremonies, and award ceremonies that honor Sailors, are embraced and properly executed;
- Assisting in the management and delivery of proper, accurate, and timely communications throughout the command(s);
- Communicating with and supporting Navy families and family support organizations; and
- Maintaining awareness of and assisting in the shaping of the health of command programs designed to ensure a professional command culture and climate.

Those filling a CSEL position are considered the senior most enlisted by precedence at their unit and at units falling under their area of responsibility (AOR), regardless of time in service or time in grade. To further add credibility to CSEL titles and positions, specialty badges are authorized to be worn on all uniforms. Service uniform regulations outline the requirements for wearing these badges.

In the Navy, all CSELs assigned to flag/general officer staff also serve as members of the MCPON leadership mess. In this capacity, they support the MCPON in the formulation, implementation, and execution of policies ensuring warfighting readiness of Sailors and their families as well as in the formulation, implementation, and execution of policies concerning morale, welfare, job satisfaction, discipline, utilization, family support, and training of all Sailors across the Navy. The MCPON leadership mess convenes as required, and attendance at MCPON leadership mess functions are by invitation as specified by the MCPON.

9-1 WHAT DOES IT TAKE TO BECOME A GOLD BADGE COMMAND MASTER CHIEF?

I am often asked, "What does it take to become a Gold Badge Command Master Chief?" There are many factors involved to answer that question, but the biggest reason for me was an inspirational leader who I was fortunate enough to work for, Boatswain's Mate Master Chief Mark Schweiger.

Most enlisted people in the Coast Guard have the potential to be a Command Master Chief. It often only takes a great leader to recognize that potential and push the person to reach higher. Master Chief Schweiger pushed everyone who worked with him to be their best; however, many of us didn't appreciate what he was doing for us at the time. As it is with many great leaders, you can't truly understand how helpful they are until well after they have made their impact on you.

The Coast Guard is the best organization to work for. We're small enough that great leaders, like Master Chief Schweiger, can devote time to develop junior people on a personal level. I'm sure if you reflect on your best leaders, they are the people who pushed you to be a better person instead of being the easiest to work for. Master Chief Schweiger first set the example for hard work and dedication, then spelled out his expectations for the crew and never wavered in those expectations, even when we couldn't appreciate what he was doing for us. He recognized his crew for their hard work and never took credit for himself.

As I've advanced through our service, I came to appreciate another of Master Chief Schweiger's key leadership traits. He consistently modeled maturity to his crew and focused on what is truly important in life, not just the Coast Guard mission. Personally, he helped me focus my goals on long-term outcomes that involved taking care of my family and helping me to become a better person. He constantly asked us to think about what was truly important to us, which helped keep us on the right track. He never got too busy to a do a daily check to be sure we were focusing on our long-term goals....

If you want to be a leader worth remembering, like Master Chief Schweiger was to me, set high standards for yourself, set high standards for your crew, communicate those standards and help your crew reach the maximum of their potential. Do not let your crew take the path of least resistance. Push them to work harder than they thought they could.

—*13th MCPOCG Jason Vanderhaden*

Being Fully Utilized

Whether you are serving as an SEL or within one of the flag staff divisions, there are many unique attributes you possess that your staff should strive to take advantage of. You bring decades of experience dealing with enlisted policy issues and utilization from a variety of perspectives and positions within the chain of command. Unlike senior officers, who cycle in and out of command positions over the course of their careers, you have consistent "front office" experience because you are consecutively assigned at the command level of leadership. You also occupy a unique position outside the chain of command that allows you to stand back from the organization, figure out what works and what does not, and then influence change. You can access, observe, and advise all officers and enlisted personnel within the commander's sphere of influence. You have been promoted to the highest possible pay grade, so you no longer have advancement acting as a potential behavioral barrier to unfettered advice. You have attended advanced professional military education and executive education courses and seminars and understand how organizations function at the strategic level. Most importantly, you are well networked, increasing their command's connections and information powerbases, thus improving the command's capacity for effective communication.

Still, there are senior and flag officers and members of their staffs who think SELs should be the command and tactical-level problem-solver across their force rather than serve as an engaged operational- or strategic-level asset. For example, some SELs have had supervisors tell them, "Go do what master chiefs do," or they have had their role captured as "heads and beds." Additionally, some perceptions exist that SELs are trying to be the "number two" in command. Because of what they do, SELs must often challenge existing norms and processes, which can create conflict. Undoubtedly, some audiences have had bad experiences with an SEL at some point in their careers that negatively shaped their perceptions. Some of our peers do not live up to the expectation of their roles, but the majority do and cannot not be defined by the poor performance of a few. The visibility and bad press highlighting those SELs who fail to adhere to standards further shapes perceptions. Similarly, many senior officers and SELs do "get it" but still miss the chance to leverage the SEL position to its full potential. So how can and should SELs be effectively utilized? Feedback from enlisted members and officers help form a framework for how to you can best engage and influence as an SEL working for a flag officer.

Speak to the Force on Behalf of the Command

One of the privileges and most rewarding roles of being an SEL is getting out and speaking with a wide variety of audiences, both officer and enlisted. In this capacity you serve as a sort of brand ambassador. During engagements ranging from site visits to recognition banquets, you will communicate your commander's roles, responsibilities, and objectives. This not only reinforces what is going on and what the organization does, but it also helps translate the commander's intent. A critical part of speaking to the workforce is to pass on messages that support the commander's strategic communication plan. Since you have the unique experience of having served as junior enlisted, you can often package the message in a way that translates well. You can also speak on behalf of your service leaders since you will attend meetings and symposia that provide insight on broader policy affecting service personnel and their families.

Serve as the "Eyes and Ears" for the Command

Organizations, leaders, and managers can't fix what they can't see. You should frequently visit subordinate units within your AOR to meet with personnel and facilitate discussion. The concerns and recommendations you receive can be reported to your commander and staff but are often routed to the Chief of Naval Operations and Commandant of the Coast Guard via the MCPON/MCPOCG, making your senior enlisted networks, in effect, an advisory board to the senior policymakers in your service. In this capacity, you observe and report to your command and service on behalf of your force. Commanders often do not have the time—despite their desire—to engage in frequent small-group discussions; however, you do, and thus can

[9-1] The author meets with a fleet CPO mess. Engagements like these offer an SEL the opportunity to communicate on behalf of the boss, but they also serve as a venue to identify policy and resourcing issues to bring back into headquarters' governance discussions.
PHOTO PROVIDED BY AUTHOR

get the story behind the PowerPoint briefs and stoplight charts that your commander typically sees. Once you have spoken to the force on behalf of the command, you should engage in discussions to solicit feedback and identify areas where communication is inadequate or where policy could be revised in the best interest of enlisted personnel and their families.

Examples of broad questions you should consider asking include "What do you need?"; "How can I help?"; "What did we get wrong with a given policy change or recommendation?"; and "What can I provide clarification on?" Answers to such questions provide your commander and staff valuable insight and feedback. During visits, take a fix on behaviors and conditions you observe that might indicate where resources are inadequate or where leadership attention is lacking. You can provide some valuable "watch team backup," and your unique perspective or background might help identify root causes that other leaders miss. It is critical that you maintain transparency when reporting issues observed in the fleet. This "observe and report" role is one that some officers may find threatening due to your direct access to the boss; communication is key to prevent this misunderstanding. You should ensure that a unit's commanding officer knows you are visiting and provide any specific unit concerns you note to the unit's leadership. The intent of these visits should not be to identify command discrepancies; rather, the intent should be to gather a broader pulse on issues such as the health of the force, the effectiveness of communication, and fiscal effects on readiness. Then provide sound recommendations to the commander.

Engagement with External Stakeholders

As an SEL serving on a staff, you will engage with military and civilian stakeholders outside of your command structure. Through these engagements you will share information and raise awareness of what our people and organizations do while forging relationships that provide resources for the enlisted force. Many partners have the same challenges that we do, so the relationships can lead to productive exchanges of ideas regarding potential solutions. You should work to build strong relationships with allied and partner nation militaries and other U.S. government and civilian organizations such as the USO or Navy League to understand and promote their programs and the value they bring service members and their families. When your commander integrates you into these events, it shows partner leadership and the high value the U.S. military places on its enlisted force. Your participation in these engagements should be a priority with a defined intention—engagement with a purpose.

Commander's Confidant

It is commonly understood that you are one of a small group of people with the experience, access, and trust to provide your boss candid feedback, especially on matters relating to their personal behavior, including perceptions. As mentioned earlier, you don't have advancement hanging over your head and thus should not be influenced by artificial barriers to telling the truth. You also serve to consult your bosses on how effectively they use their power and influence. You have many opportunities to observe leaders as they engage, observe the response of the organization, and provide leaders feedback and advice for improvement or let them know they are on target. Just understand that the command has many other "front office" staff (chief of staff, flag aides, etc.) who have as much, if not more, intimate access to your commander. Do not feel challenged by this. Develop good working relationships with these key staff and see them as a resource to help you fulfill your role much better.

Mentoring and Advising Officers and Enlisted Personnel throughout the Chain of Command

Because of your unique position outside the chain of command, you are vested with the ability to provide advice to all officers and enlisted personnel in the command. You will attend meetings with the command and staff and sit on many other councils and committees. You have the experience to provide advice ranging from how the commander could better communicate with his units to how a fellow SEL could be more effective. You should work to ensure the wide range of programs and resources available to shape readiness and success are promoted, compliant, and effective, and you should serve as a positive and engaged mentor for SELs within your scope of influence.

Although these are five broad roles for SELs, they do vary depending on the billet being filled. The scope of engagement at each level should align with the scope of responsibility, authority, and accountability of your commander. As you progress to billets of increasing influence, the scope of your roles and the stakeholders with whom you engage should be expected to evolve as well. SELs today now serve on a much broader scale than perhaps in previous generations, influencing and advising DoD and service commanders and their staffs at the operational and strategic levels, so you should consider and understand the full value you can provide in these billets. If you are currently serving as an SEL or are thinking about this career path, you should understand how your role and influence change in these billets to ensure you are providing maximum value to your commanders.

Screening for Senior Enlisted Assignments

Many assignments that will be available to you involve screening processes because of the high degree of competence and skill required and the influence these positions have on organizational success and reputation. Each service has specific policies, instructions, and processes to identify, nominate, and select candidates, and because these can change frequently, I will not cover them in depth in this guide.

Boards and panels are restricted to using only the information contained in your service's official personnel and performance records and not word of mouth. For all intents and purposes, if it's not in your records, it didn't happen. Because your official records are the only things the board considers, it is to your advantage to view the records that will be considered by the board to which you are applying. Although infrequent, errors in records do occur. Accurate and complete records and candidate packages are critical to successful screening for these positions. Your record and any associated screening package is a personal responsibility of and a direct reflection on you as a candidate. It is ultimately your responsibility to maintain your record. You should review the program instruction and messages that will outline the sources of information used by panels and boards charged with making significant personnel decisions.

Nomination packages are normally required for command and flag-level positions. Again, your service instruction will outline what is required in these packages, but they normally include biographical information, careers summaries, photos, personal statements, and endorsements. This is where your writing skills will come to good use. Once your package is assembled, make sure to pass it by a mentor who can review and identify weaknesses or gaps.

Some positions will also require you to conduct an interview with the flag officer you will be working with. A couple of suggestions here: First, take time to review the command mission and find out from current staff what the commander's priorities and goals are and what lines of effort are being worked on. From there you can think through how your knowledge, skills, and abilities can best serve to help accomplish those priorities and objectives. When researching a new assignment, realize the importance of reviewing the position description to ensure you understand its responsibilities, the scope of its authority, and any unique accountability associated with the job or duty.

At times it may be easy to lose sight of how your position fits into the larger organization. Take time to consider things from the command's perspective. Doing so will help you align your focus and effort with theirs and, ultimately, with what the organization needs. During your one-on-one time with them, bounce your activities and priorities off them to ensure alignment. These conversations will be illuminating and may help you better focus your effort. You must know the responsibilities and authorities of your OIC, CO, or commander. *Command at Sea* (Stavridis, Girrier, and Kacher 2022) is a "must read" for those senior enlisted who are serving, or desire to serve, in senior enlisted positions.

Next, review the background and career path of the officer who will be interviewing you and look for areas of commonality. This is easy if you have served with the officer in the past. But if not, you should explore further. Have you served in the same warfare community before? Perhaps you grew up in the same state or attended the same college. This is good information to help with making the interview process smoother. Take some time to get insight from the incumbent senior enlisted leader and any front office staff. You may find that they have insights and guidance you can use in the interview.

The steps above can help prepare you to best answer questions that may come up. Some interviews will be more conversational while others may be more question-and-answer. And although you are being interviewed, you should consider the perspective that you are interviewing your potential future boss, so you should be prepared to ask questions to identify areas of potential conflict or disagreement prior to assignment. You should also work to identify the expectations that officer has of you and how they envision you will best integrate into the staff and governance.

Be patient. From scheduling to final notification, the interview process can take several weeks. And although you are anxious to find out if you are the selection for the position, keep in mind that the admiral or general and their staff are busy, and this process is one of many things happening in the command. Your service has an office that will be tracking these interviews, and they are in the best position to pulse the staff on the status of the nominative process.

In most cases, you can expect that one of the front office staff will notify you by email or phone call to set up a call to notify you of the outcome. Usually, those not selected will be notified first, and then the selected individual will be notified last. If not selected, be professional and thank the officer for the opportunity; you may find yourself interviewing with that officer for another opportunity in the future. They may also recommend you as a candidate to a fellow flag officer who they think would benefit from your knowledge and experience. If you are selected, work with the flag aide to set up a follow-up meeting as necessary.

Commissioning Programs

If you find yourself more interested in technical management, there are career paths to pursue with a commission as a naval officer. Although many (if not all) interested candidates can expect some ribbing from their fellow Chiefs, these programs offer great opportunities to pursue increased leadership positions and responsibilities not afforded to senior enlisted leaders. Selection to these programs also brings significant pay increases. You should pursue the opportunity that best leverages your knowledge, skills, and abilities while providing you the career satisfaction and quality of life you desire.

LDO and CWO are two separate programs that provide your service Navy officer technical managers and technical specialists who exercise leadership in key positions throughout the service. Combined, these two communities make up more than 11 percent of the officer corps. Both programs provide the opportunity for outstanding senior enlisted personnel to compete for a commission. Currently, a college degree is not required to apply; however, a more educated force and a recognition of the professional benefits of education will certainly make a college degree required for future promotion.

- *Limited Duty Officers* serve as officer technical managers of the line or staff corps. They progressively advance within broad technical fields related to their former enlisted ratings. They fill leadership and management positions at the ensign through captain level that require technical background and skills not attainable through normal development within other officer designators. LDOs serve as, but are not limited to serving as, division officers, department heads, OICs, XOs, and COs.
- *Chief Warrant Officers* possess the authority and are qualified by extensive experience and knowledge to direct the most difficult and exacting operations within a given occupational specialty. In addition, CWOs have the leadership ability of commissioned officers, so they are expected to effectively communicate up and down the chain of command. Possessing a college degree will significantly increase your chances to earn a promotion to the warrant officer ranks. It is not a requirement to hold a college degree to secure this promotion; however, it will make you stand out among your peers. Although intended primarily as technical specialists, CWOs may also serve as division officers, department heads, and OICs. All warrant officers are grouped by specialty for the purposes of appointment and assignment.

If you are interested in either of these programs, you should start with knowing exactly what you are applying for, including what jobs will you be required to fulfill. Unfortunately, many candidates do not know what

[9-2] Chiefs in formation at a pinning ceremony. They are the Navy's future Senior Chief and Master Chief Petty Officers and should be looking forward to positions of increased responsibility beyond that of a divisional Chief. U.S. NAVY PHOTO BY TIMOTHY SCHUMAKER

their designator is or what their responsibilities would be. For example, a boatswain's mate who applies for LDO likely will follow a career path of ship's boatswain, assistant first lieutenant, amphibious detachment officer in charge, Board of Inspection and Survey, and so on. You can also expect to be assigned to a seagoing billet, so it is important to know what you are signing up for. You must ask yourself (and your spouse), "Is this a good fit for us?" and make sure your family is on board with your decision.

LDOs and CWOs are selected for appointment by In-Service Procurement Selection Boards. Each service runs its process differently, but the details are included in your appropriate service message. Board membership includes officers of the line and various staff corps to allow the senior member of the board to establish internal panels with a good knowledge of the requirements of each occupational specialty. Each member of the board is sworn to select the best-qualified candidates without prejudice or partiality. The board considers applicants for appointment in the designator(s) they have requested. If a candidate requests consideration in more than one designator, the board recommends the individual for appointment only in the designator for which she is considered best qualified. The board recommends candidates for appointment in numbers not to exceed the quotas furnished by their service. However, the board is not obligated to select the numbers provided if, in its opinion, sufficient numbers of applicants are not qualified for appointment in a particular designator.

To get started, review your service's commissioning program instruction/manual. Navy candidates should read *Enlisted to Officer Commissioning Programs Application Administrative Manual* (OPNAVINST 1420.1B) and applicable naval administrative messages, and USCG warrant officer candidates should read *Appointing Warrant Officers* (COMDTINST M1420.1) and applicable Navy and Coast Guard messages. Go over them carefully during your application process, making note of sections applicable to you as an individual candidate. These are your source documents for submitting an application; only language or policy promulgated by a more current service message for the current application cycle will override what is written in this directive. More specific information and guidance can be found on applicable service websites.

Next, check your applicable personnel records for completeness. Look for missing or misfiled evaluations, qualifications, awards, and so on. Make corrections as soon as possible. Understand that your application is your résumé to the board demonstrating your potential for selection as an officer. The format is standardized as selection board members must sort through hundreds of them, and it is easier if they are all alike. Think of your package as one of many applications for the same great job—you have to beat out the competition. You won't get extra points for excess. Do not include information that is already in your service record unless required by your service application requirements.

There are no "required" or "right" correspondence courses. A good blend of technical and nontechnical courses will help, especially if done over a number of years and not just since you decided to apply. Consider taking enlisted rating courses of the other source ratings that are also in the normal path of advancement for the designator for which you are applying.

Know who your command coordinator is if you have one. They are your primary point of contact for all questions you might have. Additionally, your command coordinator will select the interview appraisal board members and help schedule the applicants' board. You are not allowed to "shop" for your own appraisal board members—it will be a controlled process led by your command coordinator. Seek out a mentor whom you can consult with, such as an LDO or CWO in your desired designator. They can assist and ensure your application is ready for submission. Listen to what they say—they've been there. Make sure your command coordinator is part of any dialogue when you have discussions that pertain to your package or questions you might have about the application process. You can also find great guidance and insight in the article "So You Want to Be an Officer," by Chief Boatswain's Mate Jeff Bayless, U.S. Navy (Ret.) (Bayless 2021).

Once selected, candidates will attend a service-specific leadership course. In the Navy, the Limited Duty Officer/Warrant Officer/Chief Warrant Officer (LDO/WO/CWO) Academy is a four-week course designed to complete the transition of prior senior enlisted Sailors for their new roles in the wardroom. For USCG candidates, the Chief Warrant Officer Professional Development (CWOPD) course is designed to assist newly commissioned CWOs in transitioning into the commissioned officer ranks. The course curriculum focuses on leadership, service etiquette, customs and courtesies, communication (oral and written), and the necessary administrative skills needed to become an effective Coast Guard officer.

Anchor Up

What are your career path aspirations? What is the potential others see within you? What does your family think? Do these all match up?

Growing into New Roles

Even as an experienced Chief, it takes time to grow into new positions of responsibility and influence. You will come across situations you are not familiar with and make mistakes, but you will learn from them and become a better leader and manager. Even if you've had the opportunity to fill in for a more senior person, actually being assigned to the position and having the responsibility for the decisions and outcomes can be unnerving at first. But you have resources, and you should consider the following tips when assuming a new position of responsibility.

- Take time to review the applicable documents and articles that outline your roles, responsibilities, relationships, and scope of authority. Review organizational charts, which will help you understand your relationship with other leaders and staff members. Knowing these responsibilities and limits will help you manage expectations and avoid creating confusion and friction. Recognize the limits of your authority and your place within the chain of command. As your tour progresses, periodically review your responsibilities and authorities to ensure that your focus and effort remains consistent over the length of the assignment. If you do not consider how to wield new positional power and influence or choose to simply default to the leadership style or approaches that worked for you in your previous billet, you risk being less effective and even disruptive to the efficiency of your unit or team.
- Take time to consider who your new influence targets will be up, down, and across—this should be up to about seven key people. Meet with them as soon as you can once you've assumed your role. Take time to ask them what is going well and what needs to improve. Discuss expectations on communication and which decisions you have the authority to make. As you advance and are assigned to increased positions of responsibility and authority, you will lead through other people and you will have influence on organizational decision-making, so your direct influence targets change. A good rule of thumb is to consider who is now directly above you and below you in the chain of command and which peers are leading in similar positions in your command (fellow department LCPOs, for example). These are the people with whom you should focus on building relationships and with whom your influence will work to shape the efforts of the indirect influence targets who work for them.
- When assuming a new leadership or management position, take your time before you decide to make substantial changes. Take time to watch how things are running and talk to your people to get a sense of how they feel, both about what is going right and about what they think could be improved, and bounce that off the perspectives of your peers and leadership teams. Although you may

have to make or recommend that your leadership make drastic changes if things are not going well, you may find that things are running just fine, and you just need to help keep things going and engage in process improvement.

- You may find yourself hesitant to make needed decisions immediately for fear of being wrong. This as a natural feeling, but you have a responsibility to make tough decisions even if you are occasionally wrong or ineffective. When you make a poor decision, admit your mistake, accept the responsibility, and take steps to avoid repeating the error. Doing so will increase the trust and respect your people have toward you as a leader, and you will find the leaders above you will usually support you. Again, rely on your networks of people who have been there and done that. A quick phone call typically won't hinder the decision-making process.

- Find the balance between supervising too much and too little. Some leaders feel that supervision consists of ordering subordinates to do all the work while they sit back and do nothing. Those leaders who won't occasionally dirty their hands are more of a liability than an asset because morale problems are certain to develop. On the other hand, you may find yourself inclined to continue to perform the duties of your role as an operator of equipment or a maintenance technician, failing to step back and take on the supervisory role. You find you may be sticking to your old job and avoiding any effort to supervise and instruct others at lower rates. As you should understand by now, learning to delegate is a skill you will have to develop and get used to. It will allow you to best juggle the many "balls" you will be responsible for. It won't happen overnight, but eventually you will embrace this concept and your work center will benefit from it.

Selection to Chief does not mean that you have arrived or that you should be comfortable. Assignments exclusive to senior enlisted rates offer opportunities to lead, to command, and to influence the organization at its highest levels. Access to influential military and civilian leaders, their staff, and HQ program managers will expand your capacity to influence the organization well beyond the unit level. You will be able to shape discussions and organizational decisions that have impacts on dozens and potentially tens of thousands of personnel and family. You may have the opportunity to serve on boards that shape broad policy, reward employees, select candidates for special assignments, and effectively ensure the future health of your service. You may even work with joint and interagency partners to shape behaviors across organization and national lines. Take time now to pause and consider your career options and aspirations.

Ten

Preparing for and Succeeding in Transition/Retirement

> Work diligently every day like you're staying in but always plan like you're transitioning out.
> —*U.S. Coast Guard Chief Petty Officer*

Whether you find yourself retiring at twenty or more years of service or choosing a new career path prior to that, transitioning from the military and military culture is a huge undertaking that will require an immense amount of focus.

Many transitioning service members find out that, regardless of the advice they received, there were many experiences associated with the transition process they had to learn about by going through it. Many companies really want to hire you, but your success with transition directly correlates to the amount of work you put into it. Transitioning will affect everyone in your family, and each person experiences different emotions, thoughts, and feelings. While you may think that the path is clear, communication is crucial, and you need to talk things out with your leadership, family, and mentors.

There are so many resources and tools available to you these days that it can be overwhelming, but here are a few pieces of advice that you can and should do today to give yourself that needed edge when transitioning into and succeeding in civilian life.

Create a Plan

There are several "lines of effort" you will be managing simultaneously—completing your service's required transition training and counseling, job seeking, creating and submitting your VA disability claim, turning over your job to your relief, and a potential move to a new location. The more senior you are, the more complex this list may be. Regardless, you must be actively engaged in this evolution of leaving the service; it requires thought and risk management.

There are a ton of administrative things to think about, such as making time to review your draft DD-214 and allowing more time to conduct a second and final review just before you retire. You should expect to run into some obstacles along the way, which is why you want to give yourself plenty of time to handle them. Do yourself and your family a favor by talking about this and coming up with a plan that suits your needs and goals.

In the *Petty Officer's Guide* there is advice on how to manage procrastination... that advice is of particular importance during your transition. It takes time to network, save money and pay off debt, get an accurate medical diagnosis, get the needed degrees or certifications required, and research the places you may want to live. Transition can be difficult and stressful if you wait until the last moment but with a well-thought-out plan, it can actually be an exciting time.

Think about What's Next

The person you are today is not the same person you will be tomorrow. There is no magical moment when you suddenly become a civilian and everything changes. Your old habits, mindsets, and actions will persist. However, every day presents an opportunity to embrace your new reality. To do so, you must understand that you have room to grow, and that's okay. It's a process, so take it easy.

Life moves slower outside of the military, but that doesn't mean it's dull. It's just different, and you need to manage your expectations. The days of being sent to foreign lands at a moment's notice or receiving 0200 phone calls about service members causing trouble are gone. When you are with your family, you can now enjoy the absence of distractions. They have been without your undivided attention for years, and it can be a shock to everyone when you leave your phone behind for an entire day to spend time together.

Transitioning takes time, and that's a beautiful thing. You don't have to do everything today. You have the rest of your life to enjoy, and if you want to make the most of it, you must come to terms with the fact that a part of you is gone. You're going to replace it with something new and exciting. You can dwell on the loss, or you can recognize that it's part of your story and know you've learned a lot in the process. Your service is not over; it's just different now, and you can make a positive impact in a new arena using the skills you've honed over the last few decades of challenging experiences.

If you are seeking employment after you take off the uniform and are under the impression that your current position, status, or scope of responsibilities are enough to get hired, your thinking is misplaced. Just like any other project, transitioning from the military requires planning, organizing, direction, and controlling. Narrowing what you want to do involves comparing how much you want to work with how much money you want to make and adding in where you want to live and the commute factor.

You will have to open your aperture on career sectors as well. You are probably very narrowly focused on positions related to your rating or collateral duties you've held. That's great, but there are so many sectors and companies that are looking for your nontechnical knowledge and skills that you're not aware of or considering as an employment option. So how do you even know which companies to research for jobs? Start with general research on economic sectors and well-known companies such as Amazon, Nike, Google, Microsoft, and other well-known brands in the military space. Then start doing informational interviews. An informational interview is a short and informal conversation with someone working in a career field or position that interests you. It is *not* a job interview, and its purpose is not to find job openings. Rather, it's a way to explore a given field while giving you an opportunity to get an inside look at an organization where you may want to work in the future. Informational interviews are useful for a variety of reasons:

- You receive firsthand, relevant information about the realities of working within a particular position, field, or industry.

- You learn about career paths you didn't know existed.
- You get advice and guidance about how to prepare for and land your first postmilitary career position.
- You learn what it's like to work at a new civilian organization.
- You initiate a professional relationship, expand your network of contacts, and meet people who may share job leads with you in the future.

Start with people you know who have transitioned and ask them to recommend some companies or contacts in the employment spaces and sectors that you would find interesting and that you should check out. I guarantee that you have never heard of many of the companies or positions available, and learning and exploring these will open your mind and greatly enhance the scope of opportunities available to you. Start several years out from your anticipated retirement, and have as many conversations as possible with those who have made their transition, have industry knowledge and connections, and can help you think about new opportunities in this next chapter of your life.

You should also give thought to where you want to live after you retire and transition. Certain states offer financial incentives to military retirees such as no state tax on your retirement income. When you're transitioning, it's hard to fact-check everything you hear. But don't believe there's only a few states that offer exemptions on tax of military pensions. Also, each state offers benefits to veterans and retirees, so you will want to check out the state's Office of Veterans Affairs website to see what's available. One thing to consider is that if you are doing a final household goods move, schedule your pack-out date and reserve temporary lodging. You are allowed to defer your final move for up to one year. In the end, make sure to research all the potential savings and costs such as home prices, property tax, utilities, and home insurance. With that said, there are now many remote position opportunities as well, so include those in your job hunt and research.

Research Employment Options and Prepare a Résumé

Companies only care about what you can do for them for the future if they hire you, which is articulated by what skill sets you bring and what you have accomplished. They don't care as much about a position you held in the past. They also have trouble relating to positions or titles such as "senior enlisted adviser" because these positions do not exist in the civilian sector. Research, research, research! Have targeted conversations with people in the commercial sector to discuss business opportunities and where you may be able to lend your knowledge and skills to help their company.

If you're job searching, gather all the necessary data, including salary and benefits, from other colleagues in the same role, research compensation packages, and inquire about remote work options. Use caution when relying on compensation calculators, as self-reported earnings may be exaggerated, and some pay packages are estimates.

You may have heard that you must work to "demilitarize" your résumé. This is crucial to do as employers do not understand our titles or positions. It is also important to first identify the skills that you performed during your time and compare them to what the civilian company is looking for. Research can be conducted through online sites that have job postings. Look at prospective jobs that you may want to seek, including what skills these jobs require, and compare them to what you have already done. From there, identify the skill sets civilian employers are looking for and convert military terms to civilian ones on your résumé.

Ensure you clarify your past leadership roles. Know the difference between a supervisor and a manager in the civilian sector. You have not just been managing people, you have been supervising subordinate project managers and supervisors who are running different sections of operations and leading projects.

Conduct research to find what the job is paying and get an estimate of what to ask for during negotiations or interview . . . know your value!

Finally, research what current and former employees are saying about the company. Look for trends. If you see one or two comments on a website saying the company is garbage, do not get too downhearted. However, if you see a significant number of negative comments about a toxic work environment, it may give you reason to dig deeper.

For most people, writing a résumé is something reserved for the last few months in the military. But it's important to learn the skill of writing a résumé sooner rather than later. The last few months prior to retirement or separation may not be the most productive time to focus on résumé writing; there are enough stressors you will be dealing with while transitioning to civilian life. Having an up-to-date résumé is nothing new to the civilian workforce, and those of us in uniform should also have one. Until you've tried writing a résumé, you don't realize how difficult it can be to master the skill, but you should take time *now* to learn to promote your biggest asset . . . your skills and accomplishments. Your résumé is a living document, and you will receive more than a few suggestions or recommendations on writing it that will sometimes conflict with each other based on different perceptions of what the "right" résumé looks like. Take advantage of the courses offered by your service's transition assistance offices. Once you have your résumé written, you have a great foundation that you can build upon when you transfer to a new command, get promoted, or take on a new level of responsibility.

At some point it all is going to line up, and you will be given an offer. Don't give up if a job offer falls short of your salary expectations. Instead, negotiate by gathering market intelligence and prioritizing nonnegotiables. Be mindful of the company's needs to achieve a mutually satisfying agreement where both parties get around 70 to 80 percent of what they want. Companies have different approaches to salary negotiations, and some states have laws mandating pay transparency. It's important not to ask for an unrealistic salary but instead to aim for about 20 percent higher than what you want to allow for negotiation. It's important to provide evidence to support your demands and continually sell yourself as the best candidate. If you're unsatisfied with the offer, it's acceptable to make a counteroffer. If a company cannot meet your salary demands, there are other perks and benefits you can negotiate for, such as extra time off, flexible working hours, contributions toward higher education, midyear reviews, higher-level titles, and more. Stock or option plans are offered by some industries, primarily by tech companies. These plans can be very lucrative if you are able to participate, as the potential for growth and profit is high. Be sure to thoroughly investigate and negotiate for all available remunerations, benefits, and perks before walking away from an offer.

Network, Pursue Civilian Certifications, and Join Professional Organizations

Hand in hand with writing a résumé is equating your military job skills to civilian certifications, which is something we all should be able to do. One of the biggest challenges we have is explaining what we do to a civilian organization that may not be familiar with naval positions and duties. You can be confident that most civilian companies realize the intangible skills that being in the military develops—leadership, management, team building, effective communication, the ability to think and execute under pressure. Often what doesn't come through is how your rating can be used by a potential employer. Google and the USO have recently designed and deployed a search engine that matches military occupational codes to civilian postings. This will help recruiters match our experience and skills to jobs.

Civilian credentialing allows you to acquire civilian certifications for your military experience. Have you heard of Coast Guard Credentialing Opportunities Online (CGCOOL)? You can use CGCOOL to

- Get background information about civilian licensure and certification;
- Identify licenses and certifications relevant to USCG ratings and occupations;
- Learn how to fill gaps between USCG training/experience and civilian requirements; and
- Learn about resources available to help you get civilian job credentials.

Once you are certified, you can find and join professional organizations in the field you expect to work in once you separate or retire. Additionally, many nonprofit organizations offer professional development opportunities in the form of educational sessions or certifications. By participating in these sessions, you are increasing your connection and information power and your marketability by staying on top of industry trends and technologies or working toward a certification that will help you stand out within your field. Being actively involved in your association or professional society can be valuable on a wide variety of fronts, both personally and professionally. In fact, your annual membership dues may be the safest investment to make in this economy. A few hours of research into this area is sure to pay some dividends.

Get Financially Ready

One major source of transition anxiety is the prospect of not being able to find post-service employment, and with that comes the stress of wondering how to pay your bills if you cannot. Any introductory personal financial management course will strongly suggest that you have enough saved to cover three to six months of living expenses as you search for new employment. Having this amount saved will remove a great amount of anxiety from your transition; in most cases, if you follow the advice and training you will receive prior to your transition, you will find you do not even need to tap into your savings.

If you can, work to pay off as much debt as you can prior to separating or retiring. And give some thought to the "worst case" scenario in which you do not find a job within a few months. Be prepared to seek the help of credit counseling agencies who have agreements in place with most major creditors that could reduce interest rates or monthly payments until you can find employment. Once again, you will be strongly encouraged to save money, and you will be given more insight and advice regarding financially preparing for your transition.

Understand that pay is dependent on location—a given position will be paid differently depending on the local economy of that area. If you live and want to work in a rural community, your options for high pay are limited. Factor in losing some entitlements and identify if you need to travel to get a higher-paying job to offset the financial cliff from retirement. Pay attention to the financial comparison you must do during your preparation to get an idea of how much you will lose after retirement.

Get Yourself and Your Family Medically Ready

Another significant "line of effort" you will invest energy into pre- and post-retirement is your medical readiness. Your focus is not only on completing your final physicals and exams but ensuring a continuum of care into retirement. This focus starts about two years out from retirement and can continue for a year to eighteen months following it. Here is a list of things you should consider and should add to any personal transition checklist.

Consider and complete your final medical or dental exams and identify and schedule needed procedures. You will have a series of medical appointments to complete, and you should expect your initial medical appointment to lead to other more specific ones. Certain elective surgeries require minimum active-duty time remaining to be completed. You will get one final dental cleaning, so have them do a final and rigorous look at any existing fillings or any other significant dental procedures needed. As part of your final physical and exam process, consider the following referrals with orthopedics, podiatry, urology, internal medicine, cardiopulmonary/vascular, dermatology, and the sleep apnea clinic at your local military hospital. You want to get screened by experts on any potential health-care issues and keep your record active into retirement. This all applies to your dependents as well, so think about things like whether any of your children will need orthodontics prior to your retirement date, and get them done because your out-of-pocket cost for these things will increase after retirement. Schedule and complete routine physicals and eye exams for family members and make sure immunizations are up-to-date.

Make several electronic copies of medical and dental records for you and your family. This should include a CD of all X-rays, MRIs, and CT scans from radiology departments and dental X-rays. One exciting new thing about retirement is that you get a choice! But with that choice comes research. Once you retire you will have to consider things like registering at a local VA hospital if eligible, getting your first postmilitary physical with your new primary care physician and seeing how it compares to your retirement physical and getting your first postmilitary dental cleaning and exam and seeing how it compares to your final dental exam.

Know and Prepare for Your Veterans Affairs Benefits

The U.S. Department of Veterans Affairs (VA) Benefits Delivery at Discharge (BDD) program allows service members to apply for VA disability compensation benefits between 180 and 90 days prior to their separation date. The intent of the BDD program is to deliver a claims decision as soon as possible following separation.

Research and document all issues for retirement and VA physicals, and plan your appointment with a veterans service officer (VSO) to ensure you can start your BDD process exactly 180 days before your official retirement date. You should discuss with your primary care manager about how wording in your retirement or separation physical can help with your VA disability claim. Start on personal and buddy statements (if you plan on using them). You will have up to a year to claim any VA service-related disability items you missed during your initial physical. VSOs will help you write and submit your benefits claims to the VA. Their services are free. They will help you gather the information that supports your claim. Once the claim is filed, they will help you track the claim through the system. They can also help you file appeals for denied claims. It is important that you use a VSO. They will help you avoid the delays that missing paperwork or improperly filled out claims can cause. Search and find a VSO near you.

The VA operates the largest health care system in the country, with over 1,400 sites of care nationwide. When you become enrolled in the VA health care system, it's for a lifetime. You are instantly and automatically entitled to receive care at any VA location without ever having to register for VA health care benefits again. Learn more at http://www.va.gov. After you enroll, you can immediately start receiving your health care at a VA facility or can start at a later date—the choice is yours.

State VA offices are there to assist in identifying and accessing benefits after separation or retirement. In addition, there are a wide range of county, state, and federal benefits related to education, employment, finance, health care, housing, legal assistance, recreation, taxes, and more. Your state's VA office is there to assist you with the benefits available to the you through the state. Each state manages its own state VA office and benefit programs; therefore, some state VA offices have a greater ability to assist. For more information on your specific state VA benefits and to learn the location of state VA offices, visit https://department.va.gov/about/state-departments-of-veterans-affairs-office-locations/.

Research Insurance Plans

Research and secure life insurance, investments, long-term health-care insurance, and education investments for your children.

Begin researching your medical, dental, and vision insurance changes and options, including enrollment in the Federal Employees Dental and Vision Insurance Program (FEDVIP). Research medical and dental providers in the location you plan to live after retirement or separation. You will have to think about who takes the insurance you are planning on using post-transition. You have options such as Tricare Prime, Tricare Select, or a civilian employer-provided insurance plan. Use your Tricare information and referral service and health benefits officers to help you think through these decisions.

Consider and decide on any additional life insurance you want to buy *before* your retirement and VA physicals. You want to be as healthy as you can for commercial insurance to keep premiums low. Consider the following sequence—get commercial insurance physical, then do your separation physical, and then do your VA physical.

Also, some employers will offer you a life insurance option that covers the amount of your salary at no cost and provides an option to buy more at a small premium, so think about that during your job research.

Finally, research and decide on whether you will choose the Survivors Benefit Plan. The Survivor Benefit Plan (SBP) allows a retiree to ensure, after death, a continuous lifetime annuity for their dependents. The annuity, which is based on a percentage of retired pay, is called SBP and is paid to an eligible beneficiary. It pays your eligible survivors an inflation-adjusted monthly income. If you select this, you will pay premiums for SBP coverage upon retiring. Premiums are paid from gross retired pay, so they don't count as income. This means less tax and less out-of-pocket costs for SBP. The premiums are partially funded by the government, and the costs of operating the program are absorbed by the government, so the average premiums are well below the cost for a conventional insurance policy. For most retirees, SBP is a good choice, but the government contribution is based on assumptions in average cases and may not apply equally to every situation. The maximum SBP annuity for a spouse is based on 55 percent of the member's retired pay (or in the case of a member who retires under career status bonus [CSB]/REDUX, the retired pay the member would have received if under the high-three retirement system). However, a smaller number may be elected. Eligible children may also be SBP beneficiaries, either alone or added to spousal coverage. In the latter case, the children receive benefits only if the spouse dies or otherwise becomes ineligible to receive the annuity. Eligible children equally divide a benefit that is 55 percent of the member's elected base amount. Child coverage is relatively inexpensive because children get benefits only while they are considered eligible dependents. If you are divorced, review your divorce decree to see if you are required to provide this benefit to your ex-spouse.

Take Advantage of Transition Resources, Mentors, and Mentoring Programs

You should be familiar with the Transition Goals, Plans, Success (Transition GPS) program. This weeklong course provides useful information on the issues and challenges you will face during the process of retiring or separating from the service. For those who are retiring, you can request to attend the program as early as twenty-four months prior to your date. All others preparing to separate can request to attend as early as twelve months before their separation date. Spouses are also highly encouraged to attend. Command career counselors (CCC) can provide specific information including dates and locations. Workshop resources include résumé writing, landing a federal job, social networking, and searching for a job.

The information provided in Transition GPS courses can be overwhelming, but a wealth of additional resources is out there to help with your transition to civilian life, such as *The Military Advantage: The Military.com Guide to Military and Veterans Benefits* (Howell 2017), which can be a great complement to any transition assistance course.

If face-to-face learning suits you best, the Fleet and Family Support Center (FFSC) offers courses and counseling on information you will need to be successful in securing employment following your time in the military. Topics include skills and personality evaluations, résumés, the use of social media to job hunt, interview techniques, and job searches. These courses are great because they require only a few hours of your time. Keep an eye out for the FFSC schedule of events. Your CCC or CSEL should also be able to provide information on these courses.

Finding a person who has recently retired or is a few months ahead of you in the transition process will provide you great insight and a sounding

254   Chapter Ten

[10-1] The Department of Labor principal deputy assistant secretary for policy for veteran's employment and training services meets with transitioning Sailors who have attended the Fleet and Family Support Program's Transition Assistance Program.
U.S. NAVY PHOTO BY KRISHNA "KRASH" JACKSON, NBSD PUBLIC AFFAIRS

board to bounce questions off. Talk with others who are going through the transition process or who have recently completed it. You will gain great insights into many of the "tricks of the trade" that often do not get passed on. It is much more difficult to identify your employment goals or create a résumé in a vacuum or without help. You have built up a vast amount of experience, which has developed you into a huge resource to others to provide solutions and to fix problems. During your transition process it is important to realize that you have much to learn, and others can help you learn it. Mentors can be a great help to narrowing what you want to do, such as asking people (through LinkedIn, for example) you know from past military assignments who have already transitioned to look at your résumé or help identify job opportunities.

Also consider using a mentorship program such as Veterati, American Corporate Partners, and Hire Heroes USA. These are great resources to talk to other people who have already done what you are about to do and ask them how it went and what to look out for. They are also a good resource for determining what jobs in the civilian sector equate to your skills. You can connect with former military staff officers or senior enlisted who have applied and worked at multiple jobs and who will review your résumé. For example, Veterati enables you to choose your mentor and can help those who are struggling to identify where to go in the corporate world. When contacting mentors, write down your questions prior to the call so you can get as much out of the call as possible. Consider checking out Corporate Gray, whose mission is to connect those who have served in the military with employers nationwide. They do this in three ways: via their military-focused job fairs; through their website, Corporate Gray Online; and through their career transition book, now titled, *The Military to Civilian Transition Guide* (Savino 2024). More information can be found on their website: https://www.corporategray.com/welcome.

As you can see there is a lot to consider, plan, and manage during your transition to your next chapter. Plan your terminal leave and house hunting permissive temporary duty (PTDY) appropriately (if done right, you can find that you have up to ninety days) to allow time to finish your transition lines of effort, travel, decompress, focus on family, rekindle friendships, and really find out more about YOU!

And although you still have a job to do and you should not aim to be on the retired-on-active-duty (ROAD) program, you should plan your turnover (or have someone fill your role) to allot yourself time to focus on your transition to the greatest degree possible. Although some take the mindset that they will work until their final day, your transition process comes with several service-mandated lines of effort, and those will consume much, if not all, of your workdays during your final months on active duty. Don't feel guilty for taking this time to focus on your transition. Again, this should be an exciting time in your life, and transition and retirement from the military doesn't have to be hard—you've had much greater challenges. Use the advice offered in this chapter and use resources such as the Navy Retirement Guide (https://www.navyretirementguide.com/) and your services websites and courses, and I'm sure you will find success!

Retirement Ceremonies

As a Chief Petty Officer you may be asked to sponsor a retiree from your division, or you may be asked to fill any of several other roles that are part of the tradition of a retirement ceremony. Retirement ceremonies vary according to the command, personal wishes, and circumstances, of course, but all are marked by solemnity and a sense of reverence and gratitude for the sacrifices your shipmates have made over their years of service to the nation.

Attendance for these ceremonies should be strongly encouraged (it is appropriate to designate retirement ceremonies as a place of appointed duty) for all military personnel, and they are open to civilian personnel wishing to attend. The conduct of the ceremony should be in the traditional sense using existing guidance. As an official command event, the ceremony will be conducted in an appropriate location that reflects credit upon the U.S. Navy or Coast Guard.

Although discouraged, the retiree has the option to elect no ceremony or to have a less formal version. If so elected, the retiree should still be provided their awards, letter of appreciation, and certificates by the command.

The Role of the Sponsor

Sponsors should be selected as soon as possible after the command becomes aware of an individual's desire to have a retirement ceremony. This should be done at least ninety days prior to the ceremony. The sponsor's primary responsibility is ensuring that all aspects of the retirement ceremony are planned, organized, and executed. The sponsor takes care that all assigned tasks are on schedule and acts as the primary point of contact for all aspects of the ceremony. With that said, be sure the spouse, children, and family members are fully engaged and offered the opportunity to participate in the planning for their retiree. It's their day too. Timely submission of requests and continual follow-up are required. Sponsor responsibilities include the following:

- Identify yourself formally as the retirement sponsor and serve as the primary adviser and representative for the retiree.
- Select or develop and carefully read through the retirement ceremony checklist of plan of actions and milestones (POAM). This

should be identified in the command's 5060 Notice, which serves as the official document to establish the guidelines and responsibilities for retirement ceremonies to be conducted upon transfer to the Retired List or Fleet Reserve for all military personnel at your command. Your admin officer or LCPO should be able to help. There are many notices and POAMs readily available these days, so you should be able to get a copy of the version most recently used by your command. Part of your planning process should be developing the drumbeat of meetings for the team that will execute the ceremony and supporting functions. Hold regular meetings to discuss progress of assignments. Don't be afraid to take charge and be aggressive in planning—it only benefits the retiree you are representing.

- Identify and establish a retirement ceremony committee or group. Initiate the checklist and ensure that each task is assigned and that all assignments are fully understood.
- Have the retiree fill out a retirement information sheet and biography information sheet available from the CCC.
- Ensure that the end-of-tour award (if any) is submitted to the administrative officer for routing and approval. The ending date of these awards is usually the last day of duty prior to the beginning of any period of separation leave. The following timetable is recommended to ensure sufficient lead time is given for each award and is relative to the ceremony date not the actual retirement date:
  – Legion of Merit—ninety days
  – Meritorious Service Medal—thirty days
  – Navy and Marine Corps Commendation Medal—thirty days
  – Navy and Marine Corps Achievement Medal—thirty days
- Ensure that the retiree invites the guest speaker and obtains biographic information for the speaker as soon as possible. Work with the retiree to identify guests he or she wishes to invite, including identifying distinguished guests. This is important to know for protocol and seating arrangements. Summaries of retiree and guest speaker biographies should be completed as early in the planning stage as possible to allow adequate time to print programs and to ensure that all vital items are covered in the initial planning stages.

- Ensure that a notification is prepared and submitted for the Plan of the Week/Day. Coordinate with the retiree to see if they desire to have an article drafted for the base or command newsletter or paper, or if they would like their retirement announced on base electronic billboards. Ensure that a hometown release form is provided to the retiree and releases are made, as desired.
- Coordinate the layout of the retirement program as soon as possible and identify the printer you will submit the print request to.
- Work with the retiree to identify the official party and side boys as desired (six to eight is the norm). Identify flag passing detail if desired by the retiree.
- Ensure that the retiree is fully informed of the sequence of events. If the retiree is a fellow Chief, they may have acted as a sponsor for others in the past and may have particular wishes as to how his or her ceremony should be structured. Keep at the forefront that the retiree has a lot going on and is working on the lines of effort outlined in this chapter. Making specific time to touch base with the retiree and provide updates is vital and greatly appreciated.
- Write down all ideas throughout the planning stages and any lessons learned. These will be beneficial to the next sponsor.

Again, you should easily be able to find a wealth of checklists, 5060 Notices, retirement ceremony schedules of events, and POAMs since these ceremonies are frequently performed. Once you have those, you simply need to communicate with the retiree to understand any special requests they may have.

The Role of the Retiree

Although this is a busy time for the retiree, they do have things to do. The retiree should

- Provide a biography to the sponsor or event coordinator as requested prior to the ceremony date.
- Complete their retirement information worksheet and return it to the CCC or admin officer as required.
- Identify guests and distinguished visitors who will be attending.
- Make arrangements for post-ceremony reception (if desired).

10-1 SUGGESTED TIMELINES FOR RETIREMENT CEREMONIES

90 days   Generate information sheets for retiree and command 5060 Notice
Coordinate with CCC to order any presidential or state leader letters of appreciation

60 days   Begin luncheon arrangements and shadow-box development
If a band is involved, coordinate availability

45 days   Identify and contact event coordinator and master of ceremonies
Purchase retirement gifts
Complete first draft of retirement script and program

30 days   Select music and prepare digital files
Check all certificates for correct name and dates (presidential certificate, state governor certificate, Fleet Reserve certificate, retirement certificate, spouse and family member certificates of appreciation, flag certificates, etc.)

20 days   Purchase devices and items for shadow box
Verify availability of honor boatswain's mate and flag-passing detail
Verify receipt of flown flag

15 days   Verify official party assignments
Verify shadow-box completion
Order flowers for spouse/family members
Identify chaplain and verify availability
Identify photographer and verify availability

7 days   Draft and submit Plan of the Week/Day notification
Submit base billboard announcement to base PAO
Verify onsite logistic support including public address system, seating, and decor

2 days   Practice as many times as needed

Important Elements of the Retirement Ceremony

I've mentioned several of these, but some of these elements require further clarification.

- *Information Sheet.* The most basic information required for adequate planning will be provided by the retiring individual to the sponsor on this information sheet. This should be given to the retiree at least ninety days in advance, and the sponsor or CCC should ask to have it back within ten days. This information sheet should be completed prior to the first meeting of the retirement committee. It should contain complete biographic information, choices of music, guests, and other information of interest to the retiree. Most commands have sample information sheets readily available in a paper or digital file.
- *Ceremony Location and Floor Plan.* The sponsor should ensure that all involved know the layout of the ceremony location. Consideration for seating, side boys, and procession are all factors to consider. If a ship or hangar is the desired location, the sponsor will have to contact that command to check the planned date against the operational schedule of the unit. Inspect the chosen site well in advance of the ceremony and plan out the area. In many cases, retirement ceremonies will have been held in the location before, and the layout will already be set. Things to consider include the location of the speaker podium, area for presentations, side boys, awards table, honor guard and flag placement, and any dressing desired.
- *Master of Ceremonies.* As a sponsor, you may be asked to act as master of ceremonies for the event. The choice is always that of the retiree. Selection should be completed within forty-five days of the ceremony date. The sponsor should follow up and verify the availability of the designated master of ceremonies fifteen days prior to the event.
- *Chaplain.* The chaplain delivers the invocation and benediction at the ceremony. These are not required parts of the program. The retiree may choose not to have an invocation or benediction, but if

they do, they should also choose which chaplain they want to offer those. Be prepared to provide the chaplain's office some biographic information on the retiree.
- *Honors Boatswain's Mate and Side Boys.* This is the person who will lead the side boys and pipe the side for the retiree and distinguished guests. Obtain the services of a boatswain's mate sufficiently in advance of the ceremony and recheck availability at the twenty-day point. Have a backup identified. Side boys may be specifically chosen by the retiree or the honors boatswain may be tasked to assemble them. Be sure all side boys are informed of the time, place, uniform, and any rehearsals planned. Side boys may also participate in the flag presentation ceremony, act as ushers, present flowers, or perform other official duties requested by the retiring member.
- It has become very popular, if not standard practice, to pipe the side twice, once for the retiring member and a second time for the member accompanied by his or her spouse and children. In many cases, the Chief is present as guests in the ceremony are invited to "man the rails" and join the side boys during these two pipings ashore. Always remind official and unofficial photographers that this is one of the moments that must be captured.
- *Guest Speaker.* The retiree has the option to request a specific person as the guest speaker. If no particular person is requested by the retiree, then an individual should be agreed upon by the sponsor and the retiree. The retiree is responsible for identifying and notifying the guest speaker, and this should be done no later than sixty days before the ceremony. The sponsor may assist in preparing the guest speaker's biography.
- *Public Address System and Music.* Coordinate for a PA system and always remember to check the system out before the ceremony starts. Use it during the rehearsal to adjust the volume and placement of speakers. Generally, digital music is used for retirement ceremonies. There may be a rare occasion when live music is desired. If live music is to be used, it is important that musicians be requested as soon in the planning stages as possible.

262　Chapter Ten

[10-2] The author is piped ashore during his retirement ceremony.
PHOTO PROVIDED BY AUTHOR

- *National Ensign.* Early in the planning process, check with the retiree to determine his or her wishes regarding the national ensign to be used at the ceremony or included in the shadow box. Many retirees request the flag(s) to be flown over a location of their choice and then presented to family members at the ceremony. Depending on the location, request times will vary—some may take as long as ninety days—so it is important that the location be identified as soon as possible.
- *Guest List.* Obtain the number and names of guests the retiree wishes to invite to the ceremony no later than sixty days prior. This is often done using electronic invitations that feed into a spreadsheet. Ensure the arrangements are made to accommodate the number of guests at the site. Have the retiree ensure that accurate information pertaining to each guest is complete prior to submitting the request for invitation. Again, many electronic invitation tools enable the guest to provide their pertinent information. This list should be used to help arrange seating assignments. Also, the sponsor should coordinate all matters of security and access to the command.

- *Programs.* Each guest should be given a printed program. A final formal portrait of the retiree is traditionally included. Many retirees include photos from throughout their career. Ensure to include biographies of the retiree and guest speaker. Other items to include in the program are the Sailor's Creed, a favorite poem, or words to a song. Sponsors should also speak with spouses about any other additions to personalize the program. Sponsors should plan to have the program outlined and the request submitted to the printer no earlier than forty-five days and no later than twenty-five days before the ceremony.
- *Certificates.* The sponsor is responsible for ensuring that all appropriate certificates are on hand for the retirement ceremony. CCC's can help the sponsor with this line of effort. Extensive lead time is necessary to obtain the required signatures on all certificates. The usual items for presentation include:
  – Certificate of Retirement
  – Certificate—Fleet Reserve
  – Spouse and family member Certificate of Appreciation
  – MCPON Letter of Appreciation
  – Certificate of Appreciation for Service in the Armed Forces of the United States (bearing the president's signature)
  – End-of-tour award
  – Letters of appreciation
- *Shadow Box / Gift.* Planning should begin sixty days prior to the ceremony. Ask the retiree for any special content requirements. Purchase devices for the box twenty days prior to the ceremony and aim to have the shadow box completed no later than ten days prior to the ceremony. Consider the American flag, devices, and engraved duty stations plates for inclusion. Contact the maker of the shadow box as soon as possible to allow adequate time for construction, and take charge of purchasing all necessary contents.
- Normally the CPOA funds a standard retirement presentation like a shadow box that symbolizes and summarizes the career service of the retiring member. The sponsor should make sure this standard presentation is what the retiring member wants. Occasionally the

retiring person may prefer a different version of the shadow box or some different presentation. It is perfectly acceptable—and even desirable—for the retiring member to participate in the decision, even to the extent of paying the difference between the standard presentation and that which he or she prefers. Remember to ask the retiree if he or she wishes to contribute any special items for inclusion in the shadow box, or if a shipmate wants to contribute a new device for inclusion, something that offsets some of the expense.

Typical Sequence of Events

As I mentioned, you can easily find existing scripts for retirements that have an established sequence of events. From there you can adjust the time as needed and add or remove elements to fit the specific ceremony. Although the ceremony should honor and recognize the service of the member and family, it should take no longer than an hour. Here are a few guidelines for the flow of a typical retirement ceremony:

- Thirty minutes prior to the official start, assemble all participants for a briefing, escort visitors to their seats, and ensure the reception area is ready. Check the award table setup, color guard readiness, photographer, and master of ceremonies. Last-minute adjustments should be identified and made at this point.
- Ten minutes prior, the master of ceremonies should take position and inform guests to take their seats. Position the official party and ensure that special guests are positioned for entrance.
- Five minutes prior, the official music begins. All guests are present and seated. All doors are closed. Escorts seat special guests, including spouse, parents, children, special friends, and so on.
- One minute prior, the prelude music terminates and the MC starts the ceremony.
- The official party arrives.
- Parading of the colors and playing of the national anthem.
- Benediction is read, if desired.
- Opening remarks and introduction of the guest speaker, then guest speaker remarks (ten to fifteen minutes).

- Presentation of personal awards, certificates, and shadow box (ten minutes).
- Presentation of family awards (five to ten minutes).
- Remarks by the retiree (ten to fifteen minutes).
- Flag passing detail if desired (ten to fifteen minutes).
- Reading of the CPO retirement creed.
- Going ashore, to include the reciting of "Old Glory" and piping the side.
- Conclusion, information on the reception, and receiving line.

Think about Staying Connected

The U.S. Navy's Chief Petty Officer Retirement Creed reads,

> You have on this day, experienced that which comes to all of us who serve on active duty in OUR NAVY. I say "OUR NAVY," because your departure from active duty in no way terminates your relationship. By law and tradition, *U.S. Navy Retirees are always on the rolls, ever ready to lend their service when the need arises*. The respect that you earned as "The Chief" was based on the same attributes that you will now carry into retirement. You should have no regrets. Do not view your retirement as an end of an era but rather as orders to a new and challenging assignment, to a form of independent duty. Remember well that you have been, and will always be, an accepted member of the most exclusive of all fraternities—that of the U.S. Navy Chief Petty Officers. The active-duty Chiefs salute you, your retired Chiefs welcome you. I wish you the traditional "Fair Winds and Following Seas."

There will be many things you don't miss about your military service, but one thing that many retirees and veterans express is that they miss the camaraderie and the feeling of belonging. You have a choice on how much you want to stay connected to your "tribe" after retirement.

Membership in base and state CPO Associations offers a great opportunity to continue to give back in a new way. And beyond your CPO mess-based associations, you have many opportunities to become a member of other organizations. Many, if not all, of these organizations provide advocacy,

[10-3] Retired MCPON James Herdt, the ninth MCPON, is briefed prior to touring the Trident Training Facility on Naval Submarine Base Kings Bay.
U.S. NAVY PHOTO BY MC3 AARON XAVIER SALDANA/RELEASED

provide an avenue to increase your professional development and affiliation, and serve as an alumni organization post-service so that you can stay connected to the sea services and military.

You may have heard of or participated in a conference or special event hosted by a professional organization such as the Surface Navy Association (SNA), the American Society of Naval Engineers (ASNE), the Naval Submarine League, the Fleet Reserve Association (FRA), the Disabled American Vets (DAV), the Navy League of the United States, or the U.S. Naval Institute (USNI). These are not "officer organizations"; membership and the associated benefits are there for you! Beyond many of the same benefits we describe in the section on peer networks, membership in these organizations can bring

- Access to ranking and influential leaders in the associated field or community;
- Exclusive subscriptions to professional magazines, journals, or archives;

- Increased networking and access to the organization's online job databases;
- Learning experiences such as conferences, symposia, and special events;
- Discounts on professional courses and certifications;
- Eligibility for member-only scholarships and awards; and
- Discounts on books and magazines or sponsor services such as credit cards or rental cars.

Although membership with these professional organizations comes with a fee, the benefits gained greatly exceed the cost. If you are interested in any of the benefits and opportunities listed above, do some research and reach out to a current member to get their perspective. We are sure you will find an organization out there that meets your professional and personal desires.

You can also stay digitally connected via CPO or service community social media pages, groups, and channels. You may even find yourself in a position working for the VA or one of the military-supporting organizations I've mentioned. And depending on your position, you may be invited to speak at events or smaller panels or speaking sessions with active-duty service members. It's your choice to decide how much you want to stay connected.

Some Final Thoughts

If the Chief's mess is to continue its proud legacy of leading their teams toward mission accomplishment and command excellence, Navy and Coast Guard leaders must reflect on the state of their collective CPO mess and their use. In this era of rapid change in the twenty-first century, of unrelenting mission requirements and fiscal constraints, each member of the CPO mess must look inward to build on their strengths and to correct and improve on their weaknesses just as the entire mess turns outward for opportunities to remain credible and relevant while mitigating external threats.

This may be the time to holistically evaluate how we can more fully leverage the modern enlisted force to increase organizational flexibility and better manage personnel gaps. As the enlisted force has become much more professionalized and educated, capabilities have naturally increased. Today many enlisted service members now have a degree, and it is not uncommon for them to qualify and stand watches traditionally reserved for officers, including officer of the deck (OOD) and tactical action officer (TAO). In the mid-2000s the Navy tested a "CPO as division officer" concept as it experimented with its human resource strategy. Then MCPON Terry D. Scott felt the USS *Decatur* (DDG 73) experiment recognized that today's senior enlisted personnel are capable of taking on additional authorities and responsibilities. Around the same time, the Navy almost implemented a degree requirement for CPO advancement that could have supported expanded commissioning opportunities. There was an understanding that the more educated enlisted force could be leveraged in new ways toward organizational effectiveness and efficiency. This all leads some to continue to advocate for expanding authorities for this more educated, experienced, and influential CPO mess. While traditionalists will argue that the realm of the Chief is as deck-plate leader, innovators see opportunities for expanded use of a more educated and influential enlisted force.

The Navy and Coast Guard CPO messes are not the same as they were at the time of their inception. Since 1958 we have added the E-8 and E-9 pay grades, shifted to the all-volunteer Navy, and reaped the benefits of the GI Bill and tuition assistance programs. Regardless of what lies in the future, leveraging the Chief's mess in collaboration, communication, and coordination efforts from within each command and across warfare communities will be a strategic advantage in achieving success in naval warfighting. Regardless of the era or challenge, the Chief's mess will always be expected to deliver "Results, Not Excuses!"

Appendix I

"A Short Talk with Chief Petty Officers"

1. Part IV of *The Bluejacket's Manual* is written as a general guide for Chief Petty Officers. It should be regarded more in the light of an index as to what Chief Petty Officers of different branches are supposed to know, and what qualifications they are supposed to possess, than as a book of information. Inasmuch as every Chief Petty Officer is supposed to be an expert in his own branch, an effort to embody in one book all of the information that each Chief Petty Officer is supposed to know would result in a very large volume, as it would necessarily have to cover every detail of the naval profession. Consequently, this manual is merely an index of the subjects that you are supposed to know; and it tells you where you may find the subject fully discussed.

2. Chief Petty Officers of each branch should therefore make a point of studying the subjects which relate to their particular specialty and should study them from the reference books mentioned. In doing this, Chief Petty Officers should not overlook the subjects that are laid down for them as a class, irrespective of their specialty.

3. This "Short Talk with Chief Petty Officers" will, of course, be more directly applicable to those who are just coming up for their rate than to those who have held the rate for a long time; for Chief Petty Officers of any length of service should be familiar with the duties and responsibilities of their

position. However, as the same honor, dignity and demeanor are required of all Chief Petty Officers, it is hoped that this "talk" may be of some value even to those who are already rated Chief Petty Officers, by giving them the point of view of their senior officers, by telling them how their seniors regard them, how they desire to treat them, and, on the other hand, what degree of proficiency and what general demeanor they expect of them.

4. Take your own particular case, for example. It is quite probable that you entered the service a few years ago an inexperienced and irresponsible boy or girl, without any knowledge of the Navy, of discipline, and probably without any knowledge of the special branch, or specialty, in which you are now to become a Chief Petty Officer. During the time you served through the lower ratings you were under instruction not only as to your individual duties, but also in the elements of discipline. While you were in the lower ratings, you were not supposed to be highly responsible; you were supposed to do what you were told, to acquire the knowledge requisite for the ratings you held, to use that knowledge under the direction of your petty officers, and to behave yourself and comply with the rules of military discipline.

5. Then came a great change in your status; you were appointed a petty officer. When you received this promotion, it showed that your officers considered that you had a sufficient knowledge of the details of the duties of your rating and that you were sufficiently disciplined to warrant your stepping up from a status in which you merely did what you were told to a status in which with the knowledge of what was required to be done and how it should be done, you could be trusted with the duty of taking charge of a number of Sailors and giving them order, under the general direction of your seniors. Your duty was to follow up the work and assure yourself that it had been done properly. Instead of merely doing what your immediate petty officer told you to do, you as a petty officer, had a larger field and performed your duty not by your own labor, but by directing a group of Sailors under you; and such was your status whether you were engaged in cleaning ship, painting ship, coaling ship or drilling. In each case your excellence as a petty officer was measured by the amount and excellence of the work which was accomplished by the Sailors under you, their practical knowledge, their proficiency, their thoroughness and their reliability. As time passed and as

your experience increased, you were promoted from third class to second class, and finally, to first class; with each promotion you added to your experience and knowledge, your duties broadened and your responsibilities increased; nevertheless, at all times you were more or less under instruction and under trial.

6. You have now come to the point where having served through all the lower ratings, you are supposed to be an expert in your own branch. You have training and experience, and had you not succeeded in making your officers believe that you had proper regard for orders and for discipline, you would not now be coming up for Chief Petty Officer. When you are promoted to Chief Petty Officer, your status changes even to a greater extent than it changed when you were promoted from the ranks to petty officer. The change from petty officer, first class, to Chief Petty Officer probably carries with it a greater change in status than any other promotion in your whole career. Your uniform changes, your quarters and your method of living changes; the treatment accorded you by your senior officers changes. All Chief Petty Officers welcome these changes as well as the corresponding increase in pay. But don't forget that these are not the only features of your life that change. Along with all these changes comes a very great change in your responsibilities as well as the absolute necessity for a different point of view. If you forget the changes of this nature, you altogether fail in your duties to the Government.

7. The aim of this little talk is to dwell upon this new point of view, this increased feeling of responsibility, this sense of duty which impels you to do a thing not because you have to do it, but because it ought to be done, because it is your duty to do it.

8. The position of Chief Petty Officer is one of special honor. It shows not only that you have served successfully, but that your service has met with the commendation of your seniors, that you are proficient, trustworthy and reliable. The uniform of a Chief Petty Officer shows therefore not only that you are serving honorably now, but that you have served honorably for years, and have by your own successful effort risen to the top of the petty

officers of your own branch. See to it that your entire demeanor is such as to elevate the standing of the uniform which you now wear. Make your life and your actions both on board ship and on shore such as to increase rather than to decrease the difference between the bluejacket's uniform and that of the Chief Petty Officer.

9. Your position is such that your senior officers wish to treat you as an officer. In order to be accorded this treatment you must adopt the point of view of an officer. This point of view can best be described by saying that you must cultivate a deep sense of responsibility, a high sense of duty, and live up to a high professional standard.

10. Standard. The fact that you are a Chief Petty Officer is evidence that you know how things should be done. Do not neglect to do your duty properly, do not fall to a lower standard simply because you think you will not be spoken to or reported for not doing this duty properly. Such an attitude is not surprising in a recruit; there are times when it may even be overlooked in the lower ratings of petty officer, but, as Chief Petty Officer, you have passed that stage. You are constantly under the watchful eye of your juniors. Anything they see you do, they naturally think is all right. If, for example, they see that you are careless about your uniform or about saluting, regardless of the amount of instruction they may have received, their standard is lowered. If you are punctilious, the men under you will copy the precedent you have established. If your manner is military toward your seniors, you will find the enlisted men under you more easily brought up to standard. If the Chief Petty Officers are thorough, respectful, and have a high sense of duty, the tone of the whole ship will follow. If, on the other hand, enlisted men see that the Chief Petty Officers are unmilitary, that they violate orders and regulations when officers are not around, they will feel even more than ordinarily justified in doing likewise. The tone of the ship, the tone of the service itself must come more directly from the Chief Petty Officers than from any other group of people in the Navy. You have the standard; live up to it, whether you are on independent duty, or on duty under officers; whether you are unobserved, or directly under the eye of your seniors. Live up to the standard, and you will find that those under you will be more inclined to do likewise.

11. Sense of Duty. You know the standard; you know what to do; you know the rules of discipline; of military etiquette; you know the regulations and instructions pertaining to your own branch. The Government not the officers over you pays you for your services. It pays you for doing things as you know they should be done. The sense of duty is the feeling that impels you do these things not because you have to do them, but because it is your duty to do them. And in deciding whether it is your duty, be very liberal in your interpretation.

12. Sense of Responsibility. It frequently happens that both commissioned officers and Chief Petty Officers see things that should be done, although it is clear that it is not their duty to do them; such cases, for example, that would result in confusion were the officer or the Chief Petty Officer in question to do them. If you are confronted with such a condition, take the point of view that you have reached a position of responsibility in the service; that something which should be done may have escaped notice; if this omission is clearly of such a nature that it is not your duty to remedy it, it is nevertheless, your duty to call the attention of the proper person to such an omission. Sometimes lives are lost because some manifest danger has not been pointed out. If you are in doubt as to whether it is your duty to look after something that you know should be done, the only safe rule is to do it. If you know that it is someone else's duty, call attention to it. Take the attitude that you are part of the Navy, not merely a part of your department on an individual ship; try to do a little more rather than a little less than a strict interpretation of your duty demands. Both your seniors and you, yourself, will be better pleased, and the service will benefit thereby.

13. Professional Work. As a Chief Petty Officer, you are an expert in your own department. There are no petty officers senior to you. Those below you will look up to you for information and instruction. Be sure that the information you give out is absolutely accurate. If you are weak on any feature of your specialty, study it up. It is all down somewhere in black and white. Study the best methods; keep up with all improvements. Do not feel that because you passed an examination you have finished studying. Keep yourself fully informed, and be ready to impart your knowledge and skill to your subordinates.

14. Thoroughness and Reliability. An absolute essential of your rating is reliability. This does not mean merely that you are certain to return on time for duty. It means that you may be relied upon to do thoroughly and in the manner that it should be done whatever you are going to do, however important the duty, and however general your orders may be. It means that when you report the duty finished your report may be accepted without an inspection and your senior feel that the duty has been done and everything finished as well and as thoroughly as it would have been done, had they been there personally. If, for any reason, you find that you cannot carry out your orders in every detail, report any part of the order you were unable to carry out and why you were unable to carry it out.

15. Duties. Every Chief Petty Officer understands in a general way that they are the senior petty officer on the ship in their particular branch, that their duties are of a general nature in their department and that they are required to see their department and everything connected with it kept in shipshape condition. All this, however, constitutes but a part of a Chief Petty Officer's duties. As a Chief Petty Officer, you recognize these duties, but in paying due attention to the matériel, do not overlook your duties in connection with the personnel. Too many Chief Petty Officers wholly neglect the fact that, in all probability, the most important part of their duty is the training and instruction of their subordinates. As a Chief Petty Officer you are an expert in the details of your department. Unless you recognize that it is your duty to instruct your juniors and unless you do instruct them, and unless you endeavor to include in them the knowledge of how things should be done, of how they should conduct themselves, you will have failed in your duties. Too often petty officers direct inexperienced men of Sailors ratings to carry out certain orders, and then think no more about it; later, when it is found that the work has not been done, or has not been thoroughly done, or has been done improperly, they lay the blame on the junior. In such a case it is clearly evident that the petty officer has neglected their duty. Remember always that you are an instructor, and that the instruction of your juniors is one of your most important duties; that it is your duty to instruct them not only in the details of the professions, but also in regard to their general conduct or demeanor on board ship. Not only is it your duty to instruct them; it is also your duty to enforce compliance with such instructions, and see that they are trained to do their duty properly, thoroughly, and to observe the rules and the regulations of the service.

16. Twofold Nature of Duties. Duties in the Navy are twofold in nature. Not only must you be expert in your specialty and be able to instruct others in that specialty; but in addition to this, do not for a moment forget the military side of your life. As a Chief Petty Officer it is more incumbent upon you to remember this than it would be were you in one of the lower ratings. For example, if you happen to be a Chief machinist's mate, there is no reason why you should not be able to march a squad of Sailors in a military manner, halt them, and face them smartly. Because you may be a Chief yeoman, there is no reason why you should neglect boat etiquette, or neglect to salute your seniors. If you happen to be a Chief pharmacist's mate, that is no reason why you should not know and observe uniform regulations, or orders concerning ship routine. Each Chief Petty Officer should take pride in knowing, in observing, and in requiring others under them to observe all of these details of ship life. Simply because you may not happen to be in the seaman branch, do not allow yourself for a moment to think that your duties do not extend to the military side of your profession.

17. Let Officers Judge Your Proficiency. It frequently happens, that, when the time draws near for a Chief Petty Officer to receive a permanent appointment, or when he or she desires a letter of commendation preparatory to taking an examination for warrant, he or she becomes very enthusiastic, and eager to expound his or her points of excellence. Let your conduct as a Chief Petty Officer be such that instead of being forced to explain your points of merit, your officers will already know them. Let your officers be the judges of your proficiency. An officer knows no greater pleasure than that of being able to give an unqualified recommendation to someone who has served under them. Your letter ought to be based on your excellent work as a Chief Petty Officer rather than upon the excellent manner in which you plead your case when you come up for promotion.

—From *The Bluejacket's Manual*, 1918 ed., pp. 711–17

Appendix II

U.S. Navy and U.S. Coast Guard Service Songs

***Anchors Aweigh*, revised lyrics 1997,**
by MCPON John Hagan

Stand Navy out to sea, fight our battle cry!
We'll never change our course so vicious foes steer shy-y-y-y!
Roll out the TNT, anchors aweigh!
Sail on to victory, and sink their bones to Davy Jones, hooray!

Anchors Aweigh, my boys, Anchors Aweigh!
Farewell to foreign Shores, we sail at break of day-ay-ay-ay;
Through our last night ashore, drink to the foam,
Until we meet once more, here's wishing you a happy voyage home!

Blue of the mighty deep, Gold of God's great sun;
Let these our colors be, Till All of time be done, done, done, done;
On seven seas we learn, Navy's stern call:
Faith, courage, service true, With honor over, honor over all.

USCG Service March *Semper Paratus* (Always Ready),
by CAPT Francis Saltus Van Boskerck, USCG

From Aztec shore to Arctic zone,
To Europe and Far East,
The Flag is carried by our ships
In times of war and peace;
And never have we struck it yet,
In spite of foemen's might,
Who cheered our crews and cheered again
For showing how to fight.

Chorus:
So here's the Coast Guard marching song,
We sing on land or sea.
Through surf and storm and howling gale,
High shall our purpose be.
"Semper Paratus" is our guide,
Our fame, our glory too,
To fight to save or fight and die!
Aye! Coast Guard we are for you!

"Surveyor" and "Narcissus,"
The "Eagle" and "Dispatch,"
The "Hudson" and the "Tampa,"
These names are hard to match;
From Barrow's shores to Paraguay,
Great Lakes or Ocean's wave,
The Coast Guard fights through storms and winds,
To punish or to save.

Aye! We've been "Always Ready";
To do, to fight, or die!
Write glory to the shield we wear
In letters to the sky.
To sink the foe or save the maimed;
Our mission and our pride.
We'll carry on 'til Kingdom Come,
Ideals for which we've died.

Appendix III

"Read, Think, Write, Publish"

ADM James Stavridis

Benjamin Franklin once said, "Either write something worth reading or do something worth writing." But I would say, "Do both!" Live well, write about it, and write it well. Life in today's military certainly takes care of the "worth writing" part of Franklin's advice by providing us a broad, rich array of worthy experiences and ideas, worthy of living, but also worthy of reading, documenting, discussing, and—above all—publishing.

Much as the sea has been the inspiration for many writers—poets, novelists, journalists, even scientists—our military profession itself is a sea of inspiration. It is ever-changing, nearly boundless, often Hollywood-style exciting, and begs to be interpreted, presented, and debated. Indeed, we already have a well-established literary heritage, from purist strategy and tactics to fiction and even science fiction, but each of us has a role to play in continuing and improving on this heritage.

And it has never been easier to get started. All you need are some ideas you care about and pen and paper . . . or more likely, just a keyboard.

Something Worth Writing

All of us who have served have observed or lived something worth writing and something that would be good for others to read. We often express these ideas and observations in wardroom discussions, which are critical elements of personal and unit development. But these discussions usually make local impact only and stay within the lifelines of the ship or unit. Publishing your thoughts for others to see, however, extends the reach of your ideas and sparks a larger discussion, a larger professional conversation. In the case of widely-read journals—whether service specific like *Proceedings* or the *Marine Corps Gazette*, or broader-reaching joint or international publications like *Foreign Affairs* or the *Harvard Business Review*—your ideas can influence a great many and inspire conversations in numerous wardrooms or even academic centers, boardrooms, and cafés.

But here is the catch: your ideas will not go anywhere unless you have the courage to "hang them out there" for others to see. Publishing can be a daunting task. In our professional lives, we can rationalize and mitigate the risks of holding station alongside an oiler in heavy seas or landing our aircraft on a pitching carrier deck; but for many, the thought of having our ideas read by others pegs the risk meter as unacceptable. Once our thoughts are out there, we feel we have lost control.

Let's face it, sometimes mentors even advise people against publishing, because it is perceived as a "career risk." Don't be afraid—have the moral courage to vet your ideas responsibly and sensibly. In virtually every case of which I am aware, even the most controversial articles (and I've written my share) are respected as attempts to contribute and respected as such.

The key to publishing and mitigating any risk is twofold: finding the appropriate venue and writing as best you can with complete honesty for that audience. Finding a venue is getting easier all the time. There are many print journals, for example, that would eagerly publish your ideas, stories, and articles, especially professional military journals. You don't have to be the CNO or a combatant commander to get them published, although one day you might find yourself in those shoes. After all, just look at three young officers who published in *Proceedings* over the years, names you might recognize: Lieutenants William F. Halsey, Chester Nimitz, and Ernest J. King. What ever happened to those guys?

In fact, *Proceedings*, or any professional journal, would become irrelevant without the youth of the force publishing ideas and taking interest in the greater professional conversation. If you look at the more exciting, thought-provoking, or innovative articles printed today, you more than likely will find young minds behind them—lieutenants, lieutenant commanders, and commanders. And the best ideas often come from unlikely sources and certainly are not the sole dominion of the "brain" or "genius" of the unit.

Options for publishing and testing our ideas are also ever-expanding. The Internet and electronic publications afford us ample opportunity to match our ideas against those of others. Blogs and Internet forums are great arenas for testing the waters, sharpening arguments, and crystallizing thoughts. Perhaps these forums even reduce the perceived risk level of publishing, lowering the "whole Navy will read this" anxiety factor.

To a certain extent this is true, and electronic forums serve a great messaging purpose. But military professionals should be cautioned always to keep the conversation aboveboard and to avoid anonymous posting while keeping classification and good judgment in the forefront of our minds. I'm sure we've all learned the lesson of the email we wish we hadn't sent—the one that got forwarded well beyond the lifelines of the ship—and that returned to haunt us. So use all the media available, but do so within the bounds of command sense, policy, regulation, and especially classification.

Something Worth Reading

Even though we have growing publishing opportunities, that does not mean writing well is getting any easier. As Nathaniel Hawthorne once observed, "Easy reading is damn hard writing." Writing is a skill that needs continuous honing through practice, study, and formal mentorship if possible. Much as physical fitness and technical proficiency require dedicated time and effort, so too does writing. In fact, writing is a key skill for all leaders, regardless of rank, and must be exercised, evaluated, and rewarded when done well.

Of course, we have to keep in mind that not all of our writing will be worth reading. All of us will create some losers—I sure have. Even the best writers have had their flops. The key is to keep writing and publishing anyway. Much as a baseball player who bats .333 (only one in three successes) is having a great season, a writer can also have hits and misses and still be successful. Of course, through bouncing your ideas off your peers and through honest editing, you should be able to turn your thoughts into a well-written argument and better position it for success. Always show a draft article to a few trusted advisers for comments and criticisms before turning it loose like a fawn in the forest for the real world.

When writing a professional article, I think Mark Twain has the best advice. "The time to begin writing an article is when you have finished it to your satisfaction. By that time, you begin to clearly and logically perceive what it is you really want to say." Rewriting is essential. But, on the other hand, do not let the perfect article be the enemy of the very good one. The perfect article does not exist! Trying to make it so will only guarantee you never publish it. By all means re-write, edit, deliberate, think; but ultimately, launch your ideas and see what comes.

Be prepared, however, to face criticism. Despite your best efforts to formulate an idea and write it well, there will be critics. But you should look at criticism as a strength of the system. It means people are reading your work, that they are thinking, and that the environment is set for overall professional development. Besides, your argument, if written well, might persuade, inform, or influence the audience just as you intended.

Taking a good idea beyond the article phase can also be rewarding and make a lasting contribution to our literary legacy. Often an article or series of articles can germinate and grow into a full-length book. And probably the best way to master your subject of interest is to research and write a book about it. In the naval service, we have many published authors whose works still influence new generations of sea-goers.

Of course, our culture has evolved over the years when it comes to writing. Alfred Thayer Mahan is a legend for his strategy classics, but after he wrote his defining opus, *The Influence of Sea Power Upon History, 1660–1783*, Mahan was admonished by a superior who said in a famously quoted fitness report, "It is not the business of a Naval officer to write books." I disagree. Don't feel you have to write a book, but on the other hand, don't rule out the possibility that eventually you may want to do so. And don't forget that Mahan ended up retiring as an admiral after all. No one remembers the officer who wrote the fitness report; but everyone knows Admiral Mahan, and the *Arleigh Burke* destroyer named for him proudly sails the seas today.

The Marketplace of Ideas

In this rapidly globalizing 21st century, our nation and our military are out competing in a marketplace of ideas. We live in a 24/7 news cycle with near instant reporting and widespread dissemination of stories. It is a teeming, tumultuous, and exhausting marketplace. There has been a tremendous push for military professionals to understand, quantify, and assess our ability to compete in this arena. On all fronts, we must excel at strategic communication—the ability to get our message out to the right audience, at the right time, with the proper effect, and in all media.

Each of us has a clear obligation to contribute to this effort, to be a part of the conversation, to help our ideas compete. Our nation was founded on ideas that just could not be repressed—those of freedom and liberty. In 1776, we launched these ideas into a world ruled by a different system. Our ideas faced stiff competition, and throughout the years we have even suffered wars to defend them—wars like today's struggle against extremists who use terrorism as a weapon, often to suppress freedom of expression. Our second president, John Adams, once wrote that the best way to defend our ideas was through using our minds: "Let us tenderly and kindly cherish, therefore, the means of knowledge. Let us dare to read, think, speak, and write."

So, dare to read and develop your understanding. Carve out the time to think and form new ideas. Dare to speak out and challenge assumptions and accepted wisdom if your view differs from them. Have the courage to write, publish, and be heard. Launch your ideas and be an integral part of the conversation. Why? Because it makes our nation and our profession stronger. In the end, no one of us is as smart as all of us thinking together.

> **ADM James Stavridis, USN (Ret.)** is a 1976 distinguished graduate of the U.S. Naval Academy who spent over thirty-five years on active service in the Navy. He commanded destroyers and a carrier strike group in combat and served for seven years as a four-star admiral, including nearly four years as the first Navy officer chosen as Supreme Allied Commander for Global Operations at NATO. After retiring from the Navy, he was named the dean of the Fletcher School of Law and Diplomacy at Tufts University in 2013. In addition, he currently

serves as the U.S. Naval Institute's chair of the Board of Directors. He has written articles on global security issues for the *New York Times*, *Washington Post*, *Atlantic*, *Naval War College Review*, and U.S. Naval Institute *Proceedings* and is the author or coauthor of several books, including *Command at Sea*, 6th ed., and *Destroyer Captain*.

—From U.S. Naval Institute *Proceedings* 8, no. 134: 16–19.
Reprinted with permission. © 2008 U.S. Naval Institute.

References and Recommended Reading

References

Bayless, Jeff. 2021. "So You Want to Be an Officer?" *U.S. Naval Institute Proceedings* 147, no. 1 (January): 1415. https://www.usni.org/magazines/proceedings/2021/january/so-you-want-be-officer.

Blanchard, Ken. 2020. "7 Common Reactions to Change and How to Respond to Them." LinkedIn, 12 March. https://www.linkedin.com/pulse/7-common-reactions-change-how-respond-them-ken-blanchard/.

Bowlin, Nicholas. 2023. "Don't Give Up the Ship: Leading after Being Crushed." LinkedIn, 31 May. https://www.linkedin.com/pulse/dont-give-up-ship-leading-after-being-crushed-nicholas-bowlin/.

Bradberry, Travis, and Jean Greaves. 2009. *Emotional Intelligence 2.0*. San Diego: TalentSmart.

Campa, Joe. 2016. "Mission, Vision, and Guiding Principles for Chief Petty Officers" (2007). In *Chief Petty Officer 365 Development Guide*, 3. Washington, DC: Office of the Master Chief Petty Officer of the Navy.

Chief Petty Officer's Creed (rev.). N.d. Annapolis, MD: Naval Public Affairs Library, U.S. Naval Academy.

Crist, Charlotte D. 1992. *Winds of Change: The History of the Office of the Master Chief Petty Officer of the Navy*. Ann Arbor: University of Michigan Library.

Department of the Navy. 1989. *Charting the Course to Command Excellence*. Washington, DC: Department of the Navy.

———. 1990. *United States Navy Regulations*. Washington, DC: Office of the Chief of Naval Operations.

———. 2012. *OPNAVINST 3120.32 Standard Organization and Regulations of the U.S. Navy (SORM)*. Washington, DC: Office of the Chief of Naval Operations.

Garner, Joel H. 1990. *Management Fundamentals: A Guide for Senior and Master Chief Petty Officers*. NAVEDTRA 10049. Washington, DC: Chief of Naval Education and Training. Accessed June 20, 2024. https://archive.org/details/managementfundam021192mbp.

Goleman, D. 1995. *Emotional Intelligence*. New York: Bantam.

Heinrich, W. H. 1931. *Industrial Accident Prevention: A Scientific Approach*. New York: McGraw-Hill.

Herdt, James L. 2001. *Chief Petty Officer's Core Competencies*. CPO 21 Core Competencies trifold (Ref NAVOP01.007). Accessed June 20, 2024. https://www.slideshare.net/slideshow/cpo-21-core-competencies-trifold-ref-navop01007/11529900.

Honea, James. 2023. *Mission, Vision, and Guiding Principles of the Chief Petty Officer*. Office of the Master Chief Petty Officer of the Navy.

Howell, Terry. 2017. *The Military Advantage: The Military.com Guide to Military and Veterans Benefits*. Annapolis, MD: Naval Institute Press.

Hudson, Patrick. 2001. "Safety Culture—Theory and Practice." In *The Human Factor in System Reliability Is Human Performance Predictable?* RTO Meeting Proceedings 32. Neuilly-Sur-Seine, France: NATO Research and Technology Organization.

Kingsbury, Paul. 2017. "Tapping the Power of the Chiefs." U.S. Naval Institute *Proceedings* 143, no. 1 (January): 1367.

———. 2022. *Petty Officer's Guide*. Annapolis, MD: Naval Institute Press.

Leahy, J. F. 2004. *Ask the Chief: Backbone of the Navy*. Annapolis, MD: Naval Institute Press.

Leuci, James L. 2015. *A Tradition of Change: CPO Initiations to CPO 365*. Washington, DC: Naval History and Heritage Command.

McComas, Lesa. 2011. *The Naval Officer's Guide*. 12th ed. Annapolis, MD: Naval Institute Press.

McKinnon, Ron C. 2013. *Changing the Workplace Safety Culture*. Boca Raton, FL: CRC.

Meilinger, Phillip S. 2008. "Ten Good Rules of Followership." In *Concepts for Air Force Leadership*, edited by Richard I. Lester, AU–24. Montgomery, AL: Air University Press.

Naval Justice School. 2009. *USN/USMC Commander's Quick Reference Legal Handbook*. Fort Belvoir, VA: Defense Technical Information Center.

Office of the Judge Advocate General. 2007. *Manual of the Judge Advocate General*. Washington, DC: Office of the Judge Advocate General.

Office of the Senior Enlisted Advisor to the Chairman of the Joint Chiefs of Staff. 2013. *The Noncommissioned Officer and Petty Officer: Backbone of the Armed Forces*. Washington, DC: National Defense University Press.

Paraventi, Maureen. 2015. "Understanding and Influencing Risk Tolerance." *Industrial Safety and Hygiene News*, 9 June. https://www.ishn.com/articles/101620-understanding-and-influencing-risk-tolerance.

Reason, James T. 1997. *Managing the Risks of Organizational Accidents*. Farnham, UK: Ashgate.

Rodney, David. 2017. *Navy Manpower Planning*. Washington, DC: Center for Naval Analysis.

Shenk, Robert. 2011. *The Naval Institute Guide to Naval Writing*, 3rd ed. Annapolis, MD: Naval Institute Press.

Stavridis, James, Robert Girrier, Jeffrey Heames, and Thomas Ogden. 2017. *Division Officer's Guide*. 12th ed. Annapolis, MD: Naval Institute Press.

Stavridis, James, Robert Girrier, and Fred Kacher. 2022. *Command at Sea*. 7th ed. Annapolis, MD: Naval Institute Press.

Stewart, Billy D. 2004. "If You're the Chief, Be the Chief." U.S. Naval Institute *Proceedings* 130, no. 2 (February): 1212. https://www.usni.org/magazines/proceedings/2004/february/lf-youre-chief-be-chief.

Tucker, Lester. 1993. "History of the Chief Petty Officer Grade." *Pull Together: Newsletter of the Naval Historical Foundation and the Naval Historical Center* 32, no. 1 (Spring–Summer); available at *All Hands Magazine*, https://allhands.navy.mil/Stories/Display-Story/Article/1839459/history-of-the-chief-petty-officer-grade/.

Tuckman, Bruce W. 1965. "Developmental sequnce in small groups." *Psychological Bulletin*, 63(6), 384-399.

Van Der Veer, Norman R. 1918. *The Bluejacket's Manual*. New York: Military Publishing.

Vaughan, Diane. 1997. *Challenger Launch Decision: Risky Technology, Culture, and Deviance at NASA*. Chicago: University of Chicago Press.

Recommended Reading

Abrashoff, Michael D. 2012. *It's Your Ship: Management Techniques from the Best Damn Ship in the Navy*. New York: Grand Central Publishing.

Benning, Scott A. 2017. *Power of Positive Leadership*. North Charleston, SC: CreateSpace.

Carnegie, Dale. 1936. *How to Win Friends and Influence People*. New York: Simon and Schuster.

Collier, Peter. 2006. *Medal of Honor: Portraits of Valor Beyond the Call of Duty*. New York: Artisan.

"Chief Petty Officer Resource Links." *Goat Locker*. Accessed 30 April 2018. http://www.goatlocker.org/cpo-resources.html.

Collins, Jim. 2001. *Good to Great (Why Some Companies Make the Leap . . . and Others Don't)*. New York: Harper Collins.

Cutler, Thomas J. 2005. *A Sailor's History of the U.S. Navy*. Annapolis, MD: Naval Institute Press.

Department of the Navy. 2004. *OPNAVINST 3500.39B Operational Risk Management*. Washington, DC: Office of the Chief of Naval Operations.

———. 2014. *Navy Military Personnel Manual*. Washington, DC: Office of the Chief Naval Personnel.

———. 2017. *OPNAVINST 1740.5D United States Navy Personal Financial Management Program*. Washington, DC: Office of the Chief of Naval Operations.

Furnham, A. 1997. *The Psychology of Behavior at Work*. Hove, UK: Psychology Press.

Greene, Robert. 1998. *The 48 Laws of Power*. New York: Viking.

Hersey, Paul. 1985. *The Situational Leader*. New York: Warner.

Joint Service Committee on Military Justice. 2016. *Manual for Courts-Martial United States*. Washington DC: Joint Service Committee on Military Justice.

Kacher, Fred W., and Douglas A. Robb. 2019. *Naval Officer's Guide to the Pentagon*. Annapolis, MD: Naval Institute Press.

Kingsbury, Paul. 2016a. "Harnessing the Influence of Senior Enlisted Leaders." *Joint Forces Quarterly* 81 (March 29): 70–75.

———. 2016b. "What Makes the CPO Mess Tick." *U.S. Naval Institute Proceedings* 142, no. 4 (April): 1358.

Koonce, Bob, and Matt Digeronimo. 2016. *Extreme Operational Excellence: Applying the US Nuclear Submarine Culture to Your Organization*. Parker, CO: Outskirts Press.

Kroll, C. Douglas. 2010. *Coast Guardsman's History of the U.S. Coast Guard*. Annapolis, MD: Naval Institute Press.

Lencioni, Patrick. 2002. *The Five Dysfunctions of a Team: A Leadership Fable*. San Francisco: Jossey-Bass.

Lewin, K., R. Lippit, and R. K. White. 1939. "Patterns of Aggressive Behavior in Experimentally Created Social Climates." *Journal of Social Psychology* 10: 271–301.

Mack, Royal W., and William P. Mack. 2004. *Naval Ceremonies, Customs, and Traditions*. Annapolis, MD: Naval Institute Press.

Maslow, Abraham. 1943. "A Theory of Human Motivation." *Psychological Review* 50, no. 4: 370–96.

Maxwell, John. 2022. *The 21 Irrefutable Laws of Leadership*. 25th ed. Nashville: Harper Christian Resources.

McChrystal, Stanley. 2015. *Team of Teams New Rules of Engagement for a Complex World*, with Tantum Collins, David Silverman, and Chris Fussell. New York: Penguin.

McKenna, Richard M. 1948. "The Post-War Chief Petty Officer: A Closer Look." U.S. Naval Institute *Proceedings* 74 (December): 1481–84.

———. 1963. *The Sand Pebbles*. New York: Harper & Row.

———. 1984. *The Left-Handed Monkey Wrench: Stories and Essays by Richard McKenna*. Annapolis, MD: Naval Institute Press.

McLean, Ridley. 1902. "Hints for Petty Officers." *The Bluejacket's Manual*. Annapolis, MD: Naval Institute Press.

Naim, Moises. 2013. *The End of Power*. New York: Basic Books.

Nelson, Bob. 1993. *1001 Ways to Reward Employees*. New York: Workman Publishing.

Office of the Chief of Naval Personnel. 2014. *Navy Military Personnel Manual*. Washington, DC: Office of the Chief of Naval Personnel.

Office of the Master Chief Petty Officer of the Navy. "MCPON releases 'Zeroing in on Excellence' initiative." *Military News*, November 14, 2012. https://www.militarynews.com/norfolk-navy-flagship/news/quarterdeck/mcpon-releases-zeroing-in-on-excellence-initiative/article_7b65078f-fef4-5fc1-8216-8d2e0f4ae8fd.html.

Office of the Secretary of the Navy. 2015. *Department of the Navy Correspondence Manual*. Washington, DC: Office of the Secretary of the Navy.

Ostrom, Thomas P. 2006. *The United States Coast Guard: 1790 to the Present*. Oakland, OR: Red Anvil.

Phillips, Donald T. 1992. *Lincoln on Leadership*. New York: Grand Central Publishing.

Powell, Colin. 2012. *It Worked for Me: In Life and Leadership*, with Tony Koltz. Toronto: HarperCollins.

Raven, B. H., and J. French. 1959. "The Bases of Social Power." In *Studies in Social Power*, edited by D. Cartwright, 150–67. Ann Arbor, MI: Institute for Social Research.

Rielage, Dale C. 2022. *Navy Staff Officer's Guide: Leading with Impact from Squadron to OPNAV*. Annapolis, MD: Naval Institute Press.

Rohn, Jim. 2017. "Rohn: 7 Personality Traits of a Great Leader." *Success*, May 3. https://www.success.com/article/rohn-7-personality-traits-of-a-great-leader.

Savino, Carl S., and Ronald L. Krannich, PhD. 2024. *The Military to Civilian Transition Guide: Secrets to Finding Great Jobs and Employers*. Corporate Gray. https://www.corporategray.com/book/transition-guide-2024/index.html.

Sinek, Simon. 2011. Start with Why: A Powerful Way to Lead with Purpose. London: Portfolio.

United States Life-Saving Service Heritage Association. 2007. *They Had to Go Out . . . True Stories of America's Coastal Life-Savers from the Pages of "Wreck & Rescue Journal."* Hull, MA: United States Life-Saving Service Heritage Association.

U.S. Coast Guard. 2018a. *Risk Management (RM)*, COMDTINST 3500.3A.

———. 2018b. *Safety and Environmental Health Manual*, COMDTINST M5100.47.

———. 2024. *Correspondence Manual*, COMDTINST 5216.4E.

Watkins, Michael D. 2013. *The First 90 Days*. New York: Harvard Business Review Press.

Willink, Jocko, and Leaf Babin. 2015. *Extreme Ownership: How U.S. Navy SEALs Lead and Win*. New York: St. Martin's Press.

Yukl, Gary. 2012. *Leadership in Organizations*, 8th ed. London: Pearson.

Index

Note: page numbers in italics refer to figures.

accountability: after career-derailing infraction, 99; of CSEL, for CPO mess decisions, 44; as guiding principle of CPOs, 26. *See also* self-accountability in CPO mess
adaptability, in project management, 167
African Americans: first Master diver in U.S. Navy, 16; first MCPOCG, 16, *17*
aggregates (type of group), 115
American Corporate Partners, 254–55
American Society of Naval Engineers (ASNE), 266
"Ancients" Coast Guard awards, 82–83
Appointing Warrant Officers, 237
associations: and increasing connection power, 81; for retirees, 266–67. *See also* Chief Petty Officer Associations (CPOAs)
audience for *Chief Petty Officer's Guide*, 2, 3

backup, forceful, importance of, xvii
behavior, appropriate, 92–95; avoidance of inappropriate relationships or fraternization, 94; and CPOs as role models, 93. 94; increased pressures of higher rank and, 92, 94; low tolerance for violations of, 93; misbehavior in CPOs, 44, 89–90; questions used to evaluate actions, 95; responsibility to meet services' ethical requirements, 92–93; techniques for resolution of ethical conflicts, 93
Black, Delbert, D., 16, 48, 82

Bonhomme Richard, 193
Boorda, Mike, 52–54
Brashear, Carl Maxie, 16
Byers, Edward C. Jr., 16

calculative organizational culture, 206
Calhoun, Charles Luther, 11
Campa, Joe R. Jr., 12, *23*, 24
Cantrell, Steven W., 74, 190
Career Compensation Act of 1949, 8, 9
career-derailing situations, 98–100; frequency of, 98; steps toward recovery from, 99–100; types of infractions, 98
Casualty Assistance Calls Officer (CACO), 110
chain of command: correcting breaches of, 64–65; CPOs as key link in, 58, 188; duty to report ethical breaches to, 68; fraternization and, 94; proper respect for, 21, 24, 33, 57, 122; representing sailors to, 58, 123; SELs' unique position outside of, 67, 227, 231
Challenger disaster, 208
change management, 125–32; certifications in, 133; common situations requiring, 125; communication in, 129; creating vision for change, 126; customer focus in, 128; definition of, 125; embedding and solidifying change, 126; five steps in, 125–26; focus on controlling what you own, 131–32; implementing change, 126; management of your attitude toward, 130–31; matching

individuals to roles in, 130; overcoming resistance to change, 132–33; preparation for change, 126; reviewing and analyzing, 126; roles of CPO in, 127; skills needed for, 127–29; stress management in, 132; as team leader, 114; types of change, 125; types of reactions to change, 129–31
chaplains, 69, 109, 259, 260–61
charge book, 33–34, *35*
Charting the Course to Command Excellence (Department of the Navy), 36, 52
Chief: commissioning of, 48, 52–54; CPO donations in honor of, 48
chief, as term: attention commanded by, 18; history of, 6; mess pay grades included in, 2
chief of staff (COS), functions of, 175
Chief Petty Officer (CPO): selection process for, 30; teams' high expectations of, 152; trend toward greater education and expanded authority, 268. *See also* command climate; conduct of CPO; CPO mess; guiding principles of CPOs; influence of CPOs; manager, CPO as; responsibilities of Chief Petty Officer; retirement
Chief Petty Officer Associations (CPOAs), 48–50; activities and events of, 49; balancing activities of with official duties, 50; rules regarding, 49
Chief Petty Officer Leader Development Course, 103
Chief Petty Officer Retirement Creed, 265
Chief Petty Officer Scholarship Fund (CPOSF), 48–49
Chief Petty Officers' Association (CPOA) [Coast Guard], 48, 263
Chief Petty Officer's Creed, vii, 5, 24, 86. See also *Teaching to the Creed* modules
chief staff officer (CSO), functions of, 175
Chief Warrant Officer (CWO): commissioning program for, 235; duties of, 160, 235; post-selection leadership course, 238; selection board for, 236–37
Chief Warrant Officer Professional Development (CWOPD) course, 238
circadian rhythm: and fatigue management, 213–14; and sleep, 212
CMC for a Day program, 155
CMC/COB Course, 104
Coast Guard: awards offered by, 82–83; CPO Association, 48; heroic action by CPOs, 15–16, *17*; and honor of service, 14; on leadership core competencies, 127–28; mishap reporting systems, 198; pay, in 20th century, 8. *See also* Master Chief Petty Officer of the Coast Guard (MCPOCG)
Coast Guard Correspondence Manual, 136
Coast Guard CPO Academy, 103
Coast Guard Credentialing Opportunities Online (CGCOOL), 248
Coast Guard Senior Enlisted Leadership Course, 104
coercive power: expert/information power as, 139; helping young officers to understand and use, 80
coercive power of CPOs, 84–86; appropriate uses of, 84; educational resources on, 85; judge advocate's advice in, 85; knowledge required for use of, 84–85, 86; through advising of commanding officer, 84
cohorts (type of group), 115
college courses/degrees: commissioning programs and, 235; in strengthening of mental domain, 100–101
Command Career Counselor (CCC), 109
command climate: attention to needs of crew and families, 187–88; *vs.* command culture, 186; command philosophy in, 186–87; communication and, 186–87; good, policies leading to, 187; good management and, 187–88; leadership's influence on, 186; management of, as key CPO function, 186; negative effect of toxic boss on, 68–69; programs and resources designed to improve, 155–57. *See also* communication to manage command climate
command climate surveys: negative, all-hands debrief on, 70; as tool for managing command climate, 153
command culture, *vs.* command climate, 186
Command Financial Specialist (CFS), 109
Command Managed Equal Opportunity Manager, 109
Command Master Chief (CMC): base, differences from fleet duties, 172; communication with, 48; relationship to ISIC CMC, 46–47; relationship with flag or general officer staff, 47; and Senior Shore Leadership Course (SSLC), 172

command philosophy, and command climate, 186–87
command senior enlisted leader (CSEL): awareness of factors affecting CPO mess effectiveness, 50; benefits of explaining decisions by, 44; benefits of officers' support of, 56; and CPO mess initiation/CCTI process, 33; creation of positions, 10–11; experience and security of position to wield influence, 67; influence over policy and decisions, 67; Keystone Course for, 104; leadership in CPO mess deliberations, 39; and organizational/flag leader positions, 223–25; positions included under, 223; respect due to, 42–44; responsibility for healthy wardroom-CPO mess relationship, 57; specialty badges for, 225; tools for correcting errant CPOs, 45–46; typical duties of, 224–25
Commander, Navy Installations Command (CNIC), 171–72
commissioning programs, 234–38; application process, 237; Chief Warrant Officer (CWO) program, 235; choice of program, 234; college degree and, 235; command coordinator's role in, 237–38; courses and, 237; Limited Duty Officer (LDO) program, 235; mentors and, 238; percentage of officers' corps originating in, 235; selection board for, 236–37; service record, checking for errors, 237; sources of information on, 237, 238; understanding future duties before applying, 235–36
commodore, as title, 174
communication: about meetings' purpose, 148; in change management, 129; clear, importance of, xvii; and command climate, 186–87; by commander, of command philosophy, 186–87; CPO as facilitator of, 139–40; developing plan for, 48; explaining reasons for orders, 145; importance of encouraging, 136; in introducing unpopular policies, 89; with leadership, rules for, 145–46; and misinformation, 135, 139, 140; and noise, 151; in project management, 165; and putting bottom line up front (BLUF), 145–46; responsibility to give frequent feedback, 144–45; in safety/risk management, 195, 197, 200–201, 202–3; in transitioning from military, 242; verbal and nonverbal, 144–45

communication, strategic, 150–52; audience and, 151; choice of venue for, 151; CPO role in success of, 150, 152; definition of, 150; effective, requirements for, 150–51; and noise, 151

communication skills: and active listening, 144; challenges of, 135–36; constant self-assessment and improvement of, 134, 135; and CPOs' broader audiences, 134–35; effective, knowledge required for, 141; factors effecting communication quality, 140, 143–44; importance of, 134; importance of clear verbal and written expression, 136; increased number of platforms and channels, 135–36; knowing rules and conventions of channels of communication, 141, 151; tailoring message to audience, 140–41. *See also* meetings; speaking skills; writing

communication to manage command climate, 152–57; benefits of, 157; board and council meeting attendance as, 154–55; CMC for a Day program as, 155; CMC/CSEL calls as, 154; CO's calls as, 154; daily circulation among crew and, 155–57; frequent, transparent, and authentic communications and, 152–53, 156; as key responsibility of CPOs, 152; knowledge of programs and resources and, 156; surveys and metrics as tools for, 153; two-way mechanisms of communication and, 153

conduct of CPO: compliance with military formalities, 24; conduct above reproach as example to others, 23. *See also* ethical requirements of service

conflict management, leadership and, 129

connection power: of CPOs, 60, 61, 67, 76, 78–79, 81; helping young DIVOs build and use, 60, 61; means of increasing, 81

control by negation in naval services, 22–23

COOL (Credentialing Opportunities On-Line), 168

Core Strengths assessment, 106

Corporate Gray, 255

CPO. *See* Chief Petty Officer

CPO mess: balancing hierarchical and egalitarian structures in, 41–44; ceremonial functions, importance of attending, 40; as Chief's home aboard ship, 29; collaboration in management projects, 161; complacency, costs of, 56–57; demonstrating solidarity with, 40; dining facilities ashore, 49; and discipline, enforcement of, 37; efforts to remain credible and relevant, 267; factors affecting effectiveness, leadership's need to monitor, 50; family-like equality within hierarchy, 41–42; *Hue City* scandal, 89; impact of CO and SEL on culture of, 45; inculcating safety awareness, 197; mission, vision, and guiding principles (MVPG) for, 24, 27, 38, 114; petty officers' engagement with, before promotion to CPO, 29; power from ranking, award, and disciplinary boards, 37–38; recent expressions of mistrust from Sailors, 86; respect due to command senior enlisted leader, 42–44; and translating values into behavior, 20; variations in size and facilities, 29; vital importance of, 13. *See also* self-accountability in CPO mess; wardroom-CPO mess relationship

CPO mess, deliberation in, 39–41; avoiding bad behavior, 39–40; leadership role of CSEL in, 39; respect due to command senior enlisted leader in, 42–44; value of explaining decisions, 44

CPO mess, good personal relationships in: correction of poor attitudes and behaviors, 39; importance to synergy, 36; investments in building of, 38, 40; loyalty and trust necessary for, 38–39; obligations of members to CPO community, 29–30

CPO mess, working together as team: and consistency across command, 37; ethical boundaries and, 41; as goal, 36–38; synergistic effects of, 36–37

CPO mess initiation/CCTI, 30–36; activities in, 33; charge book in, 33–34, 35; command senior enlisted leader and, 33; final night and pinning ceremony, 35; formal and informal training, 31, 33; goals of process, 31; hazing and, 33; and indoctrination of selectees to new role, 86; lessons to be learned during, 35–36; as rite of passage, 31; sponsor assigned to CPO selectees, 34–35

CPO mission, vision, and guiding principles (CPO MVPG), 27, 38; editions of, 24; expectations and values outlined in, 24; on team leadership, 114

creativity/innovation, and leadership, 129

credentials and qualifications: commissioning programs and, 235, 237; COOL (Credentialing Opportunities On-Line), 168; emphasis on shipboard and watch station qualifications, xvii; management skills certifications, 168; for post-military employment, 248

creed. *See Chief Petty Officer's Creed*

Crew Endurance Handbook, 215

Crow, Tom, 10

Crozier, Brett, 89

cultural barriers, CPOs breaking, 16

culture. *See* command culture

culture of excellence, CPO responsibility to create, xv, 25–26

customer focus in leadership, 128

cutlass: as Sailor's weapon of choice, 74; as symbol of good CPO leadership, 74

decision-making: different styles of, 181; factors affecting, 185; by flag staff, CPO role in, 180–84; and leadership, 128; performance metrics and, 181–82; prioritizing of decision types, 181

Del Black Leadership Award, 82

Delbert D. Black National Chief's Mess, 48

Department of the Navy (Coast Guard) Correspondence Manual, 142–43

detachment for cause (DFC), 98

detail, attention to, in project management, 166

Disabled American Vets (DAV), 266

DISC assessments, 106

discipline: acceptable and unacceptable types of, 68; tools for CPO mess enforcement of, 37

diversity: cultivating respect for differences and, 136; teams and, 121, 122

divisional Chief, types of interactions as, 218

divorce, survivor benefits and, 253

Drug and Alcohol Program Adviser (DAPA), 109

drugs and alcohol, health impact of, 214

Eastwind collision, 191

ecological power of CPOs, 76, 83–84

education and training: importance to command climate, 187; on risk management, 197–98. *See also* college courses/degrees; credentials and qualifications

Educational Services Officer (ESO), 110
effectiveness: *vs.* efficiency, 160; of team, as CPO responsibility, 27
efficiency, *vs.* effectiveness, 160
emotional intelligence (EI): definition of, 95–96; online tests to evaluate, 97; value for leadership, 96–98
Emotional Intelligence Assessment, 106
empathy: and emotional intelligence, 96; value for leadership, 97–98
employment, post-military: acquiring civilian credentials, 248; informational interviews and, 244–45; mentorship programs for veterans, 254–55; necessary preparation for, 244; negotiating salary and benefits, 247; professional organizations and, 248–49; researching potential employers, 244–45, 246; researching salaries and benefits, 246; sources of information on, 253; value of mentor for finding, 254. *See also* résumés
energy drink abuse, 214
enlisted personnel: change over time in characteristics of, 27–29; CPO responsibility to represent, 58, 123; increasing education and capabilities of, 267–68; pay, in 20th century, 8; role of, 13
Enlisted to Officer Commissioning Programs Application Administrative Manual, 237
esprit de corps of teams: indications of, 121; methods of enhancing, 120–24
ethical requirements of service: and CPOs as role models, 93. 94; ethical conflicts, techniques for resolution of, 93; low tolerance for violations of, 93; questions used to evaluate actions, 95; responsibility to meet, 92–93. *See also* behavior, appropriate; stewardship
excellence, culture of, CPO responsibility to maintain, xv, 25–26
expert/information power: agility as learner required for, 80; of CPOs, 76, 78–80; credibility gained from, 60, 78–79; helping young officers to achieve, 60; increasing influence of, 136; and leading up, 139; misuses of, 139; need for constant updating and broadening of, 78, 79–80; sharing of, 138; and sources of information, familiarity with, 136–37; types of uses, 138–39; withholding of information to shape behavior, 138–39

family: and decision to seek commission, 236; importance of investing time and energy in, 101–2; involvement in planning of retirement ceremony, 256, 263; modern strains on, 101; programs and resources for, 156–57; Survivor Benefit Plan (SBP) for, 252–53; treatment as part of team, 156–57
Family Readiness Fleet and Family Support Programs (FFSP), 111
fatigue management, 211–15; drugs and alcohol and, 214; importance to performance, 211–12; three guiding principles for, 212–14
Federal Employees Dental and Vision Insurance Program (FEDVIP), 252
feedback: accepting, after career-derailing infraction, 99; accepting, as more-senior CPO, 221; to crew, on command climate surveys, 153; frequent, in good communication, 144–45; on leadership, asking for, 92; to teams, 122–23
financial assistance, resources for, 112
financial management, importance of understanding, 169–70
Finn, John W., 15
flag lieutenant, functions of, 176
flag secretary, functions of, 175–76
flag staff: assisting commander as function of, 173–74; chain of staff authority, 174; civilians on staff, 178–79; N/CG codes and functions of, 176–78; relationship with flagship personnel, 179–80; staff titles and functions, 175–78; types of functions, 173, 174; variations in structure and size, 174–75, 176
flag staff, working in: adjustment time required, 173; balancing travel and office time, 183; and business process improvements, 184; importance of good relations with staff officers, 174, 182; role in decision-making processes, 180–84; time with boss and staff, importance of, 183; travel time, efficient use of, 183–84; types of interactions as member of, 218
Fleet and Family Support Center (FFSC), 253
fleet master chief petty officer (FLTCM), 11
Fleet Reserve Association (FRA), 266
flexible culture, as safety culture subculture, 206

followership skills, 90–91; attributes of good follower, 90–91; self-reflection on character traits affecting, 91
force generation and deployment, 170
force master chief petty officer, 11
fouled anchor emblem, 25
fraternization: guidance for young officers on, 64; importance of avoiding, 94
free association technique, to elicit crew feedback, 154

Gantt chart, 164
GEICO Military Service Awards Program, 81–82
General Order 43, 8–9
General Order 134, 8
General Schedule (GS), 179
general service employees, 179
generative organizational culture, 206
Glenn Defense Marine scandal, 86
goodwill ambassador, CPO role as, 86–90; and condemnation of abuse, 87; help in improving skills in, 90; lack of education or guidance on, 86; and management of conflicting loyalties, 87–90; meaning of term, 86; negative outcomes of ignoring, 86; and self-evaluation about attitudes, 87, 90; skills and knowledge needed for, 87
Google search engine for matching military occupation codes to civilian postings, 248
Greenert, Jonathan, 72, *138*
groups: definition of, 115; types of, 115–16
guiding principles of CPOs, 22–28; evolution over time, 27–28; list of, 26–27; self-sufficiency as, 22–23; skills development and improvement, 27; Van Der Veer's "A Short Talk with Chief Petty Officers" on, 23–24; as yardsticks for self-evaluation, 27. *See also Chief Petty Officer's Creed*; CPO mission, vision, and guiding principles (CPO MVPG); integrity; professionalism

Halsey, William "Bull," 51, 279
health: medical readiness when transitioning from military, 249–50; Military Health System Nurse Advice Line, 112–13; resources for medical advice, 112–13; Veterans Affairs health care system, 251
health of crew: CPO's concern about, 210; fatigue management, 211–15; stress management, 210–11

Heinrich, W. H., 204
Herdt, James, 24, *266*
heroic action by CPOs, 15–16
Hire Heroes USA, 254–55
history of CPO rank, 6–9; acting *vs.* permanent appointments, 7–8; creation of, 5, 6, 7; creation of CMC, FLTCM, and FMC ratings, 11; creation of MCPON rating, 10–11; creation of Senior Chief (E-8) and Master Chief (E-9) ratings, 9–10, 268; in nineteenth century, 6–7; pay, in early 20th century, 8; in twentieth century, 8–9
Hogan Assessment, 106
Honea, James, 24–25
Horne, Terrell E. III, 15–16, *17*
Hue City, 89

implicit leadership theory (ILT), 91
influence of CPOs: lasting impact on others, 12; as mentors and teachers for young officers, 51, 52–54, 63, 73; writing as essential tool for, 136. *See also* power base of CPOs
influence of more-senior CPOs: excepting feedback and, 221; expertise and personal power as basis of, 218; learning of new tactics, 220; mentoring of subordinates, 220; need to alter influence targets and style, 216, 239; new types of obstacles to consider, 220; as part of larger web of influence within command, 219–20; seeking advice from successful predecessors, 219, 220–21; systems, processes, and culture as venues for, 217; time required to understand power bases and influence tactics, 217–18, 219; types of knowledge needed for, 218–19; variations depending on position, 220; working through subordinates, 216, 220
information power. *See* expert/information power
informed culture, as safety culture subculture, 205
Ingham, Harrington, 107
initiation/CCTI. *See* CPO mess initiation/CCTI
In-Service Procurement Selection Boards, 236
inspections, readiness for, 167
institutional expertise, as CPO responsibility, 26

296   Index

integrity: as guiding principle of CPOs, 26; importance of valuing, xvii; owning and correcting mistakes, xvii

Johari Window, 107
Joint Professional Military Education (JPME) courses, 20
JPME. *See* Joint Professional Military Education (JPME) courses
just culture, as safety culture subculture, 206

Keystone Course, 104
Kingsbury, Paul A., 20, 60, 75
Kirton Adaption-Innovation Inventory (KAI), 107, 130
knowledge, professional: CPO responsibility to stay current on technology, 13, 19–20; education programs, 20; maintaining high level of, xvii. *See also* technical mastery

LCPO. *See* leading chief petty officer
leadership: asking for feedback on, 92; as central function of CPOs, 53–54; and conflict management, 129; and creativity/innovation, 129; customer focus in, 128; cutlass as symbol of, 74; and decision-making skills, 128; deckplate leadership, 26; and dedication to mission, xvi; demotivational types of, 80; development of other leaders, 187; effect of followers' "leader prototypes" on perceptions of, 91–92; fair, 80; guidelines for development of (Kingsbury), 75; importance of demonstrating, xvii; knowledge as basis of, 113; management by walking around, 56, 58; managing change and, 127–28; need for continued improvement in, 75; officers' expectations for, 53–55; power base as necessary for, 60; and problem-solving skills, 128; in project management, 128, 165; resources for improving, 75, 108; and risk-taking, 129; schools and courses on, 103–5; self-assessment tools for, 105–8; self-learning resources for, 75, 108; skills needed for, 127–29; strategies for improving, 113; in strengthening four domains of resilience, 100–102; training of relief and, 32; in war, as CPOs' greatest role, 54. *See also* influence of CPOs; influence of more-senior CPOs; team leadership

leading chief petty officer (LCPO): influence over policy and decisions, 67; types of interactions as, 218
learning culture: as safety culture subculture, 206; training of relief and, 32
legacy of CPO career, training of relief and, 32, 255
Limited Duty Officer (LDO): commissioning program for, 235; duties of, 235; management responsibilities, 160; post-selection leadership course, 238; selection board for, 236–37
Limited Duty Officer/Warrant Officer/Chief Warrant Officer (LDO/WO/CWO) Academy, 238
LinkedIn Learning program, 108
Luft, Joseph, 107

Mallo, Glenn, 32
management fundamentals, 160–62; efficiency *vs.* effectiveness, 160; increasing demands with higher rank, 160–61, 162; interdependence of four phases of, 161
manager, CPO as: budgeting and cost management, 163, 164; and command climate, 187–88; CPO mess collaboration in, 161; four elements to consider in, 162–65; importance or written communication skills in, 141–42; increasing demands with higher rank, 160–61, 162; limited resources and, 158; management skills, 165–68; managing big projects, 162–65; manpower management, 170–71; need for self-evaluation and improvement in, 160; organizational management, needed skills for, 168–73; and process management, 128; and project management, 163; quality management in, 164–65; resource management, 163; resources for information on, 158; scope management, 163, 164; self-assessment checklist for, 159; self-assessment tools for, 105–8; self-learning resources for, 108; skills certifications, 168; skills needed for, 20, 158, 162; time management, 163, 164, 165–66; types of management responsibilities, 161. *See also* change management
Manual of the Judge Advocate General (JAGMAN), 85
Master Chief Petty Officer (MCPO): positions for, 222; rating, creation of, 9–10; responsibilities of, 19, 160, 186

Master Chief Petty Officer of the Coast Guard (MCPOCG): creation of office, 11; first African American serving as, 16, *17*
Master Chief Petty Officer of the Command (MCPOC), 11, 16
Master Chief Petty Officer of the Navy (MCPON): creation of office, 10–11; first, 16, 48; MCPON leadership mess, 225
MBTI. *See* Myers-Briggs Type Indicator
McKenna, Richard, 18
Medal of Honor, CPO recipients of, 15, 16, *17*
meetings: appropriate venue for, 148, 149; rules for, 147–49; scheduling of, 149
mental domain: definition of, 100; practices to strengthen, 100–101; self-learning resources and, 108
mentoring: and career success, 226–27; commissioning programs and, 238; importance of, xvii; in post-military job search, 254; as senior enlisted leader, 231–32; in transition from military, 254. *See also* officers, CPOs as mentors for
Military Health System Nurse Advice Line, 112–13
Military OneSource, 112
mishap reporting systems, 198
mistakes, owning and correcting: after career-derailing infraction, 99; as duty, xvii; as senior enlisted leader, 240
moral failures of officers: minor, correction of, 67–68; serious, responsibility to report, 68
morals, definition of, 92
mottos of CPO mess: "Anchor Up," 15, 22; "Ask the Chief," 4, 15, 22, 78–79; qualities needed to fulfill, 15, 22–28; "Results, Not Excuses," 4, 15, 22, 268
Myers-Briggs Type Indicator (MBTI), 105–6

National Chief's Mess, 48, 82
National Defense University Keystone Course, 104
Naval Justice School, Senior Leader Legal Course (SLLC), 85
Naval Submarine League, 266
Naval Supply Systems Command (NAVSUP), 171
Navy Capitol Hill Workshop, 105
Navy Core Values, 103
Navy Inspector General's Office, 71

Navy Leader Development Framework (CNO), 103
Navy Leadership and Ethics Center CMC/COB Course, 104
Navy League Awards, 81
Navy League of the United States, 266
Navy Manpower Planning (Rodney), 171
Navy Memorial National Chief's Mess, 82
Navy Senior Leader Seminar, 104–5
Navy Total Force Manpower Policies and Procedures, 171
Navy–Marine Corps Relief Society, 112
normalized deviance: factors leading to, 208–9; responsibility to identify and resolve, 209

officers: benefits of supporting CSEL, 56; expectations for CPOs, 53–55, 58. *See also* chain of command; flag staff; toxic boss; wardroom-CPO mess relationship
officers, CPOs as mentors for: on boundaries, roles and responsibilities, 71–72; on chain of command, 64–65; clarity about desire to help, 64; correction of deficient attention to duties, 65; correction of excessive interference, 65; correction of moral failures, 67–68; on development and use of power, 59–61; and development of officer's unique qualities, 59; educational tactics in, 72; on fraternization, 64; LCPO and SCEL influence over officers' policies and decisions, 67; metrics for success of, 72; reaching out to struggling officers, 55; on relating to their people, 65–66; responsibility to correct, despite resistance, 62–63, 64, 66; strong influence of, 51, 52–54, 63, 73; training for future command roles, 59; typical areas of weakness in young officers, 64; as unwritten expectation, 59; usefulness for junior and senior officers, 73
OODA (observe, orient, decide, and act) loop, reducing time spent in, 13
Operational Fleet Response Plan (OFRP), 170
Optimized Fleet Response Plan, 170
organizational culture, spectrum of types, 206
organizational management: importance of understanding, 168; skills needed for, 168–72; variations in specific processes and, 173

298   Index

organizational skills, in project management, 166

Papp, Robert, 54–55
partner nation militaries, building relationships with, 230
pathological organizational culture, 206
Patton, Vince W. III, 16, *17*
Pearl Harbor attack, CPO heroism in, 15, 16, *17*
personal development as CPO, 27–28
personal power (character): credibility gained from, 60, 76, 80; helping young officers to achieve, 60
physical domain, strengthening of, 101
Pierce, Lloyd, 14
planning, programming, budgeting and execution process (PPBE), 169
PMI Authorized Training Partner Program, 108
political correctness, and good-natured fun, 123
positional power: of CPO, 76, 77–78; toxic boss's overreliance on, 88
power base development, teaching young officers about, 60–61; attention to boundaries, roles and responsibilities, 71–72; as essential for leadership, 60; honest criticism of weak areas, 61; types of power bases, 60; as useful knowledge at all levels of career, 60
power base of CPOs: CPO Power and Influence Model, 76; ongoing work to strengthen, 77; strength of, and influence over less-experienced officers, 61; types of, 76, 77–87; using for benefit of your units or larger service, 77
pride in service, Chiefs legacy and, 18
problem-solving skills: and leadership, 128; in project management, 166; self-assessment for, 107
procedure, knowing and complying with, xvii
process management and improvement, 128
professional development, importance of, xvi
Professional Military Education (PME), importance of, 20
professionalism: basic elements of, 22; as guiding principle of CPOs, 22, 26
Project Management Professional (PMP) certification, 168

public affairs officer (PAO), 150, 220
Public Health Service Commissioned Officers Corps service song, 18

qualifications. *See* credentials and qualifications
quality management system (QMS), 165

rating force master chief (RFMC), positions for, 223
readiness generations model, 170
Reason, James, 204–6
recognition, motivational power of, 83
Region Legal service Offices (RLSO), 111–12
region master chief, duties of, 172
relationships, inappropriate, 94
relief for cause (RFC), 98
relief. training of, 32, 255
reporting culture, as safety culture subculture, 205
resilience, four domains of, 100–102
resources: career counseling, 109; chaplains, 109; on coercive power of CPOs, 85; CPOs and, 111; for equal opportunity issues, 109; for family support, 111; for financial assistance, 112; on four domains of resilience, 102; importance of knowing about, 108–9, 110; in-command, 109–10; on leadership, 75, 108; for managers, 108; for medical advice, 112–13; Military OneSource counseling and referral services, 112; for personal financial help, 109; for personal legal services, 111–12; for sexual assault cases, 110; suicide prevention programs, 110; for support of families of casualties, 110; for training and education, 110; for treatment of drug and alcohol abuse, 109; for voting assistance, 110
responsibilities of Chief Petty Officer: anticipation of problems, 58; commanding officers' expectations, 58; expectations for results, 56–57; formal establishment of, 10; as greater in U.S. Navy than other navies, 5; as linchpin between officers and enlisted, 37; literature on, 1–2; overview of, xvi–xvii, 13, 19–20, 24; questions CPO's should ask themselves, 56; readiness of all personnel and spaces, 36–37; to represent sailors to chain of command, 58, 123; taking initiative on new programs and procedures, 58; taking

ownership of, xvi; threat awareness, 13; understanding role in creating successful outcomes, 20; warfare readiness, 13, 25–26; to work with wardroom to achieve goals set by senior officers, 52. *See also* behavior, appropriate; culture of excellence; goodwill ambassador, CPO role as; guiding principles of CPO; knowledge, professional; leadership; manager, CPO as

résumés: help from mentor with, 254; preparation in advance, 246–47; translating military accomplishments into civilian terms, 245–46, 248

retirement: associations for retirees, 266–67; Chief Petty Officer Retirement Creed, 265; hometown announcements, 258; Navy Retirement Guide, 255; staying connected after, 265–67

retirement ceremonies, 256–65; 5060 Notice for, 256–57; awards, lead times for, 257, 2643; chaplain for, 260–61; family involvement in planning of, 256, 263; guest list for, 257, 258, 262; guest speaker, 261; guidelines for, 256; honors Boatswain's Mate and backup, 261; important elements of, 260–64; information sheet for, 260; master of ceremonies for, 260; national ensign presentation, 262; and photographers, guidance for, 261; as place of appointed duty, 256; plan of actions and milestones (POAM) for, 256–57; post-ceremony reception, 258, 265; program for, 257, 258, 263; public address system and music, 261; retirees' options for, 256, 263–64; retirees' responsibilities in, 257, 258; securing location, and planning floor plan, 260; sequence and timing of events, 264–65; shadow box preparation and presentation, 259, 262, 263; side boys selection and duties, 261; sponsor's role in planning of, 256–59

reward power, helping young officers to understand and use, 60

reward power of CPOs, 76, 81–83; available awards, 81–83; opportunities to use, 81; and recognition, motivational power of, 83; researching available awards, 83

RFC. *See* relief for cause

risk management: components of process, 196; and cost of mishaps, 172, 190–91; CPO activities to strengthen, 197; CPO involvement in decision-making on, 196–97; and evolving attitudes about safety, 215; excessive risk tolerance, factors leading to, 207–8; fatigue management and, 215; higher-level leadership and, 192; identification and mitigation of risks, 192, 196; importance at all levels, 190; importance of understanding, 172–73; inadvertent encouragement of at-risk behavior, 209; knowledge needed for, 192; maintaining awareness of, 197; modeling of, 193, 194; and normalized deviance, 208–9; as one pillar of safety management system (SMS), 196–98; and organizational hazards, 192; and organizational *vs.* personal risk tolerance, 207; in project management, 166; risk management models, 172; risk to forces *vs.* risk to mission, 196; role of every person in, 196. *See also* safety management system (SMS)

risk tolerance: excessive, factors leading to, 207–8; organizational *vs.* personal, 192, 207

risk-taking, leadership and, 129

rites of passage, function of, 31

safety: evolution of attitudes toward, 215; as value rather than program, 194

safety assurance: CPO activities to strengthen, 199; evaluation of safety management system effectiveness, 198; four approaches to, 200; mishap reporting systems and, 198; as pillar of safety management system, 198–200; relearning, with higher levels or responsibility, 200. *See also* risk management

safety climate: definition of, 203–4; importance to safety management system, 203

safety culture: Accident Causal Chain ("Swiss cheese") model of, 204–5; definition of, 204; early "blame the worker" approach, 204; five subcultures of, 205–6; and high performance, 206; importance to safety management system, 203; and information flow, trust and accountability, 206; research on, 204–6; responsibility to assess and improve, 207; strong, outcomes of, 204

safety management system (SMS): applicability to all levels of organization, 202; four pillars of, 193; importance of safety climate and culture to, 203; purpose of, 193; as relatively new, 193–94; risk management pillar of, 196–98; safety assurance pillar of, 198–200; safety policy pillar of, 194–95; safety promotion pillar of, 200–203. *See also* risk management

safety policy: CPO activities to strengthen, 195; as pillar of safety management system, 194–95

safety promotion: communication in, 200–201, 202–3; CPO activities to strengthen, 203; as pillar of safety management system (SMS), 200–203; training in, 200–202

The Sand Pebbles (McKenna), 18

schools and courses on leadership, 103–5

Schweiger, Mark, 226–27

Scott, Terry D., 268

SEA. *See* Senior Enlisted Academy

SELC. *See* Coast Guard Senior Enlisted Leadership Course

self-accountability in CPO mess, 44–46; "and watch-team backup," 44; CPO misbehavior, rarity of, 44; importance of maintaining, 42, 43; mechanisms for correcting deficiencies, 45–46; monitoring of peers' performance, 44; practices and values necessary for, 38

self-assessment: about impact on others, 12; of attitude toward change, 130–31; of attitudes as goodwill ambassador, 87, 90; of character attributes, 21; of communication skills, 134, 135, 158; of core strengths, 106; DISC assessments, 106; of emotional intelligence, 97, 106; to evaluate behavior, 95; guiding principles of CPOs as yardsticks for, 27; importance of honesty in, 3–4; of "leading across" skills, 39–40; of managerial skills, 105–8, 159, 160, 165; and playing to strengths while compensating for weaknesses, 19; principles used as yardsticks for, 27; tools, for leaders and managers, 105–8; for toxic leadership, 88

self-sufficiency, as guiding principle of CPOs, 22–23

Senior Chief Petty Officer (SCPO): and management of command climate, 186; positions for, 222; rating, creation of, 9–10; responsibilities of, 19, 160

Senior Enlisted Academy (SEA), 20, 103–4

senior enlisted leader (SEL): management responsibilities, 160–61; and opportunity for influence, 240–41; relationship to immediate superior in command (ISIC), 46–47; types of interactions as, 218; unique position outside chain of command, 67, 227, 231. *See also* command senior enlisted leader (CSEL)

senior enlisted leader, career paths: acquisition of skills necessary for, 221; direct-level leadership and management positions, 221–22; executive/command leader positions, 222–23; maintaining focus on next step, 217; mentoring and, 226–27; new positions, growing into, 238–41; organizational/flag leader positions, 223–25. *See also* commissioning programs

senior enlisted leader, leveraging positions to full potential, 227–32; commander's confidant role, 231; decision-making and, 240; engagement with external stakeholders, 230–31; freedom from promotion concerns, 227–28; influence targets, identification of, 239; learning to delegate, 240; mentoring and advising officers and enlisted persons, 231–32; mistakes, owning of, 240; potential resistance to, 228; reporting force concerns to command, 229–30; review of documents on roles and scope of authority, 239; speaking to force on behalf of command, 228–29; taking time to consider substantial changes, 239–40; valuable knowledge and experience brought to, 227–28; value of good relationships to key staff, 231

senior enlisted leader, screening for assignments as, 232–34; interview preparation, 233–34; nomination packages, 232–33; notification of decision, 234; personnel records, checking for accuracy, 232

Senior Enlisted Legal Course (SELC), 85

Senior Executive Service (SES), 178–79

Senior Leader Legal Course (SLLC), 85

Senior Officer Course (SOC), 85

Senior Shore Leadership Course (SSLC), 172

separation. *See* transitioning from military service, as honor, 14

Sexual Assault Victim Advocates, 110

shore installation management, 171–72

"A Short Talk with Chief Petty Officers" (Van Der Veer), 23–24, 59

skills required by CPO: as goodwill ambassador, 87, 90; need for constant improvement in, 75–77. *See also* communication skills; followership skills; leadership; manager, CPO as; problem-solving skills
sleep: as biological imperative, 211–12; circadian rhythm and, 212
SLLC. *See* Senior Leader Legal Course
social domain, strengthening of, 101–2
social media: being a goodwill ambassador on, 87; and increasing connection power, 81; staying connected to service community through, 267
speaking skills, 146–47
spiritual domain, strengthening of, 102
sponsor: in CPO mess initiation /CCTI, 34–35; of retirement ceremonies, 256–59
stakeholder management, in project management, 167
Standard Organization and Regulations Manual (SORM), 47
standards, high, maintaining, xvii
Stevens, Mike, 131, *131*
stewardship, in project management, 166
strategic thinking, importance of, 168–69
stress management, 210–11; health effects of stress, 210; stress continuum used to identify stress levels, 210
Suicide Prevention Coordinator, 110
supply and material management, 171
Surface Navy Association (SNA), 266
Surface Navy Association awards, 82
Survivor Benefit Plan (SBP), 252–53

Teaching to the Creed modules, 24, 33
team: characteristics of, as group, 116; dynamics of, and training of relief, 32; stages of development in, 117–20; typical percentage of productive members, 120
team leadership: adjourning stage, management of, 119–20; building team identity, 118; communicate trust and approval, 122, 123; communicating goals and responsibilities, 117, 121, 122; and delegation, 123; development of team trust and interdependency, 118, 124; diversity and, 121, 122; encouraging input from team, 124; encouraging productive dissent, 119; feedback on progress of work, 122–23; friction with- in team in early stages, 118; and good-natured fun, 123; managing change and, 114; managing team conflict, 119; morale and esprit de corps, 120–24; providing necessary resources, 122; stages of team development, 117–20; two dimensions of, 116; types of groups and, 115–16. *See also* change management
technical mastery: as CPO responsibility, 13, 19–20, 26–27; in project management, 167
Tomich, Peter, 15, *17*
toxic boss, 68–71; documenting of behaviors and correction efforts, 69, 70; formal reporting of, 70–71; frequency of news reports on, 68; gathering allies for confrontation with, 69, 70; insecurities underlying, 69, 88; meeting with, to discuss problem, 69–70; negative command climate surveys, all-hands debrief on, 70; negative effect on command climate, 68–69; responsibility to take action, 69, 71; self-assessment questionnaire, 88; stress of confronting, 71; typical behavior of, 68–69
tradition: ceremonies and, 78; charge books and, 33–34; CPO mess and, 30, 33. *See also* retirement ceremonies
training: continuous, importance of, xvii; opportunities, importance of understanding, 171; on safety/risk management, 200–202; of your relief, benefits of, 32
Transition Goals, Plans Success (Transition GPS) program, 253
transitioning from military: advanced planning, need for, 243, 249, 255; family and, 242, 243–44, 250; financial preparation for, 249; forward-looking attitude in, 244; health insurance options, 252; and house hunting permissive temporary duty (PTDY), 255; information resources on, 253; "lines of effort" in, 242, 243; medical readiness checklist, 249–50; mentors, value of, 254; military's transition resources and, 253; Navy Retirement Guide, 255; networking with other recent retirees, 253–54; place of residence, research on costs of, 245; as process requiring time, 243–44, 255; researching insurance plans, 251–53; state and federal benefits for

retired military, accessing, 251; Survivor Benefit Plan (SBP), 252–53; terminal leave, use of, 255; turnover planning, 32, 255; Veterans Affairs benefits, claiming of, 250–51. *See also* employment, post-military

travel, as flag staff, 183–84

Uniform Code of Military Justice (UCMJ), on toxic leadership, 71
United Service Organizations (USO): awards offered by, 81; search engine for job seekers, 248
unpopular policies, strategy for introducing, 89
U.S. Naval Institute (USNI): benefits of joining, 266; Enlisted Essay Prize, 18
USN/USMC Commander's Quick Reference Legal Handbook (Naval Justice School), 85

Vanderhaden, Jason, *143*, 226–27
Veterans Affairs, Department of: claiming benefits from, 250–51; health care system, 251
veterans benefits, sources of information on, 253
veterans service officer (VSO), 251
Veterati, 254–55
Voting Assistance Officers (VAOs), 110

Walker, Bob, 11, 48, 49
walking around: and command climate, 155–57; and deck-plate leadership, 56, 58

Walsh, Loretta Perfectus, 16, *17*
wardroom, written guides for, 51
wardroom-CPO mess relationship, 52–57; communication and trust, importance of, 55, 71; cooperation to achieve goals set by senior officers, 52, 55, 57; CPO mess's expectations for support, 55–56; dysfunctional, as damaging to overall success, 55, 56–57; effect on CPO mess reputation, 73; expectations for CPO leadership, 53–55; expectations for CPO results, 56–57; healthy, CSEL's responsibility for maintaining, 57; importance of developing, 71; as one of mutual support, 52; questions CPOs should ask themselves, 56; questions officers should ask themselves, 55–56
warrior mentality, importance of, xvii
watchstanders, and fatigue management, 211–15
Watson, Dennis G., 65–66
women: first CPO, 16, *17*; first enlisted woman in Navy, 16
writers, composers, and intellectuals, CPOs as, 18
writing, 141–44; as essential tool for influence, 136; as key skill in administrative role, 141–42; resources for improving, 136, 142–44; seven common forms of written communication, 141–42; use by seniors to judge you, 144

"Zeroing in on Excellence" approach, 131, *131*

About the Author

Paul A. Kingsbury, FLTCM (Ret.), served thirty-one years in the Navy, culminating with his final assignment as the fleet master chief for U.S. Fleet Forces Command. He has published several articles in military journals and received awards in both the U.S. Naval Institute General Essay and Enlisted Essay contests. He is the author of *Chief Petty Officer's Guide*, 2nd ed., and *Petty Officer's Guide,* and is a coauthor of *The Bluejacket's Manual,* 26th ed. He is the host and producer of the *Cutlass* podcast. He serves as the director of uniformed service relations for the Blue Cross Blue Shield Association.

The Naval Institute Press is the book-publishing arm of the U.S. Naval Institute, a private, nonprofit, membership society for sea service professionals and others who share an interest in naval and maritime affairs. Established in 1873 at the U.S. Naval Academy in Annapolis, Maryland, where its offices remain today, the Naval Institute has members worldwide.

Members of the Naval Institute support the education programs of the society and receive the influential monthly magazine *Proceedings* or the colorful bimonthly magazine *Naval History* and discounts on fine nautical prints and on ship and aircraft photos. They also have access to the transcripts of the Institute's Oral History Program and get discounted admission to any of the Institute-sponsored seminars offered around the country.

The Naval Institute's book-publishing program, begun in 1898 with basic guides to naval practices, has broadened its scope to include books of more general interest. Now the Naval Institute Press publishes about seventy titles each year, ranging from how-to books on boating and navigation to battle histories, biographies, ship and aircraft guides, and novels. Institute members receive significant discounts on the Press' more than eight hundred books in print.

Full-time students are eligible for special half-price membership rates. Life memberships are also available.

For more information about Naval Institute Press books that are currently available, visit www.usni.org/press/books. To learn about joining the U.S. Naval Institute, please write to:

Member Services
U.S. NAVAL INSTITUTE
291 Wood Road
Annapolis, MD 21402-5034
Telephone: (800) 233-8764
Fax: (410) 571-1703
Web address: www.usni.org

www.ingramcontent.com/pod-product-compliance
Ingram Content Group UK Ltd.
Pitfield, Milton Keynes, MK11 3LW, UK
UKHW032216260325
456756UK00002B/5